Justice in Practice
Legal Ethnography of a
Pakistani Punjabi Village

Justice in Practice
Legal Ethnography of a
Pakistani Punjabi Village

Muhammad Azam Chaudhary

OXFORD
UNIVERSITY PRESS

OXFORD

UNIVERSITY PRESS

Great Clarendon Street, Oxford OX2 6DP

Oxford University Press is a department of the University of Oxford.
It furthers the University's objective of excellence in research, scholarship,
and education by publishing worldwide in

Oxford New York

Athens Auckland Bangkok Bogotá Buenos Aires Calcutta
Cape Town Chennai Dar es Salaam Delhi Florence Hong Kong Istanbul
Karachi Kuala Lumpur Madrid Melbourne Mexico City Mumbai
Nairobi Paris São Paulo Singapore Taipei Tokyo Toronto Warsaw
with associated companies in Berlin Ibadan

ISBN 0 19 579063 4

Printed in Pakistan at
Mas Printers, Karachi.
Published by
Ameena Saiyid, Oxford University Press
5-Bangalore Town, Sharae Faisal
PO Box 13033, Karachi-75350, Pakistan.

CONTENTS

ACKNOWLEDGEMENTS

My foremost and heartfelt thanks are to Prof. Dr Karl Jettmar for his valuable help without which this study would not have been possible. Thanks to Prof. Dr Klaus Peter Koepping and Dr Aparna Rao-Casimir for their expert advice and suggestions.

I am extremely grateful to Prof. Dr Harald Hauptmann who readily offered me a place for working on my dissertation undisturbed, and a special word of thanks to Martin Bemmann for his immense patience in helping and answering the technical questions regarding the computers. I am also very grateful to Tanja Powell for reading the last draft of this manuscript as also to Elisabeth Sepi for the drawings in this dissertation.

For the help and encouragement by friends, colleagues, and others in the preparation of this work, I feel indebted to Tobias Becht, Susanne Bressan, Prof. Dr M.A. Chaudhary, Claudia Heibrock, Regina Heibrock, Jamal Abdul Nasir, and Prof. F.M. Malik.

In the village, I have to thank Zahid Shah, Zulfiqar Ali, and Saleem who accompanied me to the courts with immense patience and explained the conflicts in their own families and in the families of their relatives. I am also very thankful to the lawyers and their clerks and to the clerks of the courts who were very friendly and supported my research, especially Nazir Chaudhary, Tariq Mahmood, Hanif Shah, and Yasin Waraich for their cooperation. Thanks are due to those whose names are better kept secret for giving me a *parchi* for getting data and information from the police and courts. The unconditional support of my family deserves my gratitude.

Stephanie Zingel-Ave Lallemant deserves a very special thank for making my English text legible. Last but not least I gratefully acknowledge the moral support given by Taslima Katzan and her valuable suggestions regarding the structure of the study.

AUTHOR'S NOTE

All the Urdu/Punjabi words have been written in italics and in small letters. No diacritical marks have been used. It has been tried to transcribe with the nearest possible English letters. Punjabi/Urdu words, already known in English literature, have been mostly adopted. Those Urdu/Punjabi words having no equivalent in English or that cannot be easily translated have been transcribed and the nearest possible translation is given in brackets. If a Punjabi/Urdu word is very frequently used the English translation may be absent. For an additional explanation of the important Urdu/Punjabi terms a glossary has been added. It is important to mention that Misalpur is a fictional name as also the names of most of the persons and places used in this study.

CHAPTER 1

INTRODUCTION

Five decades into Pakistan's hard-won creation, in public
discourse, among jurists, anthropologists, political elite, and the
general public, there is an ongoing debate as to which of the
two, the official system of justice, or the traditional methods of
resolving conflicts, is more suitable for solving the socio-legal
problems of Pakistani society.

In most of the available ethnographic-legal literature (Cohn,
Moore, Hoebel) on South Asia, especially India and Pakistan,[1]
the official legal system seems to be branded as 'imposed',
'imported', 'alien', 'formal'. Cohn, a well-known legal anthropologist, in 1967 writes about the official system in India:

> It is my thesis that the present attitude of the Indian peasant was an
> inevitable consequence of the British decision to establish courts in
> India patterned on British procedural law. The way a people settle
> disputes is part of its social structure and value system. In attempting
> to introduce British procedural law into their Indian courts, the
> British confronted the Indians with a situation in which there was a
> direct clash of the values of the two societies; and the Indians in
> response thought only of manipulating the new situation and did
> not use the courts to settle disputes but only to further them.[2]

Similarly Moore, another legal anthropologist, writes in 1985:

> The British system, as it has developed in India (and America),
> examines one distinct dispute under 'laboratory conditions'. The
> court room is seen as a vacuum into which only carefully
> circumscribed testimony and evidence are presented and

manipulated by professionals. In theory, the disputants lose their social status and are viewed equals before the law.[3]

The same negative impression is conveyed through the different names used for the official system such as 'Lawyer's Law',[4] 'National law',[5] 'Formal law', 'Public law',[6] 'colonial law' and 'the law of the police', etc. On the other hand the non-official or the traditional system is seen, in this same ethno-legal literature, as indigenous, something coming from the society, formed by the society and for the society, and therefore better suited to it:

> In the village council, a dispute is seen as part of the environment from which it grew. The individuals, their families, the community and the histories that led to the discord are on trial. The community participates in an open discussion and the decision, arrived at by a core of respected leaders, focuses on compromise.[7]

This bias is also manifested by the different names used for the traditional part of the justice system in anthropological literature. Most commonly known are 'Local Law Ways',[8] 'Folk, Law',[9] Non-State Legal System (NSLS),[10] informal law, people's law, living law, private law,[11] and traditional justice system, or even indigenous institutions of justice. Terms like 'Local', 'Folk', etc. used in such literature have connotations of 'indigenous' and 'good'.

The colonial background of the official system is thought to be responsible for its problems. The problems of the traditional system seem to be explained—rather legitimized—through the caste, *biradari*, kinship based structure of the society. Cohn · writes about North India which is also valid for the area of the present study if we change the word caste with *biradari*:

> (…) men are not born equal, and they have widely differing inherent worth. This theme or value is basic to the whole social structure and is expressed most clearly in the caste system (...). The Chamar (cobbler) knows he is not equal to the Thakar (landlord). He may want to be equal but he knows he is not. The Thakar cannot be

convinced in any way that the Chamar is his equal, but the court acts as if the parties to the dispute were equal.[12]

Here the 'evil' of the official system seems to be the attempt to treat all the people as equal; the 'good' of the traditional system is its treatment of the people in accordance with their status and position.

This criticism of the official justice system and sympathy with the traditional system in ethnographic literature is the result, on the one hand, óf the trend of criticizing the administration of justice by the British, a trend which had already arisen during the last phase of the colonial period.[13] On the other hand, it is the trend of cultural relativism in legal anthropology which resulted in sympathizing with the 'primitive', local, or traditional systems[14] of justice.

In contrast to the findings of legal ethnologists, the legal communities (which include judges, lawyers, and others concerned with courts and law) mostly hold contrary opinions, and do not even accept the traditional methods as law. This is clearly described in several reports of the Law Reform Commission[15] whose members were all jurists. The same was expressed by many jurists interviewed by the author. Without going into details, we quote here some parts of the Law Reform Commission Reports which denounce the traditional system of justice:

It will be a retrograde step to revert to the primitive method of administration of justice by taking our disputes to a group of ordinary laymen ignorant of modern complexities of life and not conversant with legal concepts and procedures.[16]

The Commission further wrote:

(...) it is hardly correct to say that the present judicial system is a foreign transplant on Indian soil, or that it is based on alien concepts unintelligible to our people. The people have become fully accustomed to this system during more than a hundred years of its existence. The procedure and even the technical terms used by the lawyers and judges are widely understood by the large majority of the litigants.

And also:

The present day complications and delays in disposal of cases are not so much on account of the technical and cumbersome nature of our legal system as they are due to other factors operating in and outside the courts.[17]

Most of the elite and politicians of the country (except the two Martial Law Administrators who later became Presidents of Pakistan, Ayub Khan and Ziaul Haq, tried to introduce the 'improved' forms of the traditional system) support the views of the jurists. This becomes evident in the reaction and the statement of these politicians at the time of the introduction of the *jirga* (another name of the traditional system used mainly in NWFP) system in 1962 by Ayub Khan:

By throwing the honour of the nation at the mercy of the Jirga system the Government is inviting a bloody revolution.[18]

Depending upon the kind of village, the tradition and effectiveness of the traditional system in that particular village, the type of conflict and the level of the society one belonged to, the villagers would be divided on the question. As a general rule, the well-to-do and powerful are more in favour of the traditional system and the destitute more inclined towards using the official system.[19]

The present study is not interested in discussing whether the official system is imported and colonial in nature or not. Nor is it interested in proving if the traditional system is really indigenous. Its main thrust is in determining how far the two systems differ and if the difference between the two systems is as large as described and assumed by the anthropologist in the scarce literature available, or if this difference is limited only to structure and procedure.[20] The study examines how the justice system functions in practice and what role wealth, power, influence and prestige play in its functioning. It also attempts to locate the problems the legal system faces, at the lowest level, from the point of view of the receivers of the system.

Misalpur: The Ethnographic Setting

Misalpur lies some fifteen kilometers west of Faisalabad in central Punjab. According to the Population Census Report of 1981, its base population was 8,333 persons.[21] It lies directly on the main road connecting Faisalabad (the third largest town of Pakistan) with Jhang, another big town in the area. The booming cotton industry in Faisalabad (also called the Manchester of Pakistan)[22] finds its way into suburbs like this village because of the availability of relatively cheap land and labour. Industrial expansion has led to a rapid increase in its population. In fact, the usual population growth coupled with migration from other villages together with commuters from the nearby villages, to work on the power-looms, must have played a part in doubling the population of this village during the last twelve years.

The first impression of the village is that its population is divided into zemindars (farmers), *kammis*[23] (craftsmen), and businessmen. The group of businessmen is formed by those farmers and *kammis* who either own power-looms, work for the power-looms' owners, or are shopkeepers. Therefore, the division is in fact between zemindars and *kammis*.

The farmers are further divided into several *biradaris*[24] which include *Jats, Araeens, Rajputs, Gujars*, and *Dogars*.[25] However, this diversion is not (at least not at present) on the basis of profession. These *biradaries* are so represented that none makes a dominant majority in this village.

These farmer *biradaries* are known to be characterized by different attributes as also reported in the literature on the subject.[26] Some of these attributes are explained here for a better understanding of the subsequent details concerning the particular behaviour of the members of a *biradari* and the occurrence of certain conflicts.

Jats are traditionally known as farmers: hardworking,[27] ruled by passion, lacking unity among themselves. They call themselves *Chaudhries* and dismiss the claim of *Gujars* and *Araeens* to this title of honour lending hierarchy. The latter sometimes call themselves *Chaudhries* too. The *Rajputs* are known in the village for having much land, are ruled by passion,[28] but maintain unity among themselves. They call themselves *Ranas*. Both of the *lamberdars* (Revenue heads) of the village belong to this *biradari*. The *Araeens*, in the area, are known as the vegetable growers, both industrious[29] and controlled by reason. They call themselves *Mians*. Similarly, *Gujars* are known for breeding animals but also as cultivators.[30]

The specific attributes of these *biradaries* are general and not confined to this village alone. Usually, the noble or positive characteristics of the farmer *biradaries* are claimed by the members of the *biradari* themselves and the derogatory or negative characteristics are attributed to them by other *biradaries*. Every farmer *biradari* in the village considers itself superior to all other *biradaries* and none is ready to relegate itself to an inferior position in any respect. On the basis of the historical literature and the remnant characteristics, it might be concluded that in the past these *biradaries* had different professions.

The composition of these *biradaris* became more complicated at the time of Partition in 1947, when migration took place and a large number of displaced persons, as refugees from Indian Punjab, sought land and shelter in Pakistan. Faisalabad, along with a few other areas, was highly favoured for settlement because of its fertile agricultural land and for being nearer to the border.[31] The fertility of the land around Faisalabad was proverbial. There was a saying that 'if you cut a man and bury him in the land, he will grow too'. All those who could afford to, settled in the region around Faisalabad. Thus, this village has many of the original inhabitants, as well as many migrants of various backgrounds like those coming from Ambala, Ludhiana, Hoshiarpur, who speak their own dialects and have their own particular customs and traditions. This gives rise to a situation where there are people of the same *biradari* (*Jats* from Hoshiarpur, Ludhiana, Gurdaspur, or the original village inhabitants) having different regional backgrounds, following different customs, traditions and speaking different dialects of Punjabi. There is no grouping merely on the basis of refugees or original inhabitants, though sometimes the *biradaries* coming from one area do make one group. These *biradaries* are further divided into *sharikas* (sub-lineage) and *khandans* (extended family), which have their own specific customs and traditions distinct from other such groups

Kammis are categorized as barbers, blacksmiths, carpenters, sweepers, oilmen, weavers, tailors, potters, and musicians. These groups are also sometimes called *biradaries* and the division is based upon the profession. For example, the *naee* (barber) *biradari* includes all the barbers in the village and in other villages. They are sometimes further divided according to the area they live in or migrated from (many *kammi* families migrated from the Indian Punjab along with the farmers and most of them are still working for them). *Kammis*, especially those working for the farmers, are considered inferior by the latter. Their position is similar to the dependents of the farmers. They are paid from each crop at the end of a season according to the system called *seypi*, being[32] paid in kind from the major food crops with wheat, maize, etc. The amount is fixed per pair of oxen, also known as per plough, or per kitchen, or per family. In addition, farmers pay them the cash crops, like sugar, vegetable and animal fodder in varying quantities, but at will, i.e. according to the wish of the farmer and the request of the *kammi*. Besides their professional work, the *kammis* also perform different ceremonial jobs on the occasion of marriage, death, birth rituals, circumcision, etc. It will be interesting to mention here that the barber plays an important role in all these ceremonies, and is one who knows many secrets of the family and *biradari*. Barbers bring messages of deaths, marriages, births, etc. to relatives living far away. They, among others, sometimes help in finding spouses for the children of the families they serve. This is perhaps why each *biradari* has its own barber.

The barbers and the other *kammis* who performed different ceremonial duties, of course, got additional payments for these in money or in kind, or both, called *laag*. This is why the *kammis* receiving such payments were also called *laagies*. Since these *laags* were generally paid gladly and generously, the *kammis* always looked forward to such occasions. There are stories relating of how if any *kammi* became affluent and did not work properly anymore, someone from the *biradari* would arrange for him to be robbed so that he would again be rendered poor and work faithfully.

The situation has changed considerably. There were no big landholders here—even at present there are none—and the farmers were in general the well-to-do families of the village. They lived in the centre of the village, and the non-landowners (*kammis*) lived on the periphery and mostly worked for them. The status and positions of all the *biradaries* and families were relatively clearly drawn in the village, where most of the people knew each other. (This past situation is much talked about by the farmers in contrast to the *kammis*). With the passage of time, the landholdings have fragmented into subdivisions. The fertility of land has been adversely affected by waterlogging and salinity. The villages around Faisalabad have been most severely affected by this. Consequently, there has been erosion in the social status of the farmers who are without land or own smaller holdings.

The expansion of the cotton industry in Faisalabad was accompanied by the introduction of power-looms in Misalpur. The *Julahas* (weavers), who traditionally prepared cloth by working hand-driven *khadies* (looms), were the first to install power-looms. Later, they came to be called the *Malik biradari* and soon outnumbered all others in Misalpur. As such, they dominated the local council of the Basic Democracy System (explained later on) in the village to the extent of being elected as the Chairmen of village council. Besides, those households from other *biradaries* like the *Araeens*, having small holdings also gradually turned to power-looms. Consequently, the balance of power began shifting from the landowner class to that with industry and capital. Generally, most of the big *khata* (a place or factory where power-looms are installed) holders are *Maliks* (former weaver or oilmen *biradari*) or *Araeens*. Interestingly, both the candidates for the seat of Chairman of the Union Council (for further details see Basic Democracy) from Misalpur, Naeem and Karim, belonged to these two *biradaries*.

A complete change, however, has not taken place. Because of the expansion of industry, the proximity to a big city, and increase in the population, the value of land was also enhanced and those members of the landholding class who own land at a suitable place earn a lot of money. There are still many *kammis* working for the farmers on the old *seypi* system and they are the poorest class in the village.

The change in the social strata disturbed the social order of the village. The *kammis* are no longer dependent on the farmers and the hold of the *biradari* is not very strong any more. This not only gives rise to new conflicts—for example, between farmers and *kammis*—but the system of resolving them has also been disturbed. The traditional *biradari* and village elders, as also the earlier *panchayats* (council of the *biradari* or village elders and respectables) and landlords are losing their influence and position.

The physical structure of the village has also undergone pronounced changes. Previously, the village was more or less clearly divided between the zemindars (farmers) and *kammis*, with the zemindars living mostly in the centre, having *havelies* (animal-houses) on the periphery. In the centre of the village, farmer *biradaries* were settled in different parts, and these are still known after the name of the *biradari* living there such as: the *mohalla* of *Jats* or of *Rajputs* and so on. With the onset of capitalization and the disturbance of the so-called old order of the village, the structure of the village also changed. Rich *kammis* bought houses in the centre of the village wherever they were available. Farmers sold their old places and built houses in the new part of the village where the old order is not observed. The land and houses are sold here on a first come, first served basis.

Sharika, Biradari, Pind: **The Multiplex Social Organization**

Conflicts in the village, like in many traditional societies, do not generally emerge between individuals but between groups. Even those conflicts which start between individuals, sooner or later become group conflicts due to mutual obligations of the kinsmen or fellow villagers. Walsh, a colonial administrator in India in the first half of the twentieth century, wrote about the basis of crimes in the villages of the subcontinent:

> In England a very large proportion of crime is committed single-handed, and the average number of offenders per crime must be under two. The average number per crime in the United Province must be nearer ten than two, (...).[33]

For understanding the nature, reasons and types of conflicts as well as their traditional judicial treatment, it is important to know how the village society is organized into groups and their kinds. Since there is enough literature on the social organization of the Punjabi villages;[34] here it is dealt with to the extent required for an understanding of the conflicts and the process of solution of these conflicts.

In its setting, it has already been described as a multi-*biradari* and multi-head village.[35] Structurally the village community seems to open from the inside towards the outside, i.e. from the centre to the periphery, and makes different enclosures or units. These layers are based upon two criteria, i.e. of kinship and territorial ties. The former ties a villager horizontally to the *biradari*, *sharika*, and other kins even beyond the territorial boundaries, and the latter vertically with the village.[36]

This does not mean that the two types of relations or ties are equal in importance and cannot be clearly distinguished from one another. The ties based on kinship are much stronger and more durable than those of village and territory. Sometimes making a decision between *biradari* ties extending beyond village and village relations becomes difficult. The following is a discussion on the role of the above-mentioned ties in the social organization of the village.

Kinship Ties

The kinship ties which bind a villager horizontally to his fellow kinsmen are *ghar* (literally 'house', here nucleus family), *khandan* (extended family), *sharika* (patrilineage), *goot* (sub-clan, also sometimes translated as sub-caste) and *biradari* or *qoum* (clan, also translated as caste). *Biradari* is further divided into those living in the same village and then those elsewhere from the same *biradari*.[37]

Biradari, Quom

Biradari is the broadest connection for a villager in the kinship ties. The meaning of the term, *biradari* or *quom* changes not only from context to context among the same people or community, but also has other meanings for every sort of group or community or the area one is concerned with. For example the meaning of the term *quom* for nomads, or *Gujars*, Sikhs, Hindus and in Punjab, or in the Frontier Province, as also in Afghanistan, or Pakistan and so on, differs greatly.[38] A universal definition of the term is perhaps almost impossible. For the area and community in this study, 'clan', and 'ethnic group' are to some extent accurate.

A villager identifies his/her *biradari* in many different ways: The *biradari* (clan) as a whole: taking the example of Ashraf: all the *Jats*, irrespective of the area they come from, or subgroups, make up the *biradari*. The words *quom* and *biradari* and even *zaat* are used for this, *biradari* being the most frequent. It may be translated as 'clan' or 'ethnic group' in this context. It is important to mention here that the word *quom* is also used in the sense of a nation,—state identity—Pakistani *quom*, German *quom*, etc.

The second identification is based on the *illaqa* (area) one belongs to. This is a more important connection within the *biradari* than the first one and means the area of origin of an individual. Coming back to the example of Ashraf, Hoshiarpur is the district and Chanwan the village in India he comes from. This became especially important after the partition of India when many people belonging to different *biradaries* came to settle in here. The *biradaries* who migrated from one area could not settle together again in any one village. The *Jats* from Hoshiarpur form something like a 'patrilineage' for Ashraf. They not only speak a particular dialect of Punjabi, but also share customs and traditions not common in groups belonging to other areas. This linkage plays an important role especially at the time of marriages where patrilineage would be an important consideration. Besides Hoshiarpur's *Jats*, as in the case of Ashraf, other examples of *Jats* would be those from Gurdaspur, Amritsar, Baliwale, etc.

The use of the word *quom* is mostly limited to the first category. It is asked while greeting a new person:[39] Which *quom/biradari* do you belong to? (*Jat*). Which region do you come from? (Hoshiarpur/Chanwan). What kind of *Jats* are you? (Chohan). All these are further subdivisions of the *biradari*. For Ashraf in Misalpur, Chanwanwale *Jat* is the foremost connection and then comes the larger category of *Jats* taken together because his family is the only Chohan (his *goot*) in this village.

Unity and cohesion among the members of different *biradaries* is weakening, but it is still a means of power.[40] A strong and united *biradari* serves as a weapon against others. There might be different groups within the *biradari* which are based either on kinship (people having one great-grandfather and a whole group being known by the name of this grandfather like *bodu ke* or *dakhen ke*) or based on the region, *chanwanwale*, *ballywale*, *ambalie*, who in times of need act together.[41]

Goot[42]

This is the third characteristic of identification. But the importance of this is decreasing to the extent that in many cases people don't know their *goots* any more. The examples of *goots* among *Jats* would be Chohan (also found among the *Gujars*) the *goot* of Ashraf, Chadhair, Cheeme, Chathe, and so on. If there is only one *biradari* living in a village (*Jats* for example) then the *goot* becomes important and is used as a subdivision of the *biradari*. However, the word *biradari* is then used to mention this subdivision, such as Chadhair *biradari*, or Cheeme *biradari*, examples from the *Jat biradari*.

Sharika

The next category in the kinship ties is of *sharika*. It could be translated as a 'patrilineal descent group'[43] and its boundaries are fixed according to the use and situation from 'parallel cousins' to 'all the people of the *biradari* living in the same village'. In the words of Ahmad:

> Derived from the Arabic word Sharik, meaning partner, in Punjabi this word means an individual who belongs to one's biradari (kindred) or quom with whom ego competes for recognition and honour.[44]

This word has a negative connotation and is mostly replaced by *biradari* or *khandan*, depending upon the situation. *Izzat* and *sharika* are very closely related, as in sharing the *izzat* and in gaining or losing *izzat* in the eyes of the *sharika*.

As we move from the nucleus family to the extended family called *khandan*, the authority of the leader or leaders decreases— especially his hold over the resources, and the relationship between the cousins, children of those brothers who are themselves either old or already dead is weakened. At the time of the division of the land, household, and animals, there always remain some petty unpleasant memories like: one got an unusable piece of land, or a sick animal, or an unfavourable part of the house. The divisions of land, house, and animals are often readjusted among the brothers if one of them is especially dissatisfied. It is not easy to demand a redistribution and if it takes place it very often generates bitter quarrels and conflicts. Also there is real competition between the cousins for respect in the village, to the extent that the word used for cousin in Pashto is *tarbur*, which stands for enemy too, and in Punjabi the word for the families of the cousins is *sharika* and for a single person *sharik* which means 'the one who shares, the one who takes a part'. The trend of conflicts within this unit is the highest. The honour (*izzat*) is not divided equally between the brothers, most normally the eldest inherits it, but there are examples when others earn it.

If any member of a unit is threatened, the members of *sharika* are supposed to react unitedly, but later on the usual rivalry is retained. It is differentiated from *biradari* on the ground that in *sharika* only those people of the *biradari* are included who are blood relatives, i.e. from the father's side unless the mother comes from the same *sharika*. Another condition for the *sharika* is that there must be some sort of ongoing relations of ceremonial exchange of gifts, known as *vartan bhanji* in literature.[45] This is evident especially at the time of marriage, death, or other ceremonial festivals. Every *biradari*, naturally, includes more than one *sharika*, hence the feeling of unity as also competition in the *sharika* is stronger than in the *biradari*.

Khandan and Ghar

The difference and boundaries between *ghar* and *khandan*, *khandan* and *sharika*, *sharika* and *biradari* are difficult to explain in detail nor are there any fixed boundaries. Eglar, differentiating between family and *biradari*, wrote:

The line of demarcation between one's own family and the biradari as well as the essential unity of the two are expressed in a proverb: 'one does not share the bread but one shares the blame.' That is, a family owns property in common and consequently shares income and expenditures, but the biradaris, who live in different households, each with its own shared income, are affected by the wrongdoing of any one of its members into whatever household he belongs and their prestige suffers thereby.[46]

Ghar is to some extent akin to the nucleus family with children, parents, unmarried aunts, grandparents and, in some cases, all the uncles with their wives and children being included. But if the uncles and their children are not living together anymore they belong to the *khandan*. The difference between *ghar* and *khandan* could be seen in that in *ghar* there is one kitchen, and everything essential is jointly used. In a *khandan* there could still be one big house, with perhaps many shared things like a courtyard but with different separate kitchens.

A joint household consisting of a group of brothers may separate. (...) but in the compound they may have separate cooking arrangements.[47]

Those included in the *khandan* are immediate relatives from the father's side like uncles with wives and children. Those cousins included in *khandan* are the direct and immediate *sharika*. The extended *sharika* forms the immediate *biradari*. The other difference between *khandan* and *sharika* is that the latter has more negative connotations; no one would say he is my *sharik*, but to say we belong to one *khandan* is the usual way of showing kinship affiliation.

The family is the basic unit of social organization, at the same time it is also the genesis of all the conflicts. The brothers and sisters live together with their parents and after the marriage of the brothers the property is divided which gives rise to conflicts when separate households are established.

No doubt, everyone knows one another in a village, but the boundary walls of the *ghar* and *khandan* are full of secrets—family secrets. They are called the *izzat* of the family. In the presence of strangers, no quarrel takes place or is even mentioned. In the words of Moore:

> Thus a family quarrel is generally kept quiet within the family as long as possible.[48]

For example, if husband and wife are not on speaking terms because of some conflict, and a guest or visitor comes, who could even be a close relative of the wife, they would act and communicate as if nothing had happened. The strifes between parents and children are also not made public. This does not mean that they are always kept secret or remain secret. Sometimes—not too often—they become so loud and public that it is not only the neighbours who hear and see them but the whole village witnesses it. Divulgence of family conflicts and quarrels to outsiders is considered to be a betrayal of the family, especially when talked about by the women (wives of the brothers). One could say that each family and individual has an external image, in the village, which is known to everyone, and an internal family image. It would be the greatest insult for a husband, child or wife to be taunted before strangers. Very often these insults become the cause of greater conflicts on issues which when confined within the boundaries of the house would not have mattered at all, but reach enormous proportions when they become public, even leading to a divorce or a temporary separation.

The first conflict worth mentioning which arises between brothers, is after their marriage. Before marriage, disagreements among siblings are minor and are solved by mere intervention of the mother, father, or the elder brother or even amongst themselves. After the marriage of various brothers small differences among the wives as to who works more, who does not clean the house, whose relatives are treated better than those of the others, lead to the separation of the households of the brothers. This is when sometimes serious conflicts between the brothers over the division of land and property take place. Disputes between the mother or sister and wife are very common and often lead to separation, divorce (due to the pressure by the mother, father, sisters or brothers) or the separation of households.

A joint family with grown up grandchildren is the ideal of all the villagers. The examples of such families who manage to keep together are always quoted. As already mentioned quarrels between the mother-in-law and daughter-in-law are very common. There are different reasons given, such as a mother-in-law wanting to avenge what happened to her as a daughter-in-law; to keep her influence over the son and to show her authority, etc. Living together is a source of strength and honour for the family in the eyes of the outsiders. The division of the property after the death of the father and mother is accepted and considered normal, but if it takes place during the lifetime of the father, it is a source of disgrace for the family and is often attributed to the daughters-in-law of the family. In the words of Moore:

> The joint family is considered the ideal family, though after father's death, sons often divided the property. To force a division of property before Chacha's death would have been an insult to his name and would have caused a painful split in the family.[49]

Territorial Ties

The territorial affiliations cut across the lines established by the *biradari, sharika,* and other kinship ties. This, so-called, vertical unity includes people of different socio-economic status in the village and is based on common economic interests—trade specialization of different *biradaris* and the *seypi,* also known as *Jajmani,* system. These ties include *hamsaya* (neighbour), *mohalla* (quarter; an extension of the *hamsaya*) and *pind* (village) .

Hamsaya, Mohalla, or Patti

Hamsaya is the smallest unit of the vertical unity of the village. The relationship of a *hamsaya* is very important in the context of the village. The exchange of freshly prepared food and other edibles is a daily routine. The importance in Islam of *hamsaya* is also referred to by the villagers.[50] *Hamsayas* share the walls, streets and many other things, which may, however, lead to several conflicts between them.

Similarly a village is divided into different *mohallas* or *pattis*[51] which are very often named after the dominant *biradari* or family living there. *Mohalla* is the extension of *hamsaya*. The relation of the *mohalla* is especially important from the point of view of women, as this may be her only access to others, especially since her social connections and ties, if spread over the whole village, are not seen very positively. Slocum and others observed in the villages near Lahore:

> The relationship with neighbours, who in a majority of cases are also relatives, are generally close and informal. Men have frequent contacts with persons other than those of the neighbourhood, but the contacts of the women in every day life are primarily confined to women and children in the neighbourhood.[52]

Similarly he wrote about *mohalla* or *patti* (street):

> Separated in these respects, the residents of different patties develop 'in-group' 'out-group' feelings which may be latent, but become evident in matters such as representation in the village panchayat. Open hostility may also exist and factions may sometimes be formed on patti basis (...).[53]

Although neighbouring women of one *mohalla* very often become 'ceremonial' sisters, the common reasons for disagreements are the children who play together, the cleaning of the street at the entrance; animals straying into the houses of others. These incidents could sometimes lead to serious conflicts but, as a rule they are limited to the exchange of hot words. Not

Diagram No. 1 showing the social organization based on kinship and territorial relations from the point of view of one family.

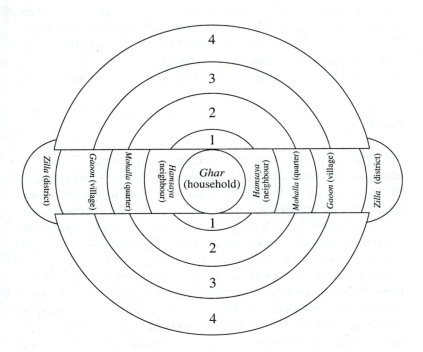

1 *Khandan* (extended family representing paternal uncles, aunts, and their children).

2 *Sharika* (patrilocal patrilineage)

3 *Biradari* (lineage, clan) of first degree; includes *goots* (generally translated as sub-castes) within one *biradari* or those of t he *biradari* who migrated from or belong to the same village, district area. For example *Chemee, Chathee, Chadhair, or Chanwanwalee, Ambersaree, Gurdaspuree,* etc. among the *Jats*.

4 *Biradari* of the second degree, people belonging to the same *biradari* like *Jats, Araeen, Gujars, Rajputs,* etc.

being on speaking terms for some time normally resolves the issue. The neighbours have common walls and roofs. The question of boundaries, if the walls are to be constructed anew, the sharing of the costs of the construction of the walls, use or misuse of the common walls often give rise to more serious conflicts. Still more serious and even more dangerous hostilities arise when young boys and girls fall in love with each other and run away. The exchange of gifts, and the necessities of life also give rise to minor antagonism especially if someone does not want to lend his or her things and if at the time of return they are broken, etc.

Pind

The village is administratively considered a unit. There are economic interests attached to this unit where the villagers have to act as members. For example the supply of irrigation water, road construction, schools, hospital, and other such benefits are common to the whole village. If the rains fail, animal sacrifice or charity—distributions of sweet cooked porridge—is made on behalf of the whole village. At a wedding especially that of a peasant family all the different *biradaris*, especially of the *kammis* do special jobs. In intra-village sport contests the honour of the village is usually at stake. This concept of unity becomes even more strong if the village concerned is inhabited by only one *biradari* and more so if it has one leader. The village is a collection of different *biradaries*, *sharikas*, and *khandans*. Broadly speaking even the whole district becomes a sign of identity and importance and very often people are called according to the names of the areas they originate from, such as Faisalabadi, Sialkoti, Lahori. Sometimes the province one hails from becomes an affiliation.

The two types of ties explained above are not alternatives but complementary in the social organization of the village community. It is very difficult to determine which affiliation predominates. One's *hamsaya* could be, and very often is, one's close relative since they share the same property. Non-relative neighbours are said to be better than relatives living far away because they share one's pleasures and sorrows. The ceremonial relationship, like ceremonial sisters, mentioned already, is not only extended to children and real relatives but also in some cases to the whole *mohalla*. Different streets or *mohallas* are named after the dominant *biradari* living there, like *jatan da mohalla*, the region, if it is a subgroup of the *biradari*, like *chanwan walyan da mohalla* or the *goot* of the sub-*biradari* as *chadhairan da mohalla* or it could be even after the name of a famous man of a family as, *budu keyan da mohalla*. The world of men is outside; the fields, or the *haveli* or business or working place (shops, or power-looms), and they make friends and ceremonial relations there.

As one moves from the centre to the periphery of links and ties, every following unit includes predecessors (*khandan* includes more than one family and *biradari* includes several *khandans*) and at every higher level cohesion, authority of the leader, secrecy, feelings of duty and responsibility, and closeness of kinship ties decrease. *Ghar* and *mohalla* are the best examples of the above-mentioned characteristics.

There is solidarity against the outside; *ghar* (the nucleus family) against another *ghar*, *khandan* against another *khandan* and *biradari* against another *biradari*, as also one *mohalla* against another *mohalla* and one village against the other village. A well known village saying puts it thus: 'I against my brother, I and my brothers against our cousins, and we all against the *biradari* and our *biradari* against the other *biradari* and so on'. This could be taken as a general principle but there are also some exceptions.

The social organization of the village is shown in diagram no. 1. Here, two types of ties, i.e. kinship and territorial ones are put together. It is important to note that the different units, steps or stages of ties of the two cannot be compared nor seen as parallels. Questions like whether the neighbourhood follows or preceeds the *khandan* or what is the position of *mohalla* to *biradari* cannot be asked. The two must be seen, on the one hand, independently, both of them having a centre which opens towards the periphery with respect to the feelings of unity etc., but, on the other hand, for understanding the community they must be seen together. They not only share a common centre, but the stages of the ties are also interwoven and sometimes one is preferred to the other like *hamsaya* instead of *biradari*, etc. The conclusion we could draw from this is that there is a centre called *apna* (own),[54] which becomes weaker and weaker as we move towards the periphery until we reach *ghair* (other).[55] This is demonstrated in diagram no. 2 (p. 78).

This diagram represents the point of view of an individual or a family. A village consists of several hundred *ghars* and *khandans* all of whom make similar diagrams intersecting with each other in one or another form. The result of this intersection and interaction could be called the social organization of the village.

Conflicts arise either within or between these different units. The nature and reasons of these conflicts are different in different units as are also the solutions to these problems. As a general principle it could be said that while moving from the *ghar* towards the *biradari*, from *hamsaya* towards *pind*, from *apna* towards *ghair* one moves from an atmosphere and situation of hierarchically oriented, own, informal, respect, and status relationship towards anonymous, strange, formal, and unknown. These terms must be considered value free—an informal and known relationship does not mean a harmonious relationship, with or without less problems or conflicts. It could be quite the other way round but to this point we shall come later on.

Legal Pluralism: The Reality of Multiple Choice

An important aspect of the South Asian legal systems[56] in general, and the village legal systems, as also the case with the area of present study, in particular, is that at least theoretically the people have a variety of legal options. It consists of different systems and subsystems, as also noted by Adamson Hoebel, a famous legal anthropologist, about Pakistan's legal system some three decades ago:

> The legal system of Pakistan does not constitute a neatly integrated whole; it is made up of an undetermined multiplicity of subsystems. Many of these are disjunctive in their relations to other. Most obvious among these systems is the Formal National law which arches as an ethereal dome above all the lesser systems. (...) Deeply imbedded in the village and tribal areas of Pakistan is a vast array of local folk systems of law varying from village to village and area to area. (...) Folk Law, too, is a relatively uncharted universe. (...) Ideologically, it incorporates Islamic law, but the folk ignorance of Islam is in fact profound. The Great Tradition and the Little Traditions are, as is to be expected, two different things.[57]

The main systems or subsystems, as also identified in the above quotation, could be named as: the official justice system, and the traditional justice system including the religious system. These systems function, at times, as independent systems and have their own subsystems, for example the traditional system has nuclear family, extended family, *biradari* (lineage), and village (containing different *biradaries*), etc. The customs of these different institutions are very often different from one another. Sometimes the official, the traditional, and the religious systems are used by the people, and these function as subsystems and they become part of one system. The multiplicity of the legal options and the constraints in their selection could be illustrated with the help of an example.

Ashraf's distressed wife came to the fields and said that Goora and his sons had forcibly occupied their *haveli* (animal-house) and had driven out their animals. It had been in Ashraf's use for more than forty years. His animal-house was situated at a place officially meant for a pond at the time not in use. Ashraf was not the only one using this place as his animal-house. Nearly one-fourth of the village occupants used this common village land. The roots of the conflict were actually laid forty years earlier when Ashraf constructed his animal-house on the land. Some prominent families of the village tried to stop the construction.

Ashraf and his brothers, who were young and strong at that time, resisted all such effort, and managed to construct the animal-house. The position of Ashraf's family changed as he and his brothers grew old, started living in separate households, after dividing their property including the said animal-house.[58]

The question was: how would Ashraf get back his animal-house? Some of the major possibilities open to him were:

* Ashraf would use direct physical force for its recovery.
* He would go to the *panchayat* (council of the village elders and respectables) which was the traditional forum.
* He could choose to go to the police and courts, i.e. the official forum.
* The choice of going to a religious practitioner for charms and prayers was also open to him.
* The use of a combination of different possibilities or forums was also possible.

The choice between these different options and forums were, however, not as available as it appeared to be. There were definite limitations as explained below:

Use of direct physical force was the most common method and to the people the only successful way of taking a *badla* (revenge) for regaining the damaged *izzat*.[59] In a similar case, in case study two, Karim and his son, Akram, tried to recover their plot (a piece of land meant for a construction of the house) which had been forcibly occupied by Anwar, but the latter along with his sons killed Akram. Although the use of direct physical force functions as a control mechanism against the emergence of conflicts, it does not offer a solution. Force is also difficult to use by the physically and economically weaker sections of the village community.

Moreover, one cannot simply go to the members of the *panchayat* and ask them to meet. Contacting the *panchayat*, it subsequently meeting, and the effectiveness of its decisions depend upon many factors and most importantly on who the opponent was. If the opponent belonged to a higher social status group—a *zamindar* against a *kammi*—one may choose to contact the *panchayat* without the fear of damaging one's *izzat*. But if one was involved in a conflict against a physically and economically stronger opponent, the *panchayat* would not proceed against him, or its decision—if contrary, could be made ineffective. At the same time, engaging in a quarrel with one from the lower social status group is taken as an insult to the one from the higher in the village.[60] Conversely, if the opponent comes from a lower social status group—a *kammi* against a farmer—calling on the *panchayat* to proceed against him would be considered an act of cowardice. Further, it is taken in the sense of increasing the importance of the opponent.

There was yet another possibility: both may belong to the same social group (craftsman vs craftsman or landlord vs landlord), the one who approaches the *panchayat* first for the meeting to be convened shows himself to be the weaker. The best method is to let a third person, such as a relative, a friend, or a member of the *panchayat*, arrange the meeting and pretend indifference to it himself. The *panchayat* does not always meet automatically after the occurrence of an incidence. They very often do not even meet on request. A conflict must reach a certain peak before one could expect the *panchayat* to meet. Similarly, the *panchayat* need not reach a compromise or decision, and the decisions of the *panchayat*[61] were not always accepted, especially by the stronger members.

One may choose to go to the police and courts to resolve the issue. They may be approached for remedy as the first choice, or it may come after the failure of the *panchayat*. The decision to go to the police/courts involves a similar risk of blemishing the *izzat*. You often hear 'if you are a man, brave and strong, come forward and fight directly. Why do you go to uncle police?' and that the real *badla*, as already mentioned, could only be inflicted directly or by close relatives and not by the police or courts.[62] But, on the other hand, if going to the police is only for the purpose of harassing the opponent and impoverishing him, it could become a source of adding to the *izzat*, especially by winning a court case against one's rival. This competition of winning the cases in the courts between the rivals leads to frequent litigation or what Darling called 'addiction to litigation'. He wrote:

> There is one aspect of rural life in Punjab which is commonly quoted as an example of the cultivator's extravagance, and that is his almost passionate love of litigation. 'The people of the Punjab', says a report of 1925, 'are greatly addicted to litigation and the litigation is of a more serious nature than in most other provinces.' (...) It is not uncommon to hear of suits dealing with the minutest fraction of an acre being fought up to the High Court, and of criminal cases involving the expenditures of thousands of rupees.[63]

One of the reasons for this 'addiction to litigation' is also to be found in the way the justice system functions. The most important consideration dissuading a person from choosing this forum is the expenses involved. The courts are not only very expensive, but also very corrupt, hence out of reach of the poor.

The possibility of going to a *pir* (saint/religious leader), or a *maulvi* (one who officiates at prayers) for a *taawiz* (amulette), visiting the tomb of a saint or by praying directly to God for justice provide an alternative for those who cannot afford any of the above-mentioned forums. This is called the forum of the poor and have-nots, who still hold the simple belief that such means may help directly or indirectly.

The most commonly adopted strategy or method is a combination of these various means. In such cases any one of these forums may function as a pressure instrument—usually the courts and police. The compromises/decisions of the *panchayat* are made and readjusted according to the changing situation of a case in the courts.[64] The combination of forums changes if the complainant is too poor to bear the court expenditures. The blend in this case could be the traditional and the religious forum.

The choice of a forum is also affected by the characteristics and nature of the conflict. Some conflicts, especially those concerning women, demand solutions other than those for those of land and property. For example, the son of Alam killed his own sister as it turned out that she had illicit relations with the son of Goora. Limitations in such a choice are also a consequence of the type of group affiliations, party loyalties or traditional belief systems of individuals involved in a conflict. For example, the conflicts within or between *ghars*, *khandans*, *sharikas*, or *biradaries*, are generally solved within the same institution.

Legal Pluralism: Some Theoretical Considerations

Legal pluralism is the central issue in legal anthropology today. There may be differences of opinion about its definition, but there is a general consensus among the legal anthropologists that all the societies of the world are legally plural,[65] though not of the same nature or even identical. Some societies may be said to be less plural in character than others[66]—the result of de-pluralisation.[67] With respect to legal systems, the world societies may be divided into three broad categories: traditional, modern, and mixed societies.

The states with the possibility of, or tendency towards, a unitary legal system could either be extremely modern national states like those of Western Europe, having only an official justice system where only the state is capable and responsible for issuing laws; or extremely traditional (acephalous) societies—customs of the society as the only source of law—with no official justice system. The national states, with official justice systems, claim[68] or at least have the theoretical possibility of having a unitary legal system.[69] Although, according to the legal anthroplogists, even these states with the official justice system as the only recognized system are in practice legally plural societies.[70] Similarly, even traditional societies do not have a unitary system of rules.[71] It was, perhaps, this type of legal pluralism of the traditional societies which led some early anthropologists to assert that the traditional societies do not possess any law.[72]

It is not the same thing to have plural legal possibilities within the traditional or official system as it is to have both the traditional and the official justice systems with their subsystems. Most of the societies of the world and especially the post-colonial third world national states like Pakistan have both the traditional and the official systems of justice with their subsystems which is sometimes known as legal dualism.

Legal pluralism was defined by J. Vanderlinden, in very general terms, as 'the existence, within a given society, of different legal mechanisms applied to identical cases'.[73] On the question of, what these legal mechanisms are and how they function L. Pospisil, a renowned legal anthropologist, advanced the idea of hierarchically arranged legal levels. He gave the following description of the existence and functioning of the multiple legal institutions in any complex society:

> (...) every functioning subgroup of a society has its own legal system which is necessarily different in some repects from those of the other subgroups. (...) The totality of the principles incorporated in the legal decisions of an authority of a society's subgroups constitutes that subgroup's legal system. Since the legal systems form a hierarchy reflecting the degrees of inclusiveness of the corresponding subgroups, the total of the legal systems of subgroups of the same type and inclusiveness (for example, family, lineage, community, political confederacy) I propose to call legal level.[74]

Pospisil's emphasis on and claim of the universal existence of subgroups and hierarchy of legal levels is somewhat problematic. This may be valid or a more suitable idea for a unitary system society (only official or traditional system) but not for the study of societies having multiple legal systems not arranged hierarchically. Therefore, the idea of legal levels is not appropriate at least for the Punjabi village society under study. The traditional and the official systems are also not hierar-chically placed. Similarly, as far as family, extended family, and to some extent sublineage (*sharika*) is concerned, the idea of legal level may be valid but when we talk about different lineages (*biradari*) they are more autonomous groups than an inclusive entity.

S.F. Moore, another well-known legal anthropologist, presented the idea of 'semi-autonomous social fields' for the study of legally plural societies:

> It is well established that between the body politic and the individual, there are interposed various smaller organized social fields to which the individual belongs. These social fields have their own customs and rules and means of coercing or inducing compliance. The semi-autonomous social field is par excellence a suitable way of defining areas for social anthropoligical study in complex societies. The semi-autonomous social field is defined and its boundaries identified not by its organization (it may be a corporate group, it may not) but by a processual characteristic, the fact that it can generate rules and coerce or induce compliance to them. Thus an arena in which a number of corporate groups deal with each other may be a semi-autonomous social field. Also the corporate groups themselves may each constitute a semi-autonomous social field. Many such fields may articulate with other in such a way as to form complex chains, rather the way social network of indivuduals, when attached to each other, (...).[75]

The importance of this definition is its emphasis on the horizontal dimensions of legal pluralism. He considered the social subfields as semi-autonomous. The individual does not only obey the rules of the state but also other sources like the traditions and customs of his group or tribe.

The aim and objective of the present study is not only to present a morphology of the Pakistani legal system but also to see which groups and parts of society use which system or part of the system. In other words we want to find out what role money, influence, honour, and prestige, etc. play in legal pluralism. It is my contention that all of the several legal systems, at times even competing with each other, are, nearly exclusively, serving the interests of the powerful sections of the community. The weak and the have-nots of the village society seek refuge in religious beliefs, and affiliation to those who are powerful in society.

Methodology

The question was how to document this legal pluralism to find out the law in practice? Case study method was chosen as a key instrument for the collection of data. This method has a long standing affiliation with the legal anthropology where it came to be known as the most appropriate instrument for reaching at the 'real law' of a society. A case study, according to Mitchell:

> (...) refers to an observer's data; i.e. the documentation of some particular phenomenon or set of events which has been assembled with the explicit end in view of drawing theoretical conclusions from it. The focus of the case study may be a single individual as the life-history approach or it may be a set of actors engaged in a sequence of activities either over a restricted or over an extended period of time. What is important is not the content of the case study as such but the use to which the data are put to support theoretical conclusions.[76]

Gluckman distinguished between 'apt illustraton', 'social situation' and 'case studies' whereas C. Mitchell considered them as types of case phenomenon falling along a continuum of increasing complexity. 'Apt illustration', which lies near one limit, according to Mitchell is 'normally a description of some fairly simple event or occurrence in which the operation of some general principle is clearly illustrated',[77] and that: 'clearly one good case can illuminate the working of a social system in a way that a series of morphological statements cannot achieve'.[78]

The 'apt illustration', known as 'trouble cases' in legal anthropology, was described by its pioneer researchers, Llewellyn, a jurist, and Hoebel, a legal anthropologist, as the easiest way of reaching at the law, especially of an illiterate society: 'The trouble-cases, sought out and examined with care, are the safest main road into the discovery of law'.[79] *The Cheyenne Way*, a book written by these authors, was the initial and still the best demonstration, in legal anthroplogy, of this method, which came to be recognized by legal anthropologists like Gulliver:

But undoubtedly a major watershed was the publication in 1941 of The Cheyenne Way by Llewellyn and Hoebel. This book marks the beginning of modern studies in the anthropology of law, and particularly in its clear identification and detailed treatment of the case study as the unit of analysis. (...) The Cheyenne Way (1941) was a remarkable exposition and demonstration of what could be done.[80]

The other outstanding and well-known examples of this method in legal anthropology include Gluckman's work *The Judicial Process Among the Barotse of Northern Rhodesia* and Bohannan's book *Justice and Judgement Among the Tiv*. The idea behind this method is to collect as many trouble cases as possible, and study the way they were solved. When enough examples of cases had been analysed this could serve as a sort of code book of the law of the concerned society. In the words of Gulliver:

In saying this, I say nothing new. As long ago as 1942, Hoebel rightly declared that anthropologists must reach their 'generalizations from particulars which are case, cases, and more cases'.[81]

Following this approach, hundreds of cases, ranging from very simple to serious conflicts with their solutions, were gathered. A few of them are presented in the appendix with complete details, some are referred to and briefly mentioned in the text at different places and others were used to generalize the typology of conflicts in chapter two.

To achieve the objectives of the study using the case study method, two types of data were needed: firstly, data on the types of conflicts, on reasons of their occurrence, and on units or groups involved in them. Secondly, data on the process of conflict solution or the functioning of the justice system by way of traditional methods and through the official system. Neither of the two types of data could be accurately collected without staying in the village over a long period of time, collecting past stories, and consulting files of the cases, etc. More so because neither do all types of conflicts and quarrels occur in a short period of time nor are their solutions to be found immediately. Some of the conflicts go on for generations and others have long-lasting effects.

My short stays during the last three years,[82] supported by permanent mail communication with friends and relatives, providing up-to-date information on the current situation of the ongoing conflicts, personal past knowledge and experience, with the conflicts and the solution process, form the major source of the data used in this study. The stories of the conflicts from the near past, especially of those still continuing in one form or another, have also been collected and included in the analysis. The conflicts in my own family, among relatives, neighbours and friends which were observed and recorded also make an important source because of personal involvement in some of them which enabled me to examine very closely how the police and courts handled them. Different members of the *panchayats* (village council), the Chairman and the members of the Basic Democracies, partly responsible for seeking solutions to the village conflicts, were interviewed. I held discussions with other villagers about their views regarding the conflicts and their proposed solutions. Parties involved in conflicts were interviewed when possible, and the records from the court or the lawyer were collected.

In the courts, several lawyers were interviewed, who were very co-operative and extended all kinds of help. The clerks (*munshies*) of the lawyers and those of the judges and the court clerks were also interviewed and discussions were held at a personal level. While the records of the police and courts were not easily accessible, most of the difficulties were encountered at the police station from where the data were then collected through *parchi* and *sifarish* (intercession) of the Reader to the Senior Superintendent of police. A lawyer known to me, said: 'Only two methods operate in the police and courts: the language of money and the language of *parchi* and *sifarish*'. The other principle he mentioned was: 'everything (actually he meant every individual) in the courts has a price but certain things have a higher price'. One day, he came back very angry from the court of a magistrate who had advised him to buy one *pao aqal*[83] (half a pound of wisdom) from the market, since, as he was told, his opposing lawyer had good connections with the magistrate. This can happen quite often in the courts. Normally, notes were taken in a simple notebook. However, a tape recorder was also used wherever permissible. Tape recorders were especially used in the courts, which the lawyers seemed to have enjoyed.

It is also important to mention some weaknesses and limitations in the collection of data. The first weakness is that the data are not homogeneous. On one side, we have Misalpur (the village where fieldwork was conducted) as the basis of our data, especially for the traditional system but, on the other side, we have Faisalabad District and Tehsil Courts as the basic unit, where scores of villages are included. Also one police station, covers more than fifty villages. In the beginning, we tried to reduce the court data to the village concerned. However, it turned out to be virtually impossible because no records are maintained by villages. We have, therefore, tried to limit the data to the village side only, the record of the conflicts of the towns, like Faisalabad, were not taken into account. We may say that the perimeters observed were Misalpur (village), Naglan (police station), Faisalabad (Tehsil and District courts; but only the village side).

Being an ex-inhabitant of the area, and particularly of the village, some eighteen years ago, gave me some advantages, like an easy access to information. I was already known in the village, having friends and relatives, and was thus in a position to observe personal and family conflicts etc. It had some disadvantages, too. The information is, at least it might be seen so, one-sided. My role in the village was already fixed. But the question is: isn't information always one-sided?

The reactions of the villagers ranged from non-seriousness, indifference and requests for help in the courts and police because of my contact with them (police and courts), to expecting some solution to the problems of justice. My role and status in the village, as has already been mentioned, was fixed beforehand, because of my belonging to a family, *biradar*i and party, etc. Apart from the members of my own family, relatives and friends who helped me in collecting data, the people involved in litigations themselves came to tell me the stories of their conflicts requesting help.

NOTES

1. Since there is not much ethno-legal literature available on Pakistan, I have included ethno-legal literature on India in the regional literature. The other reason for treating the two sources together is that pre-independence literature has no such division.
2. Cohn, 1967, p. 154
3. Moore, 1985, p. 6
4. Cohn, 1965, p. 82
5. Hoebel, 1965, p. 44
6. Baxi, 1982, p. 331
7. Moore, 1985, p. 6
8. Cohn, 1965, p. 82
9. Hoebel, 1965, p. 44
10. Baxi, 1982, p. 331
11. Baxi, 1982, p. 331
12. Cohn, 1967, p. 155
13. The direction of thoughts initiated by officials such as Warren Hastings, Macaulay, Metcalf and others i.e. of criticizing one's own policies and emphasizing the colonial nature of the official system was continued by others: 'It was amazing (...) that anything so unsuited to a simple people as the English law should ever have been foisted upon India; (...) a monstrous injustice that Indians should be subjected to laws designed for quite different social conditions (...). All injustices by former oppressors, Asiatic or European, appear as a blessing when compared with the justice of Supreme Court.' In: Moon, 1930, pp. 52–4.

   Moon wrote: 'A simple people had become habituated to systematized perjury, had been corrupted by unscrupulous lawyers, had been taught to flock to the law courts, and to revel in the tainted atmosphere of bribery and chicanery that surrounds them. Litigation had become a national pastime and the criminal law a recognized and well-tried means of harassing, imprisoning and even hanging one's enemies. (...) It is probably impossible for sophisticated people like ourselves to provide an appropriate criminal system for a peasant society, whose customs and outlook are so entirely different from our own.' Moon, 1930, pp. 52–4.

Similar ideas seem to be put forth by Cohn and Moore with the change of expressions like 'simple people' and 'sophisticated people'. Compare this with the quotation of Cohn in the text in which he writes: 'It was evident that courts did not settle disputes but were used either as a form of gambling on the part of the legal speculators who were landlords or merchants and turned to the courts to wrest property from the 'rightful' owners, or as a threat in a dispute.' Cohn, 1967, p. 154.

14. This becomes all the more clear if we follow the discussions about the definition of law by anthropologists, dealt with in detail in the next chapter. Here we find the 'lawless primitive savages' turning into 'noble savages' who do not need the 'codified' law and the law enforcing agencies like police and courts: 'But customs are an integral part of the life of primitive peoples. There is no compulsive submission to them. They are not followed because the weight of tradition overwhelms a man (...) a custom is obeyed there because it is intimately interwined in a meticulous and ordered manner', Radin, 1953, p. 223; from Diamond, 1974, p. 256.

Uchendu wrote about the Igbo: '(...) the use of force is minimal or absent (...) there are leaders rather than rulers, and (...) cohesion is achieved by rules rather than by laws and by concensus rather than by dictation.' Uchendu, *The Igbo of Southeast Nigeria*, 1965, p. 46; from Diamond, 1974, p. 257.

So much so that we find the civilization through law condemned and the 'primitive' through custom idealized. Seagle wrote: 'The dispute whether primitive societies have law or custom, is not merely a dispute over words. Only confusion can result from treating them as interchangeable phenomena. If custom is spontaneous and automatic law is the product of organized force.' Seagle, W., *The History of Law*, 1946, p. 35; from Diamond, 1974, p. 257.

Similarly Diamond himself wrote: 'We live in a law-ridden society; law has cannibalized the institutions which it presumably reinforces or with which it interacts. Accordingly, morality continues to be reduced to or confused with legality.' Diamond, 1974, p. 257.

15. For details see Law Reform Commission Reports, 1958–59 and 1967–70.

16. Law Reform Commission Report, 1967–70, p. 102.

17. Law Reform Commission Report, 1967–70, p. 102.

18. Berry, 1966, p. 98.

19. The statement is based on the discusssions with the people in this and other villages known to the author.

20. For example Baxi writes about India: 'The lesson to draw from these ongoing explorations is not that there are no differences between the

NSLS (Non-State Legal System) and the SLS (State Legal System) but that these differences are of degree rather than kind', 1982, p. 347.

21. 1981 District Census Report of Faisalabad, p. 106.
22. 1981 District Census Report of Faisalabad, p. 3.
23. The Urdu or Punjabi terms are simply made plural by adding;-s,-es or as suitable.
24. All the farmers together are sometimes called farmer *biradari* especially by the non-farmers.
25. The details about the origin and distribution of these and other *biradaries* and castes in the whole of the subcontinent is provided in *A Glossary of the Tribes and Castes of the Punjab and North-West Frontier Province* based on the Census Report for the Punjab, 1883, by Sir Denzil Ibbetson, K.C.S.I., and the Census Report for the Punjab, 1892, by the Hon. Mr. E.D. Maclagan, C.S.I., compiled by H.A. Rose.
26. The best description of these *biradaries* living here is provided by Darling in his book *The Punjab Peasant in Prosperity and Debt*. 1925, pp. 25, 32–8, 44–5, 61, and 62. We have quoted some passages from his book, *The Budhopur Report* by the members of the Cambridge University Asian Group.
27. Darling wrote: 'jat (...) is the ideal cultivator and revenue-payer. Ploughing, weeding or reaping, he will bear the burden and the heat of the day, and at night take his turn at the well.' (1925, p. 35).
28. Darling characterized a Rajput as: 'Proud of his birth and traditions, more accustomed to fight than to till, loving the bravura of life and scorning its drudgery, (...). Many rajputs almost pride themselves on their inefficiency as cultivators, claiming that their real business is fighting and sport.' (1925, p. 33,34).
29. In the words of Darling: 'For the ant-like industry there is no one in the Punjab to touch the Araeen. (...) Though often a farmer, he is by tradition and instinct a market-gardener, and alone amongst cultivators rivals the jat. `For cattle, says the proverb, `give me the cow, and for a cultivator give me the Araeen'. He turns his milk into butter for sale, and his children have to be content with the buttermilk that remains. (...) *Mal gain, te rayat Araeen'.* (1925, p. 44).
30. Darling wrote about *Gujars*: 'A hundred years ago most of them, (gujars and dogars), were shepherds or graziers, and lazy pastoral habits still prevail.' (1925, p. 61).
31. 'The district of Faisalabad has the maximum population in Punjab, i.e. 9.9% (in 21 districts) (...)' (1981 Census Report of Punjab Province 1984, p. 7).
32. Eglar wrote about the *seypi* system: 'A seypi, or contract, is a relationship established not merely between two individuals, but between two families who become seypi to each other. (...) Usually seypi relationship between

two families were established generations ago and have been inherited by the families (...)' (1960, p. 35).

33. Walsh, 1929, p. 10.

34. Hershman, P., *Punjabi Kinship and Marriage*. Delhi, 1981. Eglar, Z., *A Punjabi Village in Pakistan*. New York, 1960. Kessinger, T.G., Vilaytpur 1848–1968, *Social and Economic Change in a North Indian Village*. Berkeley, 1974. Slocum, W.L., Jamila Akhtar and A.F. Sahi, *Village Life in Lahore District: A Study of Selected Sociological Aspects*. Lahore, 1960. Izmirlian, Jr. H., *Caste, Kin, and Politics in a Punjabi Village*. Berkeley, 1964.

Social and political organization of *Jats* of Punjab, especially the Sikhs, also have got a lot of space in literature: Jassal, H.S., *Leaders, and Leadership structure in two Villages in Punjab*, India. Michigan, 1971. Pettigrew, J., Robber Noblemen, *A Study of the Political System of the Sikh Jats*. London, 1975.

35. Pakistani (Indian) villages could be divided into several different categories with respect to the composition of *biradaris* and leadership, like one *biradari* one head, one *biradari* multi head, multi-*biradari* multi-head and multi-*biradari* one head etc.

36. For similar observations about the social structure of the Indian villages consult; Srinivas 1955, M. W. Smith 1955, and B. Cohn 1965. For example Cohn writes: 'Most individuals in rural India have two sets of predominant social relations, one that ties them to a village community which may be viewed as a vertical set of ties and one that connects them horizontally to their biradari or jati (subcaste).' Cohn, 1965, p. 82.

37. Cohn wrote about the social organization of the Chamars of North India, 'The basic social and economic unit of the Chamars is the households (ghar), which is usually a nuclear family; the households in turn are united into lineages (khandan), normally traced through the male line. We may view the Chamars' social organization somewhat as the cross section of an onion, the centre ring being the household, the next the *khandan*, the next ring the hamlet, the next the six hamlets of Senapur, the next ring the network of villages into which Chamars marry and from which they take brides - a circle of four to ten miles, and finally the named subcaste, Jaisvara, whose members spread over many of the districts of Eastern and Central Uttar Pradesh.' (1965, p. 82).

38. For further details, see Rao, 1988, 200ff, Eglar, 1960, p. 75–9, and Hershman, 1981, p. 98.

39. It is mostly avoided to ask if you already know something about him because it could also be taken as an insult.

40. Eglar, 1960, p. 47.

41. Eglar observed: '(...) all the members show great solidarity when the occasion demands it.' (1960, p. 78).

42. There is some difference of opinion about the meaning. It is very often translated as 'subcaste' but Hershman disagreed with this and translated it with 'clan'. See for detail Hershman, 1981, p. 84.

   'Parentage; lineage; race; pedigree; stock of a family; subdivision of a tribe or caste; tribe; population'; from Ferozsons Urdu-English Dictionary.

   It is in this meaning that Eglar found it: 'A biradari is a patrilineage.' Eglar, 1960, p. 75.

43. Since marriages, among close relatives from the side of the father, take place, the mother's side might also be a part of the *sharika*.

44. Ahmad, 1972, p. 106.

45. 'Literally, Vartan bhanji means 'dealing in sweets,' and it has the extended meaning of 'dealing in relationships'.' Eglar, 1960, p. 105.

46. Eglar, 1960, p. 75.

47. Eglar, 1960, p. 74.

48. Moore, 1985, p. 25.

49. Moore, 1985, p. 25.

50. Mention is made of the Hadith of the Holy Prophet (PBUH) which says that *hamsaya* is only a little short of inheritors.

51. Marian W. Smith writes about a Punjabi village in India: 'houses are divided off in some sort of order according to the *pattis*, *tarafs* or other internal subdivisions observed in the village constitution. The subdivisions of the villages have both boundaries and recognized membership, even though these may not exactly correspond.' (1955, p. 166).

52. Slocum, 1960, p. 29.

53. Slocum, 1960, p. 31.

54. Eglar wrote: However, a clear distinction is made between members of the kin group who are more nearly and those who are more distantly related. Father and son, brother and sister are called *apna*, one's own; uncles, cousins, and other more distant relatives in the male line of descent are *biradari*.' (Eglar, 1960, p. 75).

55. According to Eglar: 'In contrast to the family, the *biradari*, and the *rishtadar*, everyone else is *obr* or, alternatively, *opra*, the people who are not related and consequently who are not kin'. (Eglar, 1960, p. 84).

56. The Rajasthani villager has a variety of options available for the public airing of a grievance. Here are dispute-processing forums that represent the ideological interests of religion, the dominant caste with the village, and the state. Each forum has different economic-political origins, represents a different philosophy of justice, and has its own procedural and substantive laws: state, village 'customary,' or religious.' (Moore, 1993, p. 523). See also Cohn, 1967.

57. Hoebel, 1967, p. 44.

58. For further details of the related case of Ashraf's animal-house see case study 1.

59. The meaning and importance of *izzat* in village life is explained in detail in the analysis in chapter five.

60. This is one of the reasons that if someone from the upper social group (landlord) has grievances with someone from the lower status group (craftsmen), he will try to instigate or even bribe someone else from the lower status group to start a quarrel with the person with whom he has a conflict and promise him subsequent support.

61. Details are given in the chapter on traditional system.

62. For details consult the chapter on official courts in practice.

63. Darling, 1925 (rep.) 1978, p. 67.

64. Detail is given in chapter five (conclusion) and case studies.

65. 'Legal pluralism as the normal, quasi-universal attribute of all societies. Legal pluralism stems from sociological pluralism, and no society is completely homogenous: even segmentary societies are in a sense divided.' (Norbert Rouland, 1994, p. 51).

66. S.F. Moore who named the different systems and subsystems as social sub-fields noted the existence of different autonomies of these sub-fields in the following words:

    Theoretically, one could postulate a series of possibilities: complete autonomy in a social field, semi-autonomy, or a total absence of autonomy (i.e. complete domination). Obviously, complete autonomy and complete domination are rare, if they at all exist in the world today.' (S.F. Moore, 1988, p. 78).

67. (...) a society undergoes de-pluralization through the operation of a number of different factors. In our view all societies, in fact, remain plural, since perfect homogeneity can never be achieved, but the degree of pluralism can effectively be reduced.' (Rouland, 1988, p. 52)

68. In the words of Rouland: 'All societies, traditional or modern, are plural. However, as M. Alliot had noted, the former affirm this reality, the latter deny it. In both cases, the security of the individual resides in the pluralist nature of society, for the various groups are independent of each other. But whilst Africans openly recognize this, Europeans deny it and, encouraged by the dominant tendency in legal thought, affirm on the contrary that the rights of the individual are, or should be, protected by the state (...).' 1988, p. 43.

69. 'Pluralism is the sworn enemy of the unitary ambitions of the state and the latter has two weapons with which to do battle with it. Either the state attempts a total elimination of pluralism, or the state recognizes certain manifestations of the pluralism'. (Rouland, 1988, p. 56).

70. 'Since the law of the sovereign state is hierarchical in form, no social field within a modern polity could be absolutely autonomous from a legal point of view. Absolute domination is also difficult to conceive, for even in armies and prisons and other rule-run institutions, there is usually an

underlife with some autonomy'. 1978, p. 78. For details see Moore's Study of Readymade Women's Dresses in New York. 1978, p. 59.

71. Malinowski was the first one to advance the idea that several legal systems interact in a traditional society. He noted the existence of multiple legal systems among the Trobriands:

'The law of these natives (Trobriand) consists on the contrary of a number of more or less independent systems, only partially adjusted to one another. Each of these—matriarchy, father-right, the law of marriage, the prerogatives and duties of a chief and so on—has a certain field completely its own, but it can also trespass beyond its legitimate boundaries.' (Malinowski, 1926, p. 100).

72. For details see Radcliffe-Brown, 1952, pp. 216–17. *Structure and Function in Primitive Society: Essays and Addresses.* New York, The Free Press. And Howell, P.P. 1954, p. 225. *A Manual of Nuer Law.* London, Oxford University Press.

73. From Rouland, 1988, p. 50 (Vanderlinden 1972).

74. Pospisil, 1971, p. 107.

75. Moore, S.F., 1978, p. 56, 57.

76. Mitchell, *The Sociological Review*, 1983, 31 (2) p. 191.

77. Mitchell, *The Sociological Review*, 1983, p. 193.

78. Gluckman, M. 1961. 'Ethnographic Data in British Social Anthropology', *The Sociological Review* 9, pp. 5–17.

79. Llewellyn and Hoebel, 1941, p. 21.

80. Gulliver, 1969, pp. 11, 13.

81. Gulliver, 1969, p. 13.

82. From 1991 to 1993, one and a half to two months of every year in summer. It is also important to mention the interest and involvement of the author in personal conflicts and resolution processes.

83. *Pao* is a quarter of a kilo; and *Aqal*, according to the Ferozsons Dictionary, wisdom, sense, understanding, intellect, reason, knowledge: perhaps when we put all these meanings together a similar meaning of *Aqal* can be achieved.

CHAPTER 2

ZAN, ZAR, ZAMIN: TYPES OF CONFLICTS

The case studies have been selected with a view to providing, among others things, some idea about the variety of the conflicts arising in a village setting. Undoubtedly full justice to the reasons and the variety of conflicts cannot be done unless all the cases be given in full detail, which is not possible. To overcome this drawback to some extent, the most common types of conflicts arising in the village, which suggest a discernible pattern are presented.

According to Simon Roberts, one of the leading legal anthropologists, disputes could be classified on the basis of parties or groups involved in them, and the reasons of their emergence:

> Despite these variations in form, scale and focus, two broad distinctions have often recurred in attempts to classify disputes. One of these has involved contrasting disputes between groups and disputes within a group: inter-group conflicts and intra-group conflicts. The other has involved an opposition between disputes arising out of broken rules and those having their origin in competition over scarce and valued resources.[1]

The examples taken are conflicts within or between *ghar* (nucleus family, sometimes joint family), *khandan* (extended family), *sharika* (patrilineage), *biradari* (clan or lineage), *mohalla* (quarter or street), and the *pind* (village). The other categorization is based upon the causes of the conflicts based on well-known traditional reasons related to *zan* (woman), *zar* (gold), and *zamin* (land and property). It is the latter category that will be dealt with here.

Zan, zar, and *zamin* are the proverbially known reasons for conflicts in South Asia. Willi Steul, a German anthropologist, changed the composition of this trinity for the Pashtoon society and replaced *zar* (gold) with *sar* (head).[2] He provides interesting statistics about the proportional share of these three as causes of conflicts according to which *sar* causes 19.30 per cent, *zan* 25.43 per cent, and *zamin* 55.26 per cent conflicts.[3]

Any statistics could be misleading, because many conflicts are not brought to public notice but are solved within the groups they arise in before they may become known. Most conflicts have multiple reasons and it is difficult and would be wrong to take only one of them into account. In some cases the reasons of those are intentionally misreported, especially in conflicts involving women. But one conclusion which could be drawn from the statistics for Misalpur: that conflicts relating to land and property are not only more frequent but also more serious.

Land as a Source of Conflicts

There is a saying 'as we have no land to divide, we have no reason to quarrel'. Many different types of conflicts take place over land and property; like the division of the land, house and other property between the brothers and sisters; the disagreement arising out of the sale and purchase of land; problems arising out of tenancy arrangements; provision of passage to the fields and the division of the irrigation water; theft of crops and agricultural tools, their apportionment and the sharing of their use; animals trespassing fields of others and grazing; the use and misuse of the boundaries of agricultural fields; cleaning and maintenance of the water channels; the use and misuse of government, undefined and/or common community lands and property.

Another important characteristic of land conflicts is that they are brought to the courts more often than others, especially if they are not within the family; in fact a major proportion of the cases in the official courts is about land. Epstein, a well-known social anthropologist, wrote about the Wangala (a South Indian village) peasants:

> (...) they consider their caste and village panchayats to be the ultimate judicial authority in all matters, except disputes over land.[4]

Similarly Cohn, another well-known anthropologist, writes about North India:

> Most frequently the stated reason for going to urban courts is disputes over land.[5]

The conflicts over land even within the families are sometimes brought before the courts, which is otherwise quite unusual, especially if they become complicated. We will now see them one by one.

Conflicts over the Division of Property

The conflicts over the division of land and property mostly arise within *ghar*, *khandan,* and *sharika*. Case study number six shows how the conflicts in Ashraf's family about the division of land and other property have given rise to friction between the brothers, sisters and close relatives. Simple disagreements sometimes become complicated and long drawn. Srinivas, a renowned Indian anthropologist, provides a very detailed description of the conflicts in the family on the division of land and property from India, which is equally true for this village:

> Partition disputes generally tend to drag on. When the idea is first mooted, it is at the end of a series of quarrels for which the women, especially those who have come in by marriage, are usually blamed. The elders who are approached to effect a division of the property among the copartners usually advise them to stay together and keep their women in control. After a while quarrels again break out, and finally elders concede that it is better to divide than to quarrel

perpetually. Then a second set of quarrels occurs—how should the property be divided and who should get what? There are some conventions regarding this, but they do not prevent quarrels. After the property has been divided, one member feels that he has fared badly and he demands a redistribution. In such a case, adjustments are made with some difficulty and the document registered to ensure that similar demands are not made again. Another set of quarrels arises during the paddy transplantation season where the bunds separating the flats are trimmed, and brothers, who are usually neighbours, accuse each other of encroachment. Rights of way across a brother's field and right to irrigation water flowing through it, are other matters over which disputes occur. Such disputes go on for years. The partition of property among brothers does not promise amity and it is frequently found that adult brothers are not on speaking terms with each other. While members of a lineage show solidarity in relation to lineage, among themselves there are tensions. The narrower the lineage-span, the greater the tension.[6]

The ideal family in the village is one in which all live together, including great-grandchildren in one house, and operate the land jointly. This, according to the local traditions, happens in families where the 'good' sons have their wives under control. The wives are not supposed to know the secrets of the family, nor even the weaknesses of their own husbands. The parents and elder brothers have to be respected and obeyed and they, on their part, should be selfless. The deciding power is in the hands of grandmothers and fathers, followed by elder brothers. It is the wives, on the one hand, who are held responsible for the conflicts, but, at the same time, it is also linked to upbringing and imparting of proper value systems—such as would not make sons subservient to their wives.

In reality however, the land in most of the cases is divided either after the death of the father, or even during his life when he gets old, and his sons have their own children, each needing his own share. The division is not seen as positive but the occurrence is thus rationalized. There is a saying about how quarrels arise especially among relatives: 'put together even two pots, make a noise'.

There are no clear rules about division of property. The very demand for such a division is considered a dispute. Even the question of who gets which part of the house and land with desire to get the best portions is controversial. It is not unusual for the older brothers to misuse their authority and the respect which is due to them. There are also, however, several examples of amicable divisions where one brother readily offers the other to choose whatever portions he likes, or one brother gives his share to the other. In spite of different types of problems, brothers seldom fight among themselves and in most cases the relationship of respect is maintained.

The real disputes often take place among the wives. Subsequently, bitter memories of the division of property lead to enmity among the cousins (cousin here in the sense of the children of the brothers), i.e. how the word *sharik* in Punjabi is to be understood like *tarbur* in Pushto in the meaning of 'enemy'. Barth, a British social anthropologist who has worked extensively in Swat, writes about the Pashtoons:

> Most of all, people used to fight with their own cousins, or second cousins—what we call tarbur, which means both 'cousin', and 'enemy'.[7]

It is not only the division of property which leads to these cousin conflicts—even the honour of the family is to be shared. There is a competition between the families of the cousins to earn more respect in the village. *Izzat*, which is much sought after, is very difficult to quantify and leads to indirect conflicts.

Another problem arises when the sisters demand their share of the agricultural land which they are not supposed to. This problem is more evident in those families who have much land. That is why in such families marriage strategies are developed and efforts are made to arrange them in a way that the land remains within the family unit.

Sale and Purchase of Land and Property

The genesis of many conflicts over land in the villages lies in the contradiction between the values of the peasant which do not allow land to be bought or sold, and the official system in practice which permits this.[8]

Land is said to be the second 'mother' of the farmer, since it provides food and shelter. There is a belief that those who want to make investment in business by selling land will not succeed. In the village there are many instances where families sold their land and invested the money in a business but failed and the land was also lost: Maqbool, of *Araeen biradari*, sold his land to set up a power-loom, suffered a loss and is now a shopkeeper; considered an inferior business to that of farming, since it is considered to be a business of the *kammi biradari*. Sarwar (*a Jat*) also sold his land to start a transport business and failed miserably.

Land is the most important source of social prestige for the farmers, even for those residing and working in towns, especially among traditional farmer *biradaries*. It acquires greater significance at the time of the marriages of the children. If someone acquires land by buying new land he is not considered *khandani* (a family of long standing). Gluckman explains the difference between owning immovable property and owning chattel:

> My hypothesis is that immovable property and chattels have different functions in the maintenance, through time, of a social system as an organized pattern of relations. Immovable property provides fixed positions which endure through the passing of generations, through quarrels, and even through invasions and revolutions, and many social relationships are stabilized about these positions.[9]

That is how the connection of personal honour to land is perhaps understood in the village. Land confers special honour to its owner. Land is considered a guarantee for, or a symbol of the *khandani* for the would-be husband of a daughter or sister, as also at the time of the selection of a wife for the son.

It was under colonial rule that land became a special commodity liable to be bought and sold. In the words of Cohn:

> Literally with a stroke of the pen new rights were established. Land for the first time became a commodity to be bought and sold in a market.[10]

Its sale and purchase was not comparable to the sale and purchase of other commodities. It could only be bought and sold after the record in the Revenue Department had been changed, which gave rise to a different set of conflicts. Cheshire wrote about this special position of the land:

> A layman knows that if he desires to transfer to another the ownership of a chattel, such as a motor car or a picture, the only requirement is the making of a contract which names the parties, records their intention, describes the article to be sold and states the price paid. The moment that such a contract is concluded, the ownership of the article, in the absence of a contrary intention, passes to the buyer. At first sight it is difficult to appreciate why the same simple expedient cannot be adopted in the case of land, and not unnaturally a layman grows impatient of the long and expensive investigation attendant upon the conveyance of a piece of land with perhaps one half of the car which can be effectively sold in a quarter of an hour. (...) The movement of progressive societies has been from land to money, or rather to trade, and a legal system which acquired its main features at a time when land constituted the main part of a country's wealth can scarcely be described as suitable to an industrial community.[11]

This change of status for land and the fact that the official records had to be changed, became the source of many differences. Apart from the change of the record attendant on the sale and purchase of the land, there are some other peculiarities for example, *haqq-e-shufaah* (right of pre-emption). Both the record on paper and the physical possession are important in dealing in landed property.

If a person sells his land without his close relatives knowing about it, problems arise between the brothers who may have wanted to buy it. If they cannot buy it at that time for reasons such as lack of finances, or that the other brother did not want to sell his land to his brother, who would then have more *izzat* etc., they resort to *haqq-e-shufaah*, which in itself leads to discord not only within the members of the family but also with the one who buys it. This has become quite prevalent, leading to the practice where persons quote a higher figure on sale deeds than they actually pay. Even this strategy does not help all the time. When Ihsan Alahi, the brother of Mehbub Alahi (*Jat*) sold his land to Jamil (*Araeen*), he did not ask his brother, with whom he was angry. The parties made a sale agreement quoting a figure five times higher than the actual price. Mehbub appealed to court under *haqq-e-shufaah* but, at the same time, forcibly occupied the land, forbidding Jamil from entering the fields. Ihsan had already received the money and did not want to get involved in the conflict. He had left the village to live in Bakhar, where he had purchased new land. Jamil had to give up as Mehbub was determined to take this land at any cost. In the end, it was agreed in the *panchayat* that Mehbub would pay Jamil the money he had paid to Ihsan, and assume possession of the land, which was done.

Boundaries of the Fields

Common boundaries dividing the fields of different farmers are not marked permanently and clearly. Parties on both side cut their side of the boundaries thin to gain more land, or to annoy their neighbours, leading to encroachments. The boundaries (*wat*) get very narrow which leads to water leakages at the time of irrigation or it gets difficult to walk over these thin boundaries. This leads to several conflicts between the neighbouring farmers. Similarly, the question of putting earth on either side of the boundary, also leads to severe conflicts between the farmers in the village. Ahmad wrote about such conflicts in a Pakistani Punjabi village:

> Many farmers encroach upon their neighbour's fields by slowly moving the boundary line. It takes some time before the neighbour discovers the encroachment. Usually he reacts by setting the boundary 'in order' according to his own estimate. This inevitably leads to serious fights.[12]

We have examples of such disagreements from every other household in the village. Since using an official boundary-marking commision costs a lot of money, and running around, the villagers try to solve these disputes directly which very often leads to the use of physical force. There was, for example, a dispute of boundary between Sharif, Hussain and Alam. Since Sharif is the only son in his family, he could not cultivate his land properly; the outer boundaries of his fields were at a height and thus, not arable and were lying barren. Hussain, on the one side and Alam on the other side of his fields encroached slowly. One day as Sharif was clearing his barren fields, because his sons were now grown-up and were helping him, he found out that the boundaries were not in the right place. This led to a severe quarrel between the parties which was later on resolved through the intervention of Chadhairs (a big family of *Jats* having influence on both sides).

Irrigation Water, its Passage, and the Maintenance of Water Channels

In many parts of the Punjab, distance from the river course means that irrigation is the major source of water for the crops other than rainfall. The supply of water is limited and causes a lot of hostility. The irrigation system is based on a main network of canals supplying water from the rivers, which lead through smaller canals, to different villages. The size of the waterlets from the main to the smaller canals, known as *mogha,* is regulated by the Department of Irrigation and Canals to ensure that water reaches each and every field. It is regulated so that every farmer gets water once in a week at a fixed time. There is a common village clock (now it is the official radio time) in the village. Farmers, match their watches with it before going for their turn of water. Theoretically, it seems very simple and straightforward, but in practice, it leads to dissension. There are three main and innumerable small canals (known as *khalas*) in this village, which must be cleaned regularly of grass and earth which is brought in along with the water. The question of who cleans them, when and how well, and on which side of the canal (two different owners) this should be thrown (it takes away cultivable land), leads to quarrels.

Since water is scarce, especially in summer, some try to steal water. This requires that a watch must be kept on water flows. Since these are mudlined watercourses, sometimes mice and other animals burrow holes leading to water loss and quarrels among farmers who are suffering the loss. The fields of some farmers are lower (intentionally lowered for drawing more water) than others which can also lead to hostilities.

Conflicts arise at the time of the change between turns at drawing water. If both parties are present and match their watches there is no problem. The normal practice is that one of the parties is not present, which can lead to disputes arising from the time factor of changing water courses. In fact, there can be severe fights over minutes.

The other source of antagonism is the passage of water to the next farm, since every subsequent farmer is to be provided with a water canal, but the route the water canal should take is not fixed. There are often controversies over this, since all farmers want to get the shortest possible route as there is the necessity of cleaning canals, and providing the walking paths along them, which can be considerable.

Problems also arise where there is no official approach to the fields of a farmer. This normally means a wastage of land for the farmer who has to provide the passage which often gives rise to disputes and sometimes to serious fights. Mostly, it is a sort of exchange relation, i.e. one has to provide the water passage and the other the approach to the fields. If one causes problems, the other side retaliates.

In one such case Zulfiqar had to provide the water passage to Sharif, and Sharif had to give a bullock cart passage to Zulfiqar. In another similar situation, Sharif had to provide water canals to Husain and Alam and they both had to give a bullock cart passage to Sharif. In spite of the fact that in both cases a water passage and the approach to the fields exists, it leads to conflicts. Also Sharif's animals, while moving along this passage, eat from the crops of Hussain and Alam. In turn Husain and Alam trample the crops of Sharif, throw the earth cleared from the water canal onto the crops and steal from them. And so on.

Sharing and Stealing Agricultural Tools and Crops

Most of the farmers are poor and few of them can afford all the tools necessary for farming their lands. Therefore, they are bound to lend and borrow agricultural implements. Some of them have more and others have less tools. Moreover through usage borrowed tools can break, which sometimes leads to refusing any further lending and hence to groupings and disputes.

Stealing the crops also causes conflicts and sometimes even fights. Mostly, animal fodder or small edible items are stolen. The stealing of small amounts of edibles is not considered a theft. But what really could lead to serious confrontations is the damaging of the crops by animals, though this damage need not be severe. Ahmad wrote about Malakpur:

> Unattended cattle may cause damage to crops. This is particularly serious when the crops are ready for harvesting. The issue is fought out between the owner of the field and that of the cattle on the spot.[13]

Darling reported the story of such a dispute:

> A villager was returning one evening from his fields and, being
> obliged to stop for a moment, absent-mindedly allowed his bullocks
> to stray into a neighbour's crop. The neighbour appearing, there
> was the inevitable volley of abuse followed by blows, (...).[14]

Women and Conflicts

The conflicts about women have their origin in their lowly status,
views about the *purdah* (veil), and society's ideal about men's
izzat and *ghairat* (honour and defence of family women). The
conflicts occur due to illicit sexual relations, rapes, marriages,
dowry, and divorces, etc.

The Lowly Status of Women

The discrimination against a female starts right from birth. The
family is not congratulated at the birth of a female child. The
female child means the burden of extra vigilance as they are to
be protected and taken care of. The wives giving birth only to
female children are considered *nahis* (cursed, having no
blessings) and are very often beaten, divorced, or a second
marriage is arranged for the husband. Only the woman is
considered responsible for the birth of a daughter. Villagers
express their sympathies, in case of several daughters, with
expressions like 'basketful of daughters',[15] and 'black-faced
witches'.[16] Old women of the family, when angry, give *badduah*
(curse): 'may you have to wash the face of seven daughters' or
that 'God may give you seven daughters'.[17]

Contrary to this, sweets are offered and the family is
congratulated at the birth of a son. A proverb says 'milk and
sons are the blessings of God'.[18] Sons are considered the source
of power, strength (in case of fights) and wealth (as earning
power in the future) therefore seen as a source of increasing

izzat. They are also the carriers of the family name. They bring wives and with them dowry thus adding to the assets.

Love Affair, Elopement, Abduction, Rape, and Conflicts

Marriage, which is the only sanctioned form of sexual relationships, is arranged by the family. Usually the patriarch head of the family, the father, considers it his absolute right to decide who his offsprings should marry. Young men and women working and living together in the village sometimes fall in love with each other, but since they cannot influence the decisions about their marriages they are left with the only option of fleeing the village.

There are two types of expressions used for such a running away of young couples: *nikal jana,* or more negatively expressed, *udal jana* (elopement) and the other form is *kad ke lay jana*, or more recently, *aghwa karna* (kidnapping or abduction). The first stresses the free will of the accompanying woman whereas the second emphasizes the dominant role of the man in the running away. The first expression may be used by the family of the man and other families sympathizing with them. The family of the woman will use the second, especially, while reporting the case to the police. Many cases of abduction registered with the police are of this type. It is considered the fault of the boy and that of his family, because the *izzat* of the girl's family is more deeply affected.

For the girl it is an absolute decision as her family lose their honour totally. The girl who runs away, if recovered, has no chance of marriage except in a family with a much lower status than hers; also she could get a husband who otherwise would not get married or has a bad character, except when the elopement or illicit relationship does not become public. It is not only the girl who is affected by this; if she has sisters they too would get part of the 'pollution' and would face difficulties in their marriage. Even after marriage they would be ridiculed by the in-laws with taunts like: 'we know the tradition of your family' which would probably be mentioned in every quarrel between the women. There are even cases in which after the older sister ran away, the others adopted similar strategies.

Different reasons are reported for elopement in the village. The parents of the girl find no 'suitable' match (same *biradari*, equal economic and social status, etc.); the parents cannot pay the dowry; the girl has the feeling of becoming old, or being ignored; there are many sisters and the older ones are still not married. Another reason is that the girls are engaged to be married to men they do not like and of course that they may fall in love.

Elopement, and love affairs are much discouraged and the sympathies of the villager are usually with the girl's family.[19] This family is, of course, also criticized for not having taken enough care of the girl. One reason for this dislike, among other reasons, may be that it serves as an example for the girls and boys of other families.

Elopements and abductions are taken equally seriously by all *biradaries,* more so by the so-called 'traditionally honourable' families of the farmers. The more respectful a person is, the more seriously such events are taken. The women of the richer traditional families are more confined to their houses and household jobs than those of the *kammi,* who have to do jobs outside the house. But this situation changes, when the *kammi* families become rich through the power-looms or other business and their women also start staying at home. It is in itself an interesting phenomenon that the so-called *kammi biradaries* are changing their profession, becoming rich and no longer feeling affliliated with their *biradaries* though they will still call themselves, for example, *Malik*. The use of the term *kammi* in such cases is reduced to the poor *kammi* families working for the farmers.

On the basis of data and observations it could be said that most of the elopements take place between *biradaries*, for example, the girl is of the *Mochee biradari* and the boy of the *Jats,* the girl is of the *Jat biradari* and the boy of the *Rajputs,* the girl of the *Jats* and the boy of the *Maliks,* the girl of the

Teelies and the boy of the *Jats*. It may also take place between girls and boys of the same *biradari*. It depends, among other things, upon the possibilities of their meeting, for example being neighbours, having adjacent *haveli* (animal-house) or agricultural fields, etc.

For a dispute or fight there may not necessarily be an actual elopement, abduction or illicit relationships; a simple suspicion is enough for serious hostilities as was also observed by Makhdum Tasadduq Ahmad (a Pakistani sociologist) in Malakpur, a Pakistani Punjabi village:

> Suspicions, often ill founded, regarding illicit liaison, arouse intense emotions and may lead to serious fighting, even murder.[20]

The whole family of the girl especially the men are affected by this insult; the father and the brothers even more. They must take revenge, otherwise they would be called *beghairat* (those who cannot defend their women and honour). There are different possibilities of revenge, killing the couple being the ideal solution: the others include, killing the boy, killing only the girl[21] or kidnapping a woman from the family of the boy. These possibilities exist if the family of the girl has the same or nearly the same socio-economic status. If they are poor and weak they could be even blamed for aspiring to a higher status. When the family of the girl is stronger and richer, the same blame is given to the boy and revenge is even more certain. In any case such girls, after they have been recovered, are very soon married off to a man of the father's choice.

Marriage Conflicts

Conflicts arise on and through the selection of marriage partners. Such marriage conflicts are mostly within the extended family (uncles and aunts from the mother's and father's side) on the question of who marries whom. Case study six, 'The conflicts in the family of Ashraf', serves as an apt illustration.

The example of such discord within the extended family provides information of how different interest groups form within the family. For example the father may want to arrange the marriage of his children with his relatives, while the mother may want it with hers.

Betrothals in infancy between children are very common. They take place, mostly among very close relatives, at the time of birth, and in some cases even before the birth of a child; sometimes differences in age between the future husband and wife are not taken into account and one may be older by as much as twenty years. This creates trouble later if both or one of them should want to marry someone closer their age. M. T. Ahmad wrote about Malakpur:

> It is not unusual for parents to betroth their children before puberty. Sometimes a boy who has received education develops an outlook different from that of his elders. He may refuse to have a 'rustic' wife, thereby causing a serious blow to the honour of her parents. Sometimes, however, the refusal may come from the girl's side. This happens when the boy does not measure up to the expectations of her parents.[22]

Childhood engagements, if broken later on, are one reason for disputes; even the selection of one girl or boy is taken as the rejection of another which leads to serious differences between the brothers and sisters or other close kin. Generally, such disputes are not violent but may lead to it. Whether the first preference are the children of the mother's side or cousins from the father's side is decided on the basis of which of the two has more influence and authority in family affairs, or over the children. The economic position of the respective bride or groom, beauty, education, etc. play a role too. It is the fathers, usually, who have more authority and power in the family, whereas the mothers have more influence on the children. Thus, mothers may turn out to have more say in the marriage of their children. This is especially true when the children have grown up and there are differences of opinion between their parents causing the children to take sides. Very often this leads to the breakup of childhood betrothals with the father's relatives leading to strife.

Post-Marital Conflicts

Watta satta (exchange) marriages, i.e. giving one bride and receiving one, as brother and sister marrying brother and sister, is still common here, especially if the parents have problems in finding the partner for one of them. The reasons may vary from lack of sufficient beauty; advanced age; the financial position of the boy; and many other things considered at the time of selection. In such situations, the continuation of one marriage is dependent upon the other. It is also the fastest and easiest way of arranging marriages and is considered to take care of marriage problems and the safety of the sisters and daughters. This would mean that if the husband of the daughter or sister does not treat her well, the bride at home would also receive similar treatment. Besides exchanging brothers for sisters there is also an exchange of cousins, especially if the marriage takes place outside the circle of close relatives; but in the latter case the problems of matrimonial life are seldom shared, as with exchange marriages of brother and sister.

Exchange marriages often lead to problems like separation, divorce, fights, etc. between the husbands and wives only because the other couple has such problems, too. It is very seldom the case that if one of the marriages is dissolved, the other remains intact.

Many such marriages are solemnized against the will of the girls and boys which, also lead to problems. Cousin marriages are preferred on the grounds that if the daughter-in-law is *apna khoon* (own blood) she would assist and look after the parents especially in their old age, while it is taken for granted that the *paraee* (outsider) daughter-in-law does not have those feelings.

For a woman, the first few years after the marriage are generally the most difficult of her life. There are conflicts with her mother-in-law, sisters-in-law (still more so if living in her parents' house), brothers-in-law, very often leading to discord between husband and wife. The *saas* and *nooh* (mother-in-law and daughter-in-law) relationship is considered to be one of the worst to be. The best news a mother can give her daughter before marriage is that she is marrying into a family where there is no mother-in-law. Most of the conflicts between husband and wife in the early years of their marriage are the result of the confrontations between the man's mother and wife which very often even lead to divorce. There are quarrels with the sisters of the husband who sooner or later get married and go away. It is also said that the mothers-in-law want to take revenge of what happened to them, when they came to the house of their husband as brides. Another area of dissension is the definition of rights and authority in the house which is the mother-in-law's kingdom. The mother considers the house and her son as belonging to her. As opposed to this, the wife aspires for a similar status for herself. This 'power' conflict becomes more acute when the mother-in-law and the wife blame each other for having used *taawiz* (amulets) for gaining control over the son/ husband respectively. Some mothers-in-law resent their paying greater attention to their wives or if on her advice, he does not beat her. Husbands may have sympathy for their wives but they are not supposed to show it; otherwise, they are called *zan mureed* (hen-pecked) by their mothers or by the other people of the village. The frustrated wives also may resort to charms to ward off the exploits of their in-laws, as well as to gain control of their husbands.

This could be called the 'power-breaking' period: the power of the mother is challenged and shared and she fears losing her power which she, of course, does not want to. It might take several years, many disputes, the wife might even be beaten up several times which may in itself lead to separation and, in the worst case, to a divorce. Sometimes the wife leaves the house of her husband after some quarrel with him or with her mother-in-law and is brought back, maybe by the father-in-law or husband or even mother-in-law. In this way she acquires more power and maybe gets more rights. In such cases there are long discussions in which she is represented by her parents and brothers. The birth of children, especially male children, again adds to her prestige. The balance of power thus changes from the mother-in-law to the daughter-in-law until the former, especially in her old age, is at the mercy of the latter.

During this period of 'transfer of power', there could be several crises in the life of the wife and the worst is divorce. On her marriage, a daughter is often advised that once she goes to her husband's house, she should only leave it on her death. Such parents are the living dead, the villagers say, whose daughters are divorced or returned home. There are several other expressions for such situations. The daughters or sisters, sitting in their parents' house because of separation or divorce, are considered a stain to the honour of the family, especially the male members, thus they are taught by their mothers to bear all afflictions and not to leave the house of their husband. Many prefer death to returning to the house of their married brother.

Even if such situations are rare, there are periods of separation in the life of a woman. It is almost normal that as a result of some dispute between husband and wife or mother-in-law and bride, the latter, leaves the house of her husband several times during her life.

The procedure of *talaaq* (divorce) is in itself very simple. It can be affected by the simple pronouncement of the word *talaaq* three times by the husband, repeated successively or once each in three months. The registration of *nikah* (the ritual of marriage) and *talaaq* has been made compulsory since 1962 to 'check' irregularities (men having more than one unrecorded marriages).[23] Divorce, as has already been stated, is something that is not talked about because it is considered a blemish on the *izzat* of the family. Even the other sisters suffer and brothers having divorced sisters at home also find it difficult to find wives for themselves, since the presence of sisters at home would mean a permanent source of conflict. Finding a husband for a divorced woman is difficult. In contrast the divorced men have no such difficulties, being considered eligible even for unmarried girls. The whole situation becomes even more complicated if a divorced woman has children.

There is a difference in the perception of the institutions of marriage and divorce between the state and religion and family and society. The family, parents and society want the marriage to take place by the consent, choice, and will of the parents. The intended partners are indirectly informed and cannot, or should not, decide of their own will. For them documents and records are not only unimportant but also very often an impediment especially if the official documents (*nikah nama* and *talaaq nama*) are to be presented in court or to the police.

For the state system, since 1961, it is compulsory that marriages and divorces be recorded. Without these documents, no decision may be made by the courts and the police. For the official requirement of the marriage, also called 'court marriage' in the village, it is important that the would-be husband and wife are present with their witnesses. For the official marriage the presence of the parents is not necessary if the couple are adults according to Islamic provisions. This makes elopements possible especially when the marriage is against the wishes of the parents. This also has the support of religion since that the two who want to marry should agree. The agreement of the parents or close relatives is not mandatory.

The women (whether mothers, sisters, daughters, etc.) are considered the honour of a man which he has to protect under all circumstances. *Izzat* is a term considered to be of men but it has a direct connection to the woman who could destroy it. If the women in their above-mentioned roles do not behave in the manners approved of by the society, they destroy the *izzat* of their men which has to be restored. It is considered more prestigious than anything else to divorce, or kill, the one who has smeared it. The other means is by killing the man involved, or both, otherwise the man is *beghairat* (the one who cannot defend the women and honour). *Izzat* is not only destroyed if the woman runs away with a man but also if she does not accept the marriage arranged by the father, brother or family.

Dowry as a Source of Conflict

There are many unclear and ambiguous expectations involving dowry which lead to conflicts. Dowry is considered as the daughter's share of the property of her parents. She is not supposed to ask for her share after the death of her parents, to avoid division of landed property. The big landowners, especially, try to find husbands for their daughters who will not demand the share of their wives.

The other justification given for dowry is that since the bride and bridegroom start a new household they need all the essentials of the household. In actual practice the bride lives in a joint family, leading to the problem as to who is allowed to use the items of her dowry. If the bride has not brought enough, covering all or at least most of the household articles, the other members of the familly, especially the mother-in-law, taunt[24] her in many ways.[25] On the other hand, there are confrontations when the daughters of the family or the mother-in-law use articles from the dowry of the daughter-in-law.

Dowry is one of the important factors in the decision for taking a bride but one that is not talked about. The expectations of the parents and the boy are seldom fulfilled, whereas the parents of the girl try their best and often have to borrow money for providing a substantial dowry, which is put on display both in the village of the bride and the village of the boy. These displays, especially the one in the village of the boy, are a sign of the *izzat* of the family.[26] The dowry is much discussed in the village by the women and how much or how little is given is commented upon, and the approximate values of the items are discussed.

Some long engagements are broken because the dowry might not meet the expectations. This is especially the case within relatives among whom childhood betrothals are common. Sometimes, on the very day of the marriage, when the amount of dowry becomes known, conflicts arise and in some cases lead to the return of the bridegroom's party without the marriage having taken place. The demands of certain articles in the dowry, if not fulfilled, could also lead to the breaking up of the expected marriage or at least could create tense relations during the marital life.[27]

Miscellaneous Conflicts

Moneylending

There are many sayings about lending money like: 'If you want to end the relations or friendship, lend money' or 'Money is the enemy of friendship'. 'There is *narazgee* (the state of being angry) if you do not lend money but there are quarrels if you lend it'. Similarly: 'Moneylending needs courage and getting back requires wisdom'. These sayings show the role of money as a source of conflicts. Moneylending is quite common in village life. Among the illiterate villagers asking for a written contract is impolite and considered an insult. As a result, no written record is made. At the time of need you simply go to your neighbours, relatives or friends for borrowing some money. The money is mostly borrowed for non-investment or non-productive purposes like the marriage ceremony (dowry of the daughter and wedding receptions [*walima*] and other expenditures at the son's marriage), for celebrating the birth of a son, for giving alms and food during the death rituals, and so on. These occasions are very important in the life of a villager as these are occasions of showing and earning *izzat*. They generally spend beyond their capacity. About marriage it is said that one marries only once and it must be celebrated, perhaps that is why multiple marriages are not celeberated with the same enthusiasm. Similarly, on occasions of death all mourners and visitors are served with food. On death anniversaries also meals are generally served.

For all such occasions, it is not uncommon for people to borrow money. Refusal by the well-to-do relatives and friends to lend money is considered an insult and can end relationships. Reciprocal contacts play a very important role in the life of a villager starting from their simple daily needs like getting fire, or drinking water, and food items, to ceremonial and ritual gifts. Keeping written record is not only a question of illiteracy, it also involves the honour of the borrower since his trustworthiness is not to be doubted. So much so, that many joint business ventures are made without writing them down, later resulting in misunderstandings, especially in cases of intentional cheating and hence quarrels and fights occur. (See case study five).

When farmers sell their crops to other villagers and payments are not made immediately following the sale, conflicts can arise. The shopkeepers very often also sell on credit, sometimes even on crop basis. There are often complaints of underwriting and overwriting or vice-versa. The customers, who are mostly village women, often buy on credit with the shopkeepers writing down these purchases. Being illiterate the women are unable to verify the record. All these are different forms of moneylending and borrowing which give rise to many conflicts. The police and courts are not very helpful in getting back such loans and often force is used to get them back.

Abuses

Punjabi is a language very rich in abuses, their meanings change from tone to tone and context to context. Intimate friends very often greet each other with some kind of abuse as an inverse display of affectionate regard for each other. The same when used by others or by the same friends in a different situation and tone, can lead to bloody fights. Case study four is such an example. Dildar Hussain was a friend of Umar Din and Yasin and due to the use of abuses there was serious discord between them. The details are given in the case study. Abuses involving a mother, sister, daughter and wife are often the most serious. However, abuses are said to be the weapons of the weak.

Analysis

For further strengthening our knowledge of the ethnographic part of conflicts and for better understanding the behaviour of the villagers especially in the solution of conflicts, we must know something more of village life and its politics. Here, we shall provide an analysis of the case studies on the one hand, and the general principles of village politics, factors influencing the behaviour of the people, characteristics of the conflicts and elements which influence the functioning of the justice system on the other hand.

Izzat, Ghairat and, Conflicts

To understand *zan, zar* and *zamin* as the reasons of conflicts, we have to understand the very closely related concepts of *izzat, ghairat,* and *sharam-o-haya. Izzat*[28] is usually translated as honour, *sharam*[29] may be translated as prudery or consciousness of what constitutes shame, *haya*[30] as inner modesty, and *ghairat*[31] is the more overt expression and can also be translated as successful defence of honour and women. Their absence is denoted with terms such as *be-izzat, be-sharam,* and *be-ghairat*. The expressions used in negative situations are such as: 'mix one's *izzat* in dust', 'the family's nose has been cut', 'I cannot show my face in public' and 'there is nothing left in my *jholi*[32] (pouch)'.

Walsh, a colonial officer, summed up the meaning and importance of the expression *izzat* in subcontinent as:

> (...) influence, and reputation; all of which is summed up in that great but fateful word izzat. (...) Every Indian, from the highest to the lowest, has his izzat, or name, to keep. After his son, it is his most cherished possession, and if it is injured he is an unhappy man. And in such a sensitive race there is nothing easier to injure than the izzat. The injury may be purely imaginary, but it is no less keenly felt. (...) Moreover, he will neither forget it nor forgive the man who did it.[33]

Similarly Darling, another colonial administrator, expressed his observations on *izzat* in Punjab very appropriately:

This pride or izzat is one of the Punjabi's deepest feelings, and as such must be treated with great respect. Dearer to him than life, (...) But it binds him to the vendetta and often makes him a poor farmer. (...) One is reminded of the verse in Proverbs: 'He that is despised, and hath a servant, is better than he that honoureth himself, and lacketh bread.'[34]

Keiser, an American anthropologist, observed the concept of *izzat* among the Kohistanis of Thull:

(...) izzat depends on personal accomplishments and defines the men of worth in community; it fluctuates with an individual's fortune. One measures izzat by the adab ('respect') accorded by others. Wealth, education, piety, and elected position all merit respect and thus confer izzat.[35]

Eglar, a Turkish anthropologist who worked in a Pakistani Punjabi village in the Gujrat district, observed that *izzat* is closely connected with land:

However, while his izzet is increased by the kind of property that represents income from land, it is equally, or even to a greater degree, increased by the purchase of land. (...) He (farmer) may share food and money with others but not land, for this is the source of his izzet, and he identifies his land with his pat, laj, or patlaj, which, like izzet, are words referring to power, honor, influence, respect, prestige, and status.[36]

Izzat is positively related to wealth and power. It is also possible to have much wealth and even power but not the corresponding *izzat*. There is a saying in the village that 'the prostitutes have a lot of money but no *izzat*'. You may lose *izzat* without losing wealth. In the world of men, i.e. outside the house, in nearly every action where more than one person is involved *izzat* is at stake.

Sometimes, it is used in such a way that it does not seems have much importance. One can give others *izzat*, one can receive *izzat* and one gets *izzat* while giving others *izzat*. An example would be that if a very rich, respectable, known politician visits the house of a poor farmer or *kammi*, the rich politician has given *izzat* to the poor man but, at the same time, he earned even more *izzat* by visiting a poor man.

By being rich or poor one normally has much or little *izzat* in the eyes of the fellow villagers which could be further increased or decreased by one's actions and behaviour. For example, all the brothers, while being sons of the same father and having more or less the same right to his property and wealth, have not the same level of *izzat*. *Izzat* is actually the way individuals are assessed. What this means is that one's assessment may not be the same as that of the others. This does not mean that the others are taking note of each and every action to see if it is upto the expectations of others. But any action of one's own which does not meet the social or familial expectations is disparaged. This means that one should always be very careful about one's actions and thus one's *izzat*, and must think of others in every action and behaviour.

In spite of being rich one might have very little *izzat*, and being poor one may have much *izzat*. Khushi Muhammad, for example, belongs to a middle class family, is a retired school teacher, says his prayers regularly, takes great interest in the affairs of the village working selflessly in the affairs of the mosque, and all related matters. He commands much higher *izzat* in the eyes of the villagers than Rashid Daniyanwala, who is the richest man of the village. There are also some other examples but still, as a rule, as has also already been mentioned, *izzat* is intimately connected with wealth, except when one does something totally against acceptable basic norms of the people, as Rashid did. He is a businessman. He bought cotton seeds in a large quantity and went for *haj* after storing it. One day he was told on the telephone that the price of cotton seed had gone up. He returned immediately without performing the *haj* to earn profit from the sale of cotton seeds. He is known in the village for having said: 'I can go for *haj* next year again but the price of cotton seeds does not increase as much every year'. People express that the *izzat* is getting more and more associated with wealth as money is increasingly available in the society.

There are different types of *izzat* like, *izzat-e-nafs* (one's self-respect), one's *izzat* among the members of one's family and relatives according to different roles one has to perform, *izzat* in one's biradari, and finally *izzat* in the village. *Izzat* could also be inherited from one's forefathers, though such *izzat* can be lost just as easily. The best example of inherited *izzat* would be the *gaddi nashin* (successor) of a holy man. This inherited holiness sometimes continues for generations but the bad actions of the *gaddi nashin* (descendent and successor of a holy person), can be tarnished by his own acts.

It has already been said that since *izzat* is mostly in the eyes of others—the outside world, the world of men—women are more liable to destroy it by behaving against the social and religious norms of the society. The women also have *izzat* of their own within the confines of the household (the inside world), i.e. in the family and among relatives or in the female world with its limited contacts. But it is very important for the women that they do not spoil the *izzat* of the men (husbands, brothers, fathers, etc.) by their attitude and actions, since the *izzat* of men is the *izzat* of the family.

Women are the *izzat*, *sharam*, and *ghairat* of the entire household. They can, by their own 'bad actions', (love affairs, elopement, divorce, illicit relationships) destroy the *izzat*, *ghairat*, and *sharam* of the men of the family, make them *beghairat*, *besharam-o-haya*. Other men of the village or even relatives can, by trying to have a love affair, elopement, abduction, or by divorcing the sister or daughter, make a man *beizzat*, and *beghairat*. Loss of *ghairat* and *sharam* are mostly associated with women. Keiser noted a similar phenomenon among the Kohistanis:

> Women's behavior becomes a matter of male Muslim identity because the way women act directly impacts on ghairat, men's gift

of personal integrity from God. (...) Finally, women should always comport themselves with modesty to protect their shame (sharam) hiding, controlling, minimizing, and denying their sexuality completely if possible. Men who allow their women freedom become beghairat men.'

Further that:

Because ghairat depended so much on female sexual purity, men's identities as Muslims became vulnerable to the way other men behaved toward their women (...). A glance, a word, a chance reflection of light all had potentially devastating effects on relations between men, since all could be interpreted as attacks on ghairat.

and that:

We must outline the meaning of ghairat once again to understand why this is so, this time juxtaposing it to *aizzat*. English speakers often translate both ghairat and *aizzat* as 'honor,' but these concepts have distinct meanings in Kohistani thinking. Ghairat is perhaps best understood as honor in the sense of personal worth, integrity, or character. Ghairat is natural, a part of iman, and, therefore, a gift from God.[37]

Reciprocity

'Help others at the time of trouble so that others may help you when you are in need,' says Maryam to her sons, 'take part in the village affairs and keep yourself informed. Do not stay away if there is a conflict. You must choose a side in case of a conflict, but not in each and every conflict. If you do not go near others they would not come near you. You should attend the Baithaks (that part of the house where only men congregate) of others, and make your Baithak a place for others. Don't do it the way your father and his brothers did it. Don't show yourselves weak or cowardly otherwise no one would come near you'.[38]

Reciprocity covers all spheres of life like marriage relations, gift exchange, necessities of daily life like food, agricultural tools, household implements, etc. Eglar covered all these reciprocal relationships under *vartan bhanji*:

> (...) the fundamental rule of vartan bhanji is reciprocity: a gift should be returned for a gift, a favour should be rendered for a favour, good treatment should be returned for good treatment, and bad treatment or a practical joke in like manner.[39]

These reciprocal relations often lead to confrontations, sometimes minor , like 'you drew water from my pump but did not lend me your ladder', or 'I gave you much better clothes and more rice at the marriage of your daughter than what you brought me'. Sometimes serious conflicts arise on the question of lending or borrowing agricultural implements and irrigation as also *abats* or *mangs* (reciprocal work invitations). The reciprocal relations between friends, neighbours and relatives are changing constantly. No one can live without the help of the other in the village. The behaviour of people is very strongly controlled by these relations.

Who escorts whom to the police, or courts, who gives evidence against whom, who supports whom in the *panchayat*, and who votes for whom in the village Union Council and other elections, are questions which are decided on the basis of what was done for whom and by whom. 'One gave the other one's vote, the other shall support him in matters related to *panchayat*, police and court'. Moore noted in a Rajasthani village:

> Some months later, I spoke to one of the Nara *panchayat* leaders, who told me in private that the chaudhri had wanted to save the man who had 'sold' the woman. Several years earlier there had been a fight in his own village over who would become the next chaudhri. The accused had supported him, 'so he supported (the accused) in this *panchayat*, but not because he thought that the man was right. It was not because of justice but because of shame; he had to 'go' with him. We can't always do justice. We have to be reciprocal.[40]

This is a simple reciprocal relationship, which may be called direct reciprocity. The affairs of village life are much more complex than are visible. Political affiliations are not clear cut. In the case of a conflict between two persons of the same group, varied and complex strategies are required. The process involves taking the side of the strong party, or including one from the opposite group by persuading him to change his loyalities. What may prevail is the old adage: 'the enemy of my enemy is my friend'.

Reciprocity is not always between equals, or of the same nature. For example Naeem, one of the rich villagers, has more than a hundred workers on his power-looms. Most of them are good workers. However, some of them are *gundas* (bullies; rascals) hired to do different jobs for him. Naeem on his part not only has influence in the village *panchayat*, but also with the police and courts, and if a situation of conflict arises, and his hired bullies are apprehended by the police he may even arrange for their release. In such cases reciprocity changes to a client-patron-relationship.

'Political' reciprocity is similar. The villagers give their votes in return for favours. Those interested in politics like Naeem and Karim who are rich and influential in the village, help people in different ways in return for which they get votes. In each and every conflict and its resolution they are directly or indirectly involved.

Reciprocity becomes evident at the time of a person appearing as a witness in the courts, or when giving evidence before the police. Generally, a person decides to be a witness not for the sake of truth, or love of justice, or against a criminal who should be punished, but according to who has helped him in the past, and who could be of help in the future, or who is the relative, or a member of which *biradari*. In our case studies, whenever the witnesses were required they were mostly relatives, members of one's own *biradari* or friends or those whom one had helped. Those who appeared as witnesses had not even seen the quarrel or fight and ironically those who had seen it would not be witnesses. The reason given by the people not involved directly in the conflict but declining to be witnesses often is 'we do not want to elicit the enmity'. The enmities arising from giving evidence against others are quite common and are one of the most common reasons reported in related FIRs to the police. Ahmad reports a case from Malakpur:

> The reason of this attempted murder is that I was a witness in a case registered against H.K. (...).[41]

It is usual that after a fight or quarrel if one goes to the police, it is in the company of friends and relatives. People seldom go to the police alone, both because of the fear of the police as well as to exert influence or impression on the police, through the companions one takes. The help of relatives is unconditional because they are supposed to be reciprocal, as is evident in the case study of Ashraf's *haveli*. In another conflict, where one person of Jamal's (*Rajput*) family was murdered, Ghaffar (from the Ambalvi family) sided with the *Rajputs* against Yaseen (*Jat* family) since the same *Jat* family had a conflict with the *Ambalvies* sometime ago. Now the *Rajput* family which had good relations with the police, helped the *Ambalvies* (Goora and his sons) though this *Rajput* family had no enmity with the family of Ashraf. On the other hand Ashraf and his party had kept themselves aloof from the reciprocal village relationship. Most of the young members of their family were not living in the village anymore. There was a general impression that they would move to the town where some of them already had jobs. Therefore, there was no hope of reciprocal help from them. Not only did the other people of the village make excuses for not being able to be a witness but even the members of his own *biradari* were unwilling. In a meeting especially called for this purpose, they made all sorts of excuses and not a single one came forward to be a witness. In the end, Ashraf's own brothers became witnesses for him.

The Involvement of the Whole Community

Continuing with the example of Ashraf's *haveli*, case study one, the active conflict was between Ashraf's family and that of Goora's. First the brothers, then the other immediate relatives and then the *biradari*, friends, neighbours and distant relatives found themselves drawn into the dispute. This led to interesting alignments and alliances. The in-laws of Qasim, Ashraf's brother, who were not directly related to Ashraf, were automatically on his side.

Many village conflicts continue for generations thus leading to the involvement of the whole community. Since there are many conflicts in the village, some are active and others dormant, which might errupt later. At the outbreak of a conflict, old enmities are revived and the entire village becomes automatically involved. Taking again the example of Ashraf's *haveli* the conflict started between two families. The affiliations and allegiances of respective *biradaries* and relatives were taken for granted. Some of the members of the *biradaries* had other conflicts with other *biradaries* who on their part sided with the adversaries. For example, whenYasin, a *Jat*, sided with Ashraf, Naeem, an *Araeen*, who is an enemy of Yasin, automatically sided with the opposite group. Lalo from the *Rajput* family had no direct conflict with Ashraf's family, but some people of the *Ambalvi biradari*, who were helping Goora and his son, had earlier helped Lalo in a conflict against the *Jats*, so he in turn, helped Goora and his sons.

Political affiliations in the village also play a big role in the involvement of the community in a conflict. The whole village is divided in support of two big political parties both having their own leaders. Different *biradaries* are known for their sympathies with one party or another. If the leader of one party takes one side the other goes to the other side to keep the sympathies of their followers. It is mostly during a conflict and because of the help given on these occasions that people change their political affiliations.

This does not mean that there are no persons or families who remain neutral in a conflict. There are people, who have reciprocal relations with both sides and become neutral negotiators making conciliatory efforts. This situation is not unique to this village of Punjab, we have such and similar examples from other traditional societies. Gulliver, for example, provides us with a simple, interesting and similar model of a conflict and the process of dispute settlement among the Ndendeuli of Tanzania:

> In a dispute between neighbors A and E (who are not directly related and who do not regard each other as kin), A expects the support of his kin-neighbor B; and B may well seek the support of his own kin-neighbor C (who is not kin to A) to the side of A. But C might be similarly expected to give his support in the matter to another kin-neighbor D (who is not kin to B) on the side of E who is kin D. Thus A and E are connected: their fields of social action impinge on each other's and are mutually limiting. C is placed in a structurally intermediate position, where he may be compelled to act as mediator; B and D may seek to influence each other and to prevent their own cooperative relations (via C) from undue disruption.

He further writes:

> An actual dispute situation would, of course, be far less simple. It is certain that A and E and, indeed, any of these men would be linked in other effective ways through the kinship network; more neighbors would be involved, and the impingement of the fields of action of A and E would therefore be much more complex. As I have already remarked, a dispute is not a self-contained, isolated social event, for it occurs in the context of the continuum of community life. A or E, or both, may have supported C on some recent occasion, and they both probably participate in C's work parties and he in theirs; A and D, B and D, and B and E may also have been giving each other reciprocal assistance. And all will expect to give and obtain assistance in the future. A real dispute situation is commonly affected by the efforts of particular men to demonstrate and perhaps enlarge their influence over their neighbors

and by particular friendliness or hostility between individual men as a result of past encounters and structural relationships.[42]

It must be added that in this Punjabi village the situation is additionally complicated by the existence of official courts of justice. The courts, on the one hand, cannot take into consideration the whole complicated situation of a village conflict, hence cannot directly help to solve it. But, on the other hand, their mere existence further complicates the already complicated phenomenon.

Prehistory of Conflicts and the After-effects of Decisions

About the conflicts and their resolution in traditional societies Gulliver wrote:

> Briefly, there are three main stages: the prehistory of the dispute, the dispute itself, and the social consequences that follow settlement.[43]

Similarly Cohn observed about the resolution of conflicts in North Indian villages:

> Very often, even in the caste meetings, the case which is ostensibly the crux of the dispute is only a minor expression of a long-standing antagonistic relationship between two families or groups. Often when I discussed a case with a villager, he would start out by discussing events and disputes of twenty years ago. A specific case does not stand alone, but is usually part of a string of disputes.[44]

Equally important are the after-effects of the court decision for the people who have to live with it. Since every member of a village society is known to the other, everyone has an amount of respect (*izzat*) in the eyes of the others. By accepting a humiliating compromise one may lose his status, or honour. During and at the time of settlement of a dispute, the individual's honour always plays the most important role. In Ashraf's case study, the final situation was so humiliating that he decided to leave the village. Another consequence was that the engagement of one of Ashraf's son to a relative of Khana's family was broken. They refused to give their daughter with remarks on the cowardice of Ashraf's family unable to defend their *haveli* today could not be expected to protect their daughter tomorrow.

Gulliver wrote about the importance of considering the consequences of the dispute settlement:

> The dispute may be settled (in the sense previously outlined), but the form and content of the settlement, and its subsequent enforcement as relevant, must necessarily affect relations between the disputants and others involved in some way or other. Dispute settlement does not occur in a social vacuum, insulated from the continuous stream of interaction that makes up ongoing social life - although too often anthropological analysis seems to give the contrary, and false, impression. (...) In any case, however, the settlement in effect defines, or redefines, status, rights, and obligations, both for the disputants themselves and for the other people. Status expectations may be reaffirmed, weakened, strengthened, or altered, and all this has some effect on subsequent relationship and social action.[45]

Court decisions are supposed to be based on objective facts and are, therefore, the so-called 'objective reality or truth' and are thus made without taking into account the 'after-effects' of the decision. Besides, the social context of a village may be unknown to a particular judge, not only because many of them belong to the urban areas, but because each village represents a complex social phenomenon of its own. As Cohn states:

> (...), the Indian village is a multiplex society in which people are tied by a network of relationships, and some of these ties cannot be summarily cut by a decision of a court. People must continue to live and work together in the multiplex society.[46]

Many decisions of the courts make the conflicts more complex rather than solving them. Often court decisions do not remove the bone of contention through their judgements.

Patron-Client Relationship

Village conflicts mostly take place between people of more or less the same socio-economic status and groups, i.e. people of the same *biradari*, or *biradari* of equal status. Social expectations are that the members of the *kammi biradari* would, and are supposed to, avoid quarrelling or fighting with a member of the farmer *biradari* and vice versa. The members of the farmer *biradari* could, on the contrary, react jointly against the *kammi biradari* and say 'if we let him do this today, he would do the same to us tomorrow'. The members of the *kammi biradari* are not supposed to fight with those of a higher socio-economic status, because it would spoil the *izzat* of the higher group and, likewise, the members of the farmer *biradari* are not supposed to indulge in conflicts with the poor *kammi* since these are below their status.

This does not mean that there are no disputes or conflicts between the rich (farmer and industrialist) and the poor (*kammi*) *biradaries*. These conflicts could arise because of different reasons and situations, such as: if a member of the *kammi biradari* is not performing his traditional role anymore and especially if he is a migrant in the village and is pursuing a respectable profession like running a shop, or a business such as power-looms. There are enough examples of *kammis* especially of *Taili* (oilmen) and *Julahe* (weavers) both called *Maliks* who because of their power-loom business have moved into higher social status in the village.

The other possibility is when the members of a *kammi biradari* or those of the low socio-economic status group, like the poor in the farmer *biradaries*, become involved in a conflict against a member of a higher social status, especially if they have the patronage of an influential individual who wants to disgrace his opponent.

The whole village is divided into a lot of smaller groups always merging into bigger groups and at the end two groups emerge headed by two 'big men' affiliated to two political parties, the Muslim League and the People's Party. The members of these groups and subgroups help each other in different ways, some actively in fighting and others with their influence in the *panchayat*, courts and the police. This patron-client relationship could be in some cases very clearly seen. For example, the workers in the power-loom businesses of Naeem or Zulfiqar are helped by them in their conflicts. There are some village *gundas* (bullies, goon) who, if needed, would put things in order for the patron, i.e. fight for them.

Multi-Legal/Bi-Legal Systems and the Choice of the Forum

Moore wrote about the Indian Justice system:

> The Indian villager is faced with a dual legal system. For nearly two hundred years traditional village councils have existed side by side with the formal system of British jurisprudence. (...) Thus, in the Indian village a dispute may be resolved within the network of the extended family, in a variety of traditional councils, in the gram panchayat or at the state level. A disputant will usually rely on a combination of forums.[47]

The analysis of the case studies shows that the choice of the forum is open to the parties and the parties choose from a combination of the given possibilities. In several cases compromises were made and broken several times, then the case came to the police and courts and then back to the village and in the end to a combination of the two. It is a very common mode of operation and the villagers utilize both systems, as a pressure instrument using the official one.

This is perhaps not only typical of this village or Pakistani and Indian villages alone. Most of the countries of the Third

Diagram No. 2 showing some characteristics of the social organization from the point of view of one family.

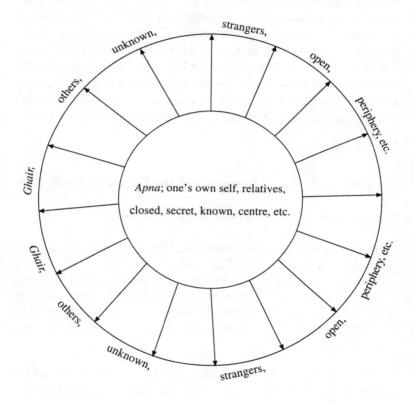

Diagram No. 3 shows the area of influence of the traditional and the official justice systems.

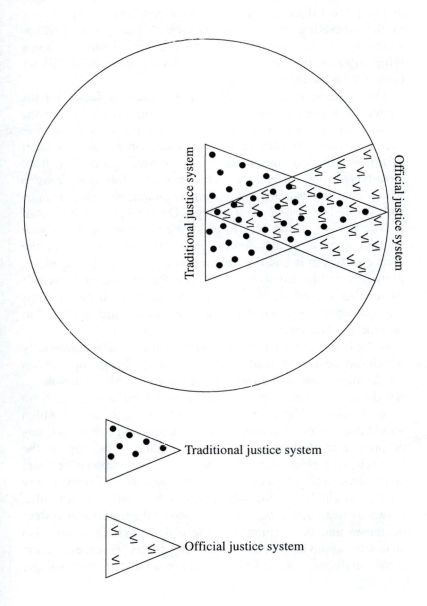

Traditional justice system

Official justice system

World which have experienced colonial subjugation find themselves in a similar situation. Gulliver in his analysis of the *Case Studies of Law in Non-Western Societies* wrote that 'Many disputes are subject to treatment by a combination of the two modes operating in different phases'.[48] One could perhaps generally say that in cities and big towns, or industrial area one relies more on the official system and vice versa. With this we come to the choice of forum.

The characteristics of conflicts is the decisive factor for the choice of forum. There are several forums available for the solution of conflicts. For the sake of simplification these have been classified into official and traditional forums, and the latter is further divided into formal and informal parts. We have already seen the different possible groups within and between whom conflicts can arise like *ghar, khandan, sharika, biradari* and, similarly, *mohalla* and village. On the basis of causes of conflicts it is not that easy to make a generalization as to what conflict goes to which forum. This generalization about the choice of forum is based more on groups involved in a conflict. Furthermore, the involvement of one forum does not exclude the further use of another. Generally speaking, if two forums are contacted simultaneously their functioning are supposed to provide the pressures.

A look at the social organization of the village community which has been presented in a very simplified form in diagram no. 2, shows that as we move from the centre to the periphery, we move into zones of familiarity and familiarity, i.e. from *apna* to *ghair*. The core of *apna* is a nucleus family which within itself represents totally hierarchical arrangements and sets of procedure (father or sometimes mother at the top of the hierarchy, the elder brother or sister above the younger brothers and sisters, etc.), denoting respect and authority. If there is any conflict at this level, it is solved within the family. As we move outwards from this centre the influence of the traditional system decreases and the influence of the official system which also stands for anonymity and therefore objectivity increases. This is shown in diagram no. 3. This does not mean that in every village, or family, this is the absolute principle. There are some villages where the village *panchayat* is more effective than in others. That could be due to the fact that the social conditions are more conducive to the state of affairs there. Similarly, there are individuals and families who adopt one system or the other. The triangles of diagram no. 3 should not be considered as straight lines, they illustrate trends. This diagram shows the ideal conditions necessary for the optimal functioning of the two systems. What is ideal for one may not be for the other. The most interesting area is in the middle of the diagram where the two triangles meet. This is where both the systems, the courts and the *panchayats*, are used, and is very often the case evident in our case studies.

This study concludes that *zan*, *zar*, and *zamin* are the originators of most conflicts, which are prolonged in direct co-ordination with the degrees of *izzat* and *ghairat* involved in any conflict. *Zan*, *zar* and *zamin* give rise to conflicts because of the unclear division and imprecise laws and rules regulating the property. Nor is there any codification of problems relating to property. Similarly, the difference between the ideal and real behaviour towards one's own and other women, also leads to conflicts. Another feature about village conflicts is that they take place between groups, i.e. between or within different units of the social organization and the choice of the forum depends upon the nature of the conflict as also the disputants.

NOTES

1. Roberts, 1979, p. 49.
2. 'Wenn auch nicht in dieser Konfliktformel, so lassen sich die haeufigsten Konfliktauslaeser dennoch in einer aehnlichen Dreiheit fassen, naemlich in zar, zan, zamin.' Steul, 1981, p. 219.

    Similar discussions are also known in this village. Some people are of the view that *zamin* and *zar* belong together and could be called capital, others say all the three could be summed up under *izzat* (honour). But the majority agrees with *zan*, *zar*, and *zamin*. In any case, *zar* cannot be changed with *sar* in this area since blood feuds are not as common as among the Pashtoons.

3. 'Von den 114 im Becken von Khost erarbeiteten Konfliktfaellen entstanden demnach 19.30% oder 22 Faelle nach Verstoessen gegen sar: 'Kopf', (...), 25.43% oder 29 Faelle nach Verstoessen gegen zan: 'Frau', (...), und 55.26% oder 63 Faelle nach Verstoessen gegen *zamin*: 'Land', (...)' Steul, 1981, p. 220.

4. Epstein, 1962, p. 145 quoted from Cohn, 1965, p. 104.

5. Cohn, 1965, p. 104.

6. Srinivas, 1962, p. 113 quoted from Cohn, 1965, p. 93.

7. Barth, 1985, p. 25.

8. Bailey made similar observation about land in the Indian villages Orissa: 'Titles to land are part of the system of private rights in land and are foreign to the village system. The system of transfers of land was initiated by, and is maintained by, the Administration. Effective title cannot be obtained in the village council, (...)' Bailey, 1957, p. 263.

9. Gluckman, 1965, p. 116.

10. Cohn, 1961, p. 621.

11. Cheshire: The Modern Law of Real Property (9th edn., 1962), pp. 5–6. Quoted from Gluckman, 965, pp. 115–16.

12. Ahmad, 1972, p. 105.

13. Ahmad, 1972, p. 105.

14. Darling, 1925, p. 69.

15. Punjabi expression: *Kuryan da tokra.*

16. Punjabi expression: *Kale munh walyan chorailan.*

17. Punjabi saying: *Allah kare satan kuryan da munh dhowain.*

18. Punjabi proverb: *Doodh te put Allah de rahmat ae.*

19. For comparison, see case study of Aslam's daughter (case study no. 3): he was helped by the neighbours and street fellows when the boy wanted to take away the girl by force. In the case of Kaloo's daughter the whole village condemned Goora Numberdar and his sons.

20. Ahmad, 1972, p. 105.

21. After they are located and if brought back home, the girl is asked by her family to tell the police and court that she was kidnapped. If she refuses the men of her family may kill her. In one such case the daughter of Kaloo *Jat* fell in love with the son of Goora Numberdar. Both of them ran away and were found by the police in Dajkot. Kaloo had already reported the kidnapping of his daughter to the police. Both, the boy and the girl, were brought back to the village. Kaloo wanted the girl to give a statement in the court that she was kidnapped by Goora's son. The family tried their best but the girl did not agree. One day before the statement was to be recorded, the girl's brother shot her dead. He afterwards went to the police and reported his action. After two months he was released. Goora's son is still in jail but without the girl's statement against him. He is expected to come back soon.

22. Ahmad, 1972, p. 105.
23. For further details see *Woman and Law in Pakistan: An Exposition of the Socio-Legal Status of Women*, by Rashida Patel. Karachi, Faiza Publishers, 1979.
24. 'Sometimes, the in-laws of the girl trouble her for bringing less dowry. They generally taunt her and sometimes even beat her.' Hooja, Dr. (Mrs.) S.L., *Dowry System in India: A Case Study 1969*, Delhi.
25. Two of the many expressions are quoted here: 'be careful it is not a part of your dowry' or, 'why did you not tell your mother to give you this if you needed it'.
26. Hooja wrote: '(...) and become associated with social status and family prestige. This association has introduced an element of competition carrying with it 'demonstration tendency'.' Hooja, 1969, p. 1.
27. For further details of dowry and problems of dowry see: Hooja, Dr. (Mrs.) S.L., *Dowry System in India, A Case Study 1969*, Dehli, and Tambiah, S.J., 'Dowry and Bridewealth and the Property Rights', in, *Cambridge Papers in Social Anthropology*, 1973, Cambridge.
28. The meanings given in Ferozson's Urdu-English Dictionary are 'honour, grandeur, glory, dignity, respect, esteem, reputation, fame'.
29. According to Ferozson's Urdu-English Dictionary it means 'shame, modesty, bashfulness'.
30. The meanings given in Ferozson's are 'modesty, shame, shyness'.
31. Here *ghairat* is the most complex and meaningful word. The meanings found in Ferozson's Dictionary are 'care of what is sacred and inviolable, sense of honour, honour, courage, modesty, bashfulness, shame, envy, indignation, enmity'.
32. Front part of the long shirts worn by the people, normally used to carry small things. The expression is especially used with reference to receiving something requested for. For example when the people go to a shrine they would pray 'Data (holy person) fill my *jholi*' or a *kammi* would say at the end of a ceremoney 'put something in my *jholi* also'. People, relatives mostly, when they go to request a daughter or son as a mate for their child, also say 'put something in my *jholi*'. It has many situational meanings.
33. Walsh, 1929, pp. 84, 85.
34. Darling, 1934 p. 50.
35. Keiser, 1991, p. 53. Enough literature exists on the use of these and similar other terms and concepts among the Pashtoons, like, Steul, 1981, pp. 136–40, 169–72; Barth, p. 1959, 81, and Keiser, 1991, pp. 42, 52, 54.
36. Eglar, 1960, p. 45.
37. Keiser, 1991, pp. 42, 52, 53–4.
38. The advice of a worldly wise mother to her sons.
39. Eglar, 1960, p. 122.

40. Moore, 1993, p. 528.
41. Ahmad, 1972, p. 102.
42. Gulliver, 1969, p. 31–2.
43. Gulliver, 1969, p. 15.
44. Cohn, 1967, p. 156.
45. Gulliver, 1969, p. 16.
46. Cohn, 1967, p. 156.
47. Moore, 1985, p. 6.
48. Gulliver, 1969, p. 21.

CHAPTER 3

THE TRADITIONAL JUSTICE SYSTEM

The traditional justice system is a simplified term for a large number of differently practised versions of folk law. These vary in macro-settings like Punjab, Balochistan, NWFP, etc. and in the micro-settings of villages. In the words of Darling, writing about Punjabi villages in the first half of the twentieth century:

> The *panchayat* has many different forms, for uniformity is as unnatural to the village as it is natural to Government. It may be confined to a single caste, (...), it may embrace a dozen villages of the same tribe; or, (...) it may go no further than invoking the help of 'white-bearded elders' to compromise a dispute. (...), it generally deals only with cases affecting a single village, (...), it sometimes takes up cases in which the parties live in different villages, (...) In single village cases, if the village is not a large one, all concerned meet in conclave and matters are decided in open assembly. But if it is too large for this, the different castes or quarters of the village depute representatives to attend meetings.[1]

Hoebel who made a legal anthropological study on Pakistan, writes about the traditional justice system:

> Deeply embedded in the village and tribal areas of Pakistan is a vast array of local folk systems of law varying from village to village and area to area. (...), it is a relatively uncharted universe. It is a law that is based, among other things, on the landlord-client relationship, on modified caste traditions, on patrilineal social structure and preferred parallel cousin marriage, on lineage opposition crosscut by opposing factions, on feud and overt violence, and on the presence or absence

of an effective village council. (...). Ideologically, it incorporates Islamic Law, but the folk ignorance of Islam is in fact profound. The Great Tradition and the Little Traditions are, as is to be expected, two different things.[2]

Cohn tried to find out some sort of formula which is universally adoptable for the whole of India on the basis of these unlimited possibilities by reducing variations in the types of villages to four basic categories:

> The classification is based on village size and the nature of dominance particular castes can utilize in settling disputes. The four kinds of villages are: (1) villages with a small population of one caste; (2) multicaste single-head villages; (3) multicaste dominant-caste villages; (4) multicaste, nondominant-caste villages.[3]

By replacing the word 'caste' with the word *biradari* for the village under study, it falls into the fourth category. The functioning of the traditional system does not depend only on the dominance or otherwise of one or more *biradaries*. It, similarly, does not only depend on the existence of a village 'big man'. It depends upon many other factors and differs from *biradari* to *biradari* and from family to family even in the same village. These differences in form and function are mainly due to the absence of a central control system, as well as, the absence of written formalities about the form and the procedure to be adopted for making it a unilineal system.

The traditional justice system operates through *khandan*, *thara*, *baithak*, *haveli*, *dera*, *panchayat*, *pirs*, saints, etc. Some details about the functioning of these institutions are given here:

Khandan (family)

Moore observed in a Rajasthani village in India:

> Intra-familial disputes are kept as quiet as possible and are generally solved within the infrastructure of an extended family.[4]

The family—nuclear, joint or extended—is structured hierarchically throughout, based on status and position. The grandfather or father and in their absence the uncle or the eldest brother is the head of the family unit, with the accepted position to adjudicate on disputes within this small circle. His decisions are respected as are his sanctions. There are fathers who are known to be cruel and there are also those who are praised for their good acts in the village. This means that there is also a check by the community and, therefore, a person is not totally free in these decisions. Good fathers, good children, and their opposite are known in the village and are also talked about as such.

One may say that there are, on the one hand, feelings of love and affection, and, on the other hand, of fear and respect. The leader or head has the authority and responsibility. The leader or head of the family has responsibility to provide food and other necessities as it is his duty to keep the family united and solve the conflicts. He has to present himself as loveable and dear, but, also as a person of authority, one whom others have to fear. The fathers keep a certain distance from the members of the family to maintain their fear and respect. This is not only true for the fathers but also for other relations like elder brothers, uncles, etc., according to their age and status and position in the family.

The members of the family obey the head because of love as also the authority and fear of sanctions. A family, as opposed to all other institutions of the traditional system, take it as their responsibility to solve all sorts of problems and conflicts between their members. The moment a conflict arises in the family, the members become active in solving it.

The solutions are the decisions of the head of the family and sometimes compromises are arrived at with mutual understanding. These decisions are not only on their own wishes, but are mostly made under the pressure from the community and even against the emotions and love for the sake of saving the *izzat* of the family or of the head. One such example would be the killing of a daughter or sister having an illicit relationship, or of those who run away with a man. If such relationships or elopements become known, or such rumours spread, then both the woman and the man must be killed. But if such relationships do not become public such a severe action is mostly avoided. This is especially true in the so-called respectable families.

Some illustrations show the role of the *khandan*. When Maqbool married a girl of his own choice against his father's wishes he was disinherited. Maqbool was already engaged to the daughter of one of the relatives.[5] He had to leave the house of his father, and returned shortly before the death of his father. The situation became difficult for the father as he had to disinherit the other son, too as he was refused the land for cultivation because of the quarrel with his wife. The father wanted his other son Muhammada, to beat his wife for quarrelling with him. Since he had only two sons, this behaviour was criticized in the village and the father gained the reputation of being a terrible man. He lived alone for quite some time since his wife had already died. He fell ill and Muhammada and Meedan (his wife) came to look after him and thus normal relations were restored after a gap of two years. Muhammada could cultivate the land of his father again. Maqbool, who had returned before the death of his father, sold his part of the land after his death, and deposited the money in the newly opened co-operative banks in Misalpur. Later he lost all his money because of bunglings in the bank. In the village it was said that it was due to the *baddu'ah* (imprecations) of the dead father.

There are many other such examples of excommunication by fathers from property and the most common reason is a marriage against their wishes, but sometimes it is also because of the bad relations between the parents and the children; in such a case, especially, the daughters-in-law are blamed. In case study six, Ashraf's family, two of the brothers, Ashraf and the elder brother Naseer, were each excommunicated by the parents, one after the other, for a year because of a quarrel between the mother and their wives, in which they had sided with their wives.

The parents always keep their relatives and *biradari* in mind and any attempt to marry outside the *biradari* is a great insult for the family. Marriages within the *biradari* against the wishes of the fathers are comparatively less troublesome than those outside the *biradari* as this could lead to the permanent excommunication of the family by the *biradari*. Marriages outside the *biradari* are very rare and are usually love marriages, or they take place when a suitable marriage partner is not available. With the passage of time and the intervention of some relatives and friends usually reconciliation is brought about.

It is important to mention that the right of excommunication is not limited to the father. If the father himself does something totally against the interest and desire of the family, then he might face the same consequences. But incidents of this kind are very rare. The reasons in such instances could be the second marriage of the father, with or without the consent of the first wife especially if there are children and even more so if they are grown up. Excommunication does not simply mean expulsion from the house, village or area. It usually also means breaking up of relationships.

No matter how frequent the quarrels between father and children, husband and wife, brothers and sisters etc. might be, going to court against each other would be the highest insult and disgrace for the whole family and is thus avoided under almost all circumstances. A third party, respected relatives, neighbours, or friends, helping in resolving conflict, is also considered a disgrace for the family.

In spite of the quarrels and fights between them they make a common cause if there is any quarrel with a stranger. Every threat from the outside makes the inner unity stronger. Brothers, even when they are not on speaking terms, if attacked and endangered by somebody from outside, come together. Similar is the case with extended families with the only difference that the cohesion or feeling of oneness is weaker than in the nuclear family. The factor of competition between cousins and the lack of a powerful leader like the father in the nucleus family, might cause some conflicts to be brought to the courts, but this is not a rule.

Thara, *Baithak*, *Haveli*, and *Dera*

There are different places for social gatherings of the men in the village. These include: a *thara* (a sort of a raised platform outside the house near the entrance, half a meter to a meter high), a *baithak* (a room at one end of the house or animal house), a *haveli* (traditionally an animal and men's house) and a *dera* (a place in the fields with many trees, one or two rooms). All these places are exclusively for men, however, sometimes a female servant may come in to clean.

Nearly every villager has a *thara* which is kept in good condition; swept every day and occasionally plastered with hay mixed mud. Because it is in the open, its use is restricted to men. *Tharas* find more use during the winter days and summer evenings. Some people even sleep here during the summer nights.Those sitting on a *thara* may come from distant streets but mostly they are the neighbours and *mohalladars* (street fellows).

Similarly many of the villagers have a *baithak*. *Baithaks* are mostly used during the summer days and winter evenings and nights. A *baithak* is a status symbol, depending on its type. A good *baithak*, for example, would have a *thara* attached to it. It could be said, in general, that since the number of *baithaks* per house are increasing, their importance as a status symbol is decreasing.

The *haveli* was traditionally meant as the animal-house but has now become a status symbol. A few well-to-do villagers have a *haveli*. It usually has a big courtyard, some rooms for the animals and one or two rooms for men.

There are only four big farmers who have a *dera* in the whole village. *Dera* is traditionally a place in the fields which only rich farmers could afford because of the land they possessed and the necessary requirements like servants. The *deras* are places of much activity in summer days. *Charpais* (wooden cots strung with rope) are arranged around the *hukka,* sometimes there are more than one *hukka*, according to the influence and wealth of the farmer and the number of visitors. *Dera* remains one of the most prestigious status symbols. They are known by the name of the farmer or the name of the family like *Shahan da dera*, Guli *da dera*, Chadharan *da dera* etc.

Smoking a *hukka* (the water pipe), or rather *hukka* 'sharing' is a common activity in all these places and it carries a great deal of social meaning for a villager. As Slocum observes:

> The men have their informal gatherings of friends in the evening. They sit together with their water pipes (Huqqa) and smoke turn by turn while discussing the matters of the day. Any news from the city is of great interest to them and every one comments on it according to his knowledge. (...) Criticism of the deviations of individuals from the traditional norms of behaviour is also common in such meetings. In important family matters advice may be sought from close friends.[6]

A *hukka* is not shared with everyone, especially not with those belonging to a lower class, for example, a *kammi*. *Kammis* are not supposed to smoke from the *hukka* of a farmer. Villagers are mostly linked to several *hukka* groups, since they are not, at least not always, mutually exclusive. In a conflict, this social togetherness would be affected, resulting in *hukka pani band karna* (literally meaning, to stop the *hukka* and water), marking the break of social relations. This could happen at the level of an individual, a family, a *biradari*, or even a village. For understanding this breaking of *hukka*-relations we must understand who smokes it with whom and where.

News is exchanged, problems are discussed and rumours are generated at the above mentioned *hukka* smoking places. If the problem is between those belonging to the same *hukka* group, these may even be solved in the discussions there. The *Chaudhary* (as the *Jats*, and *Gujars* call themselves), *Rana* (as the *Rajputs* call themselves), or a *Mian* (as the *Araeen* call themselves; they also call themselves *chaudhary* sometimes), may send for the two involved in the conflict, and after listening to the problem come to an agreement. Any one of the parties may also bring up the problem himself and solicit the help of the host. The conflicts solved here are mostly of a minor nature.

Unlike the family, it is not the duty of the *hukka* group or the host of the group to solve the conflicts, but by doing so the host gains more respect. The most common method is by complaining or talking it out until a solution, which is mostly a compromise, is found.

Panchayats, Kath, Paryah

The distinction between the two words *panchayat* and *kath* used simultaneously and alternatively, i.e. denoting a similar phenomenon, needs to be made. The word *kath* means a gathering and *panchayat*, literally, means 'a gathering of five'; but *panchayats* have functioned with more than five members. One possible difference is that the meetings of *panchayats* are normally held for one particular part of the community and have more judicial functions and the *kaths* deal with general problems and are held for the whole village. *Panchayat*, in the words of Moore is:

> A panchayat literally means a gathering of five, though today the number holds no significance. It is a term that has been used through the ages for the traditional village assemblies. The leaders, referred to as panches, are not elected or chosen in any formal way, but are men, who, being respected by the village or by the parties, are asked to assemble to help resolve the problem. It is a voluntary committee that varies in size depending on the gravity of the offense or the importance of the parties involved. There are no formal rules or format. It is a group of friends who will sit and talk-out the problem at hand.[7]

Another description of the panchayat is provided by Berreman:

> *Panchayats* are ad hoc rather than permanently constituted bodies. Their membership is recruited by invitations sent out by elders of the households involved to other interested households, who then send representatives. The membership varies with circumstances, but it is traditionally confined to the high castes. (...) Councils or

panchayats serve mainly to coordinate and express public opinion. Usually the members of the council are well aware in advance, of the facts and opinions relevant to any dispute put before them. Their decision is often a means of making official that upon which there is already general agreement.[8]

To be precise a *panchayat* is a council of any number of *mu'tabar* (trustworthy, respectable) people, summoned or meeting on their own, called by one, both or a third party, given *ikhtiyar* (authority, discretion) by one or both or none of the parties to decide a conflict.

Types of *Panchayats*

The *panchayats* could be divided on the basis of their areas of influence, a particular group they are called for, etc., into inter-village, village *panchayats*, *biradari*, *sharika* and *khandan panchayats*.

Village panchayats

Village *panchayats* differ from inter-village *panchayats*: the *panchayaties* (members of the *panchayat*) in the village *panchayat* belong to the same village. These members could belong to different *biradaries*, in a multi-*biradari* village like Misalpur, or they could belong to different groups of the same *biradari*, in a single *biradari* village, since in such cases sub-*biradaries* function like different *biradaries*. Village *biradaries* do not meet so often. They usually meet to discuss common village problems and when there is rivalry against another village. They are more often called *kath* than *panchayat*. Village *panchayats* are more chaotic as compared to the inter-village or *biradari panchayats*.

Inter-village panchayats

The inter-village *panchayats* are very rare and mostly meet to discuss very serious conflicts, in case the whole area is endangered due to the confrontation, or the meeting of such a *panchayat* could be considered as a further hope after the village *panchayat* has failed. In a conflict between *Rajputs* and *Jats*, where Phera (a *Jat*), had killed a woman of the *Rajputs*, the case was brought before the court and it became clear from the trial that Phera was going to be sentenced to death. There was a meeting of important and well known people from nearby villages who met to make peace between the two parties but failed. The other examples of inter-village *panchayats* are on questions of dispute between two or more villages on the division of irrigation water, common lands, and sports, when and if they are arranged on a village basis. Still another reason are marriage conflicts if one *biradari* is settled in two villages who have marriage relations. The members of such *panchayats* are the influential rich and well-known people of the villages or area, such as important politicians, and vary, depending upon the type of conflict.

Biradari panchayats

The most common *panchayats* are *biradari panchayats*. In case of conflicts between two *biradaries* or members of two *biradaries*, the respectables or elders of these two *biradaries* meet. In such meetings important members of third *biradaries* might also be invited. If we could replace the word caste with *biradari*, in a description of the two types of *panchayats* in India provided by Baxi, it holds true about the *panchayats* in the study of Misalpur.

> Generally, caste (Jati) panchayats deal with conflicts of interests and values within Jati-groups, including factional alliances within those groups. Village or territorial panchayats deal with conflicts of

interest cutting across caste factors, though those very factors may often play a crucial role in the 'resolution' of a conflict.[9]

He noted further:

> Jati NSLS [Non-State Legal System] primarily involves disputes and conflicts which are related to the maintenance of *Jati* ranking (in terms of ritual axis of pollution and purity) and solidarity. Ritual lapses, marital relations, commission of polluting acts, sexual deviance, inter se land disputes, credit transactions, patron-client (jajmani) relations—all those fall typically within the range of *Jati* NSLS.[10]

The *panchayats* of all *biradaries* do not function in the same ways. The procedures of arriving at a compromise and their effectiveness changes depending upon whether it is a farmer *biradari* or *kammi biradari*. For example, if there is a conflict between the barbers, shoemakers, *dehkans* (tenants), etc. then very often an intervention by the *Chaudhary*, or *Rana* or other landlord could solve the conflict. This is especially effective if both the parties are working for the same landlord. The working of the *panchayats* of *kammi biradaries* could be affected by the other *biradaries*. In such *biradari* meetings one of the influential members of the farmer *biradari* could be invited to take part. When the daughter of Aslam[11] was abducted and the meeting of the *Malik biradari* was called, Akhtar *Jat* was invited to take part in the meeting. There are *biradaries* with one head and others with none or more. Some *biradaries* are more closely knit than others. The *Ambalvi biradari* is known for its unity and effective *panchayat* in the village. There was a very rich farmer, who united his *biradari* and after his death this tradition is maintained by the other rich members of the *biradari*. The people of the other *biradaries* say that all *Ambalvies* have sworn loyality to the *biradari*. The *Araeen biradari* is also very closely knit and they also have one rich businessman (Naeem, who has been mentioned several times) as their leader. As opposed to this, *Jats* and *Gujars* are not so united; therefore their *biradari panchayats* are consequently not very effective.

Biradari panchayats deal mostly with disputes and conflicts which are a danger to the unity and honour of the *biradari*. These mostly relate to marriage affairs. It has already been mentioned that there is a *biradari* endogamy (people marry within their *biradaries*) which is rarely broken. If it happens it could lead to a *biradari* dissolution of marriage relations with a family. Elopements, abductions, illicit relationships, divorce, separation, engagement or other disputes arising out of marital relations within the same *biradari* are solved by the *biradari panchayats*. These matrimonial conflicts are best solved within the families. *Biradaries* take full part in marriage and other ceremonial occasions and on these occasions offended relatives and members of the *biradari* are reconciled: a group of *biradari* members go to the house of the offended party and beg their pardon.

It has been mentioned earlier that the *biradaries* consist of *goots* (could be translated here as a sub-*biradari*), *sharikas* and *khandans*. Their members enjoy more respect and authority as compared to the other members of the *biradari*, a fact which is indispensible for the success of the *panchayat*. These *panchayats* are more effective and deal with all kinds of conflicts. The leaders of *goots*, and *sharikas* mostly represent their members in the next higher ranking *panchayats*.

Panchayaties: Members of the *Panchayat*

The important question is who constitutes the *panchayats*? Baxi writes about India:

> While these remain to be systematically studied, a mix of any of the following variables offers some clue to authority sources of legitimation. The close correlation between age and wisdom provides one mix—the *panchayats* are often led by, even composed of, such men. Esteem, reputation, integrity, and charisma provide another mix. Economic base, as related to social status (Weber's analysis of status-groups as distinct from class is still, despite its

seminality, largely ignored in Indian studies) also invests power and authority in certain men. So does the status of being a faction leader. Although not so prevalent now, we cannot altogether ignore the hereditary or royal allocations of role and authority.[12]

The case of the *panchies* of the village Misalpur is of a similar kind. The members of the village *panchayat* are further selected from the members of the *biradari panchayats*. The members must be known for their fairness, political influence, economic resources and influence in the family, *biradari* and village also play an important role.

But the *panchies* are not always and only known for their 'positive' and 'fair' qualities, for example Moore wrote about the qualities of a member of *panchayat* in a Rajasthani village in India:

He has three brothers, two grown sons and many other relatives. Equally as important, he has money. His wealth is rumoured to be amassed by stealing cattle, blackmail and selling his influence to any 'worthy' cause. It is commonly acknowledged that fifteen years earlier, Kalif almost beat to death a Nara Brahman, Ram. He was becoming a threat to Kalif's power by acquiring a rival wealth of land and cattle.[13]

The political position is now becoming even more important since the introduction of the system of the Basic Democracies in 1959. *Panchies* (members of the *panchayat*) are the leaders of the political parties. While the *biradari panchayats* retain traditionally character enshrined to some extent, the village *panchayats* are taking on a very political character. If the characteristics of Naeem is examined who is one of the most active members of the *panchayat* it is found that he has been the chairman of the Union Council several times. He is the leading member of the Pakistan Muslim League in his area. He owns many power-looms, and is one of the richest men in the village. He is comparatively more educated having attained his matriculation (in a village where only 4 per cent of the population can read and write),[14] and, above all, he belongs to the *Araeen biradari*, the dominant *biradari*, with more unity as compared to other *biradaries* in the village. He takes an active part in village affairs and quarrels, and is known to pay a monthly 'fee' to the police on account of which he has good connections with them. He is also known to employ *gundas*.

Karim, the other important figure in Misalpur, is similar in characteristic. He is a member of the *Malik biradari*, the largest in the village, owns many power-looms, and supports the Pakistan People's Party. He became Chairman of the Union Council twice. He spends his money lavishly; tea and food is often served at his *haveli*. While relatively new in politics, he takes a keen interest in village affairs. His support comes from the *kammi biradaries* to which he belongs as well as from the Pakistan People's Party. Some *gundas* work for him also and he, too, has connections with the police.

Modus Operandi of a *Panchayat*

The first question is who can and does summon the *panchayat*? The meeting of a *panchayat* is not a matter of course, neither does it meet immediately or automatically after a dispute, fight, or conflict has occured. There is no single uniform method. Both protagonists can, usually the victim, approach it. The best and ideal situation is when the *panchayat* is arranged by a third party, for example, one of the relatives or friends or one of the *panchies*.

In practice the *panchayats* do not meet at the initiative of a poor or weak party, against the richer and stronger one. If a *kammi* comes to the *panchies* and asks for a meeting against a farmer who has abused him, he might not be able to get them to meet, but a similar request by the farmer would be accepted.[15] This means that if the conflict is between *kammis*, then the meeting of the *kammi biradari panchayat* would be more easily established, but if the conflict is between the *kammi* and the farmer *biradari* and the *kammi* wants the village *panchayat* or the *panchayat* of the farmer's *biradari* to meet, it would not be possible unless another farmer supports him. Similarly, an appeal to the *panchayat* by a poor farmer against a richer and stronger farmer would also be ineffective. This is one of the reasons why the *kammi biradaries* are against the *panchayat* system, and in spite of the official system being costly and time consuming, they take recourse to the latter, in the hope of justice.

The consent of both parties is a necessary pre-condition for calling a meeting of a *panchayat*. If the other side is unwilling then a *panchayat* cannot be initiated. As shown in instances cited earlier, villagers may refuse to act as *panchies* against the more influential disputants, on the plea that their own *izzat* would be at stake in the hands of those who had none. If, however, a *panchayat* is established through the influence of the stronger party, the poorer side of lesser status would not dare ignore any summons of the *panchayat*.

Panchayats are not immediately called after a conflict has taken place. In the beginning, some would try the police, the courts etc. Then the parties, especially the one interested in the meeting of the council, must build up a community view, which means he must narrate his problem starting with his immediate neighbours, friends and acquaintances and gauge their reaction and opinions. If others find the case sympathetic and justified, the process of lobbying starts and then the meeting of the council can take place.

There are different ways of informing the people concerned about the meetings to be convened. The *panchies* send a *choukidar* (watchman) to inform those concerned with the meeting. But this is mostly the case when the meeting is meant only for a particular group of people. The mosque's loudspeakers are also used for announcing the meeting and this is mostly done when the *panchayat* is dealing with a matter concerning the whole village. Drum beating is also used. This means a *mirasi* or *dhom* (traditional musician of the village) goes around in the village with his drum. After beating the drum for a while he announces the meeting, especially when it is meant for the whole village. Sometimes this method is used to announce the decision of the *panchayat*, to inform all those who did not or could not attend the meeting.

There is no fixed, formal proceeding or procedures for the meeting of the *panchayat*. According to the given situation and circumstances, the nature of the *panchayat* and the procedures change. Procedures of the *panchayats* are differentiated on the basis of the purpose for which they are held, e.g. some *panchayats* would decide some types of conflict; others may deliberate on the common stand towards matters concerning the whole group or community.

Punctuality is not considered necessary, nor is there any time limit prescribed. Continuous coming and going can be observed in the meetings, especially during open *panchayats* called for a common cause of the village.

If it is a matter of common interest, people start arriving at the venue early and the discussion starts at the arrival of the first few people which continues until it is felt that enough has been discussed. Everyone may take part in the general discussion and help frame the issue. Finally, someone, mostly a volunteer, tries to announce aloud what is considered to be the meaning of the gathering and in case of disagreement the voices against the summary are raised and amendments may be made. On occasions these meetings can turn into chaotic scenes of mismanagement, shouting, and interruptions. This is more true in large meetings in which all villagers or many people take part. The discussions do not always remain fixed to the point. In one meeting, several disputes or points might be discussed.

The procedure is different if the meeting of the *panchayat* is called for the resolution of a dispute between two parties. One party, usually the complainant, is required by one of the *panchies* to explain the charge. After that the accused is asked to clear his position. Generally, the two sides speak simultaneously leading to interruptions, on the spot explanations and counter accusations with the *panchies* trying to regulate the turns and proceedings, at the same time pointing out the ill-behaviours of one or the other side. After both sides have had ample time and have talked out their grievances the *panchies* carry out consultations and work out a compromise. While announcing their decision they seek agreement of both the parties. Some minor adjustments might again be made at the request of one or the other party. One of the important aspect of the proceeding here is to let the people talk out their grievances and make their *gellee shikway* (complaints to each other). The decisions of the *panchayats* are seldom a surprise, as they can already be guessed from private discusions among the people. *Panchayat* decisions are not abrupt but a gradual development in which their meeting could be seen as the last step of the process.

If a compromise is arrived at and is accepted by both parties, they are made to stand up to embrace each other and shake hands. Embracing and shaking of hands is a symbol of ending the conflict.

Methods of Punishment and their Effectiveness

The range and the area of influence of the *panchayat* is very wide and open. It covers civil problems arising out of marriage, debt, division of property, and disputes relating to these matters and at the same time it covers crimes like theft, murder, and fights, etc. As the types of problem brought before the *panchayat* are various, so are the methods of punishment and of the enforcement of its judgements. The type and nature of *panchayat*—village, *biradari*, or *sharika panchayat*—also plays a role on the type and effectiveness of the punishment. There is no agency or institution responsible for implementing the decisions of the *panchayats*. Generally coercive and physical punishments are not awarded by the council; this is left to the people themselves. The principle seems to be that when the parties, or at least one of them, are tired of fighting and interested in ending the conflict they may appeal to the council.

The decisions of *panchayats*, irrespective of the type of *panchayat*, could be divided into compromises and verdicts. Though it is difficult to draw a clear line between these two types but generally it could be said that compromises are in civil matters and cases where two parties seek help of the *panchayat* whereas verdicts are in cases of crimes like theft or cases where the interest of the concerned community is at stake. Similarly the *panchayat's* decisions are more effective against the weak and poor than against rich, influential, and strong members of the community. Likewise, compromises are less effectively implemented compared to the verdicts. *Panchayats* of lesser level, *sharika panchayats* as compared to village *panchayat* for example, are more effective in making and implementing their decisions.

Depending upon the nature of the problem there are a number of punishments a *panchayat* may award. These include ostracism, fine, disgrace, physical punishments, etc.[16] We shall take a more detailed look at these punishments:

Ostracism

Yasin ran a mill for making flour, a saw for cutting wood and a provision store in the village. He was one of the important, rich businessmen of the village. One day he was caught mixing sawdust into the wheat before grinding it into flour.

Public curiosity arose because he never ran his millstone during the day. He collected the wheat during the day and started grinding it at night. This was observed by Barkat Bibi, an old and highly respected woman in the village. She told Shafi Muhammad about it who on his part talked to some other respectables of the village and secret inquiries were made and the information turned out to be true. A meeting of the whole village was called, in which the important members of the village, Shafi, Ghulam Rasool, Fateh Muhammad, Dakhan, Sadaq *numberdar* (revenue head of the village) and Sharif (also a *numberdar*) also participated. Yasin was summoned and he openly accepted the charge against him. Different proposals were made, but in the end it was decided to excommunicate him and he was fined 5000 rupees which were to be spent on the improvement of the village pond. According to the punishment by excommunication, it was decided that no one in the village would buy provisions from him, use his saw or have any other dealings with him. It became so hard that within a month he openly wept and asked for pardon from everyone in the village. Finally another *kath* was held in which he was publicly pardoned. But even after the pardon his business never recovered and he lost almost all his property.

Amjad, the son of a tailor, and Sharifan, the daughter of a christian sweeper (both from *kammi biradari*), were reported to be caught in *delect flagranti* and blamed for having illicit sexual relations. The case was brought before the *panchayat* by some villagers. The village *panchayat*, met in the village school outside the village (the matter was said to be shameful hence not to be discussed in the village) where both the families were also summoned and they were punished and had to either leave the village or cause both the boy and the girl to be expelled from the village, called *pind badar karna*.

Social boycott is the most important and effective method of punishment. It is called *hukka pani band karna*,[17] literally: 'to stop water pipe and water'. There could be different types of boycotts like of the *khandan*, in the *biradari*, from the village or even from the whole area. The effects of the excommunication could be wide. People from other villages would not want to have anything to do with such an individual. It is one of the most severe punishments and not very often inflicted. For carrying it out it is important that the whole village, *biradari* or *khandan* co-operates. The crime must be of a very serious nature in the eyes of the people for them all to agree to social ostracism.

Fear of Disgrace

In a small village community everyone knows each other, therefore, the fear of being stigmatized as a liar, thief, or an evil-doer functions as a deterrant. When an anti-social act takes place there are a variety of punishments. The traditional punishment of a thief is reported to include, in different combinations: blackening of face, wearing a garland of old shoes, shaving of half of the head and one side of the moustaches, being driven through the village streets on the back of a donkey with others jeering at him.

Moore describes similar punishments of a thief from across the border in a Rajasthani village in India:

> I saw a man get down from a donkey (...) legs, and feet were covered with white ash. His hands were tied with a bright green sash (...) Periodically he (Sub-Inspector of Police) stopped and called out, 'This man has stolen five calves.' (...) The routine is the same. He is beaten with shoes, hands or sticks by anyone present (...) It is not ruthless; no bones are broken nor blood spilt. But it is humiliating.[18]

Fines

Fines are not awarded very often, one of the reasons being that most conflicts involve honour which is difficult to be replaced by money. The other reason being the question as to what should happen with the money since there is nothing resembling a permanent village cash-box. In some collective activity relating to agriculture, fines are imposed. For example the common water channels must be cleaned once in a while and everyone who benefits from this must take part. This is announced in the village through a loudspeaker of the mosque or a watchman and when somebody does not come he is fined. The cash from this fine is mostly consumed by the participants for drinks or sweatmeats.

Fines are, likewise, imposed and paid as a part of a compromise or compensation. In the case study in which Akram, the son of Karim, was killed and the position of Karim was also strong in the court, the *panchayat* decided that Anwar and his sons must pay five hundred thousand rupees to Karim and beg for his pardon. Additionally, none of the members of Anwar's family was allowed to enter the village again.

Other Punishments

An exhaustive list of traditional village punishments is difficult to make since it depends upon the imagination of the villagers and the circumstances. Here are some more examples of punishment taken from Misalpur:

An interesting case was reported which had an equally interesting punishment. Maqbool is a carpenter and blacksmith of the *Ambalvi biradari*. He works on *seypi* which means that at the end of the crop season he gets a fixed share from each family or per oxen-pair as has already been explained. He made good money with jobs other than the *seypi* so his interest in the low-paid *seypi* decreased. One night the young men of the *biradari* broke into his house and stole his belongings so that he would again take interest in his *seypi* work.[19]

Similarly some villagers thought that Ashraf was encroaching on the common village land and they assembled and destroyed the boundary wall of his *haveli*.

People sometimes simply invoke the wrath of God and any damage to the property, ill heath, childlessness, or other such things are explained or declared as the result of punishment.

Panchayats and Socio-political Change

There is a general impression that the popularity of the traditional system of justice, especially its formal part—the *panchayats*—has decreased to a large extent and continues to do so. There are macro-level political, historical and economic reasons for this as well as micro-level, i.e. local socio-economic factors such as, modernization, with the spread of education, the development and use of modern means of transport and communication, etc. which may be responsible for this.

Historically, the traditional system (*panchayats*) has been affected by the policies of the successive political systems and governments. In earlier times, village communities were, because of their socio-economic and political circumstances, much more self-sufficient than today and nearly all the basic needs of the community, including justice, were fulfilled locally. Cohn described it through his concept of 'little kingdoms'.[20] The British Administrator of the early nineteenth century, Sir Thomas Metcalf called the village communities 'little republics', having nearly everything they want within themselves, and almost independent of any foreign relations.[21]

The autonomy of these 'village republics' was altered a little during the Mughal period according to the assessment of the Law Reform Commission: 'At the lowest level, that is in the villages, they continued the Hindu system of getting petty disputes settled by the local panchayats...'.[22] Mughals themselves depended to a large extent on the local tribes and lineages for the administration of justice, collection of revenue and the supply of their armies.[23]

The British introduced the English style official courts of justice in Punjab. The employees of the East India Company were to control and receive the revenue directly instead of the village leaders. The traditional *panchayat* system further lost its influence due to the existence of official courts. Several attempts were made to improve the influence of the traditional system for example through the Punjab Village Act of 1922 and then the Punjab Village Act of 1939. These could also be seen as an attempt to centralize the traditional system or even an expansion of the state or the official system.

When the British left, the position of these so-called 'republics' had changed to the extent that a 'return' was impossible. Baxi wrote about those who dreamt of the old traditional *panchayat* system on the eve of freedom:

> Neither Gandhi nor his followers were unaware that they were positing an ideal picture of village self-sufficiency (...) They knew, as well as the modernists, that even if such village republics existed in the distant past, or indeed up to the Mughal rule, they were vastly affected during 1750-1850 owing to a whole variety of factors: growth of transport and communication, spread of commerce and organization of markets (...).[24]

Some efforts were undertaken during Ayub Khan's era to improve the *panchayat* system, rather to nationalize the traditional system in the form of the Basic Democracies Act of 1959. One of the main aims, in the eyes of the planners, was to enable the people to solve current problems among themselves:

> (...) they will become the nerve centre, of their areas where all local problems of development and civic responsibilities can be studied at close range and their solutions discovered and applied with concentrated attention (...) the basic democracies will, in the due course of time, replace the purely official agencies as the traditional 'Mai Baap' of the people.[25]

Voicing public opinion on the efforts to establish the 'indigenous' justice systems, the Law Reform Commission observed:

> Again, the Chairmen, not being the accepted leaders of the community, do not generally command the same respect as a village elder nor do they inspire confidence. At many places, the Chairmen were found to be very young men. At other places where they were un-educated, the general complaint was that it was the paid Secretary who managed the whole show. It is, therefore, contended that the system of local tribunals should be completely scrapped as no useful purpose is being served by it.[26]

Effects of the Centralization of the *Panchayat* System

One of the basic aims of Basic Democracies and its Conciliation Councils was to provide justice at the basic level, i.e. in the villages. The status of the members of the Union Councils, as also the nature of the institution, was neither purely traditional nor that of the formal official judiciary.

One reason why efforts to decentralize did not prove fruitful was that the members of the Union Councils did not have the respect necessary for a *panchi* but they also did not have the power and resources of the members of judiciary of the higher official levels. The only result was the creation of political factions within villages, a natural requirement of the system since the only interest of the members was to be elected. This division of the village population into groups and factions gave rise to many new conflicts in the village. Ahmad provides an example of these coflicts:

> Soon after elections a number of supporters of a successful candidate A, went near the house of B, a defeated condidate and celebrated the success of A by singing and dancing. B felt greatly humiliated and decided not to take the matter lying down. (...) One dark night N.K. and his brother who had gone to a neighbouring village were way-laid on their way back home. N.K.'s brother was fatally wounded and died a few days later (...) One night when marriage celebrations were in progress in B's house, a hail of bullets killed four persons on the spot and wounded many others.[27]

This law was annulled and replaced by the Local bodies. However, in village rhetoric the terminology can often be heard. So changing political systems, policies, and increased government intervention have adversely affected the *panchayat* system over the years. The other socio-economic factors which affected the functioning of the *panchayat* system are discussed below:

Capitalism Replacing Feudalism

The socio-economic and political structure of the village is undergoing and has undergone an enormous change. The big farmers lost their dominant position due to smaller landholdings and deteriorating quality of land. The continuous division of land within the successive generations led eventually to small landholdings. Similarly, agricultural land became a victim to water logging and salinity. The two *numberdars* (revenue heads) of Misalpur, who were once important, are now seldom consulted in the *panchayats* or other important village affairs.

As opposed to this, the *kammis* were not bound to the land like the farmers. They left their traditional professions and worked in the factories, started businesses like power-looms, shops, or even got educated and started working in offices. Most of the power-loom owners in Misalpur are either *kammis* (*Mochies, Maliks,* i.e. shoe makers, weavers, and oilmen, etc.), or small farmers (especially *Araeens*). Even those *kammis* who did not change their profession at least stopped working on *seypi* (a system according to which the craftsmen are paid by the farmers) and some opened up professional shops like barbers, laundries, carpenter etc. In this way they earned money faster as compared to the farmers who get money from the sale of their crops at harvesting times, i.e. at the most twice a year.

This change is also clearly visible in the last four elections for the post of Chairman of the Union Council. One of the rival candidates was a *Malik* (a *kammi biradari*) and the other an *Araeen*.

This is not limited only to Misalpur, similar changes are also reported from other parts of the Punjab. M.T. Ahmad gives an example from Malakpur, North Punjab:

A significant feature of those elections (B.D. Council's election 1959) was that a newly enriched *lohar* contested for a seat in the Union Council. This was a new factor in the political struggle in so far as the *kammis* had challenged the *Awans* as equal.[28]

In the old system, zemindars were the members of the *panchayat* who not only decided disputes and conflicts within and between the farmer *biradaries* but mostly also conflicts in the *kammi biradari* since they were totally dependent on the farmers for their living. It is not that *kammis* are taking the place of zemindars but that there is a change in the hierarchy of the village. The key role is now played by those with capital. It could still be the farmers but only those having capital. This has shaken the older institutions of social control such as *panchayats* and other village councils. As long as the status and position of the villagers was fixed and clear and the chances of improving this status and position were scarce, the *kammi* and non-farmers accepted the farmers as their lords. The system was at least more effective. Similar observation was also made by M.T. Ahmad:

> Rigid social stratification manifested in the existence of a number of castes, each with well defined role and status. The position of the caste was discernible not only through its worldly possessions but also through social limitations set upon the lower castes. Normally the lower castes could not have the external symbols of prestige such as fine dress, nor could any one of them raise his status through hard work. For instance a cobbler could normally be at best a very good cobbler. This was functional in the sense that it apparently kept people contented however low their status.[29]

Effects of Modernization

Modernization has also affected the functioning of the *panchayat* system. Nearly each village in the country is now connected by metalled roads and means of transport have increased. Education is spreading as is the awareness of one's rights. The other means of communication like telephone, radio, television also play their roles in the general awakening and recognition of one's rights.

Industrialization, urbanization, and increasing population leads to large and anonymous settlements. For a successful functioning of the *panchayat* system, personal relations and knowing each member of the community is a basic requirement. The urban centres, industrial settlements and the large villages are not suitable for the functioning of the traditional types of institutions.

Folk Islam

Islam influences the official system, the traditional system and it offers, in certain cases to some people, an alternative forum for the dispensation of justice. The main concern of this part of the study is the part Islam plays as an alternative institution of justice in the larger context of justice in practice. The way the villagers use Islam as a forum of justice, it forms a part of the larger category, the traditional justice system.

The courts, as an institution of the official justice system, are only influenced by 'Official Islam', i.e. the Islam of Quran and Sunnah, followed by the *fiqah* (Islamic jurisprudence), the latter mainly serving as precedence. The judges, especially of the High Court and Supreme Court do sometimes interpret a verse of the Holy Quran or a hadith according to their own understanding which may be even against the *fiqah*,[30] (*Ijtihad*, *Ijma*?) Such decisions of the High Courts or Supreme Court afterwards serve as precedent for the lower courts. There is also a Shariat Bench at the level of the High Court and Supreme Court.[31]

The State on its part takes steps to implement Islam through laws in the justice courts. According to the Constitution of Pakistan: '227 (1): All existing laws shall be brought in conformity with the injunctions of Islam as laid down in the Holy Quran and Sunnah. (...) and no law shall be enacted which is repugnant to such injunctions.'[32] To meet these requirements the Constitution made the provision for the composition of the 'Council of Islamic Ideology' also called 'Islamic Council', whose functions, among others, are: 'to advise (...) whether a proposed law is or is not repugnant to the injunctions of Islam; (c) to make recommendations as to the measures for bringing existing laws into conformity with the injunctions of Islam (...)'.[33] Therefore, the work of the Council of Islamic Ideology requires research. The recent examples of Islamic influence on official justice system are the introduction of laws and punishments like *Qisas-o-Diyat* and Hudood Ordinance.[34] The Federal Shariat Court and the Shariat Court Bench of the Supreme Court see to it that the Islamic laws be put into practice.

As far as traditional system is concerned, there are no institutions in this village for carrying out the implementation of Islamic laws based on the Quran and Sunnah or to decide whether an action is Islamic in nature or not. The Imam of the village mosque may be consulted but this is seldom done. The

State laws and decisions of the courts have nearly no influence on the day-to-day activities of the villagers, their methods of decision-making or arriving at compromises. These customs and traditions are considered good and Islamic without asking whether they confirm the spirit of the Great Tradition, i.e. the Quran and Sunnah or not. Some of these customs may be in conflict or at least not quite in accordance with the official interpretation of Islam and official justice. For example the idea of the consent of either parents or guardian in a marriage becomes more important than the consent of the future husband and wife.[35] Marriages without the consent of the parents, e.g. when elopement cases are brought before the village *panchayats*, are considered as abductions of the girls. The sympathies of the villagers are with the parents and seldom with the girl and the boy. (For details see our case study 'The elopement of Aslam's daughter'.) For official justice, as also for Islam, the consent of the husband and wife is more important. Similarly, the mere suspicion of an attempt at illicit relationship, leads to murders. The daughters may or may not get a share in the property of their parents. But this should not be taken to mean that all the customs and traditions are not in accordance with Islam. Being Muslims, the villagers are by and large directed by Islam.

As this study is mainly concerned with justice in practice it is beyond its scope to deal in detail with the influence of Islam on the system of justice. Similarly the details of Islamic system of justice fall outside the range of this study. The concentration is on how Islam in practice, in the day-to-day life of the villagers, helps them in seeking justice. The villagers call it the forum of the have-nots and/or the court of God. The have-nots include those who cannot afford to go to the courts, cannot influence the members of the *panchayat* for initiating a meeting against a more influential member of the community, and could be further extended to include women suffering the tyranny of their husbands and in-laws. E. Moore went a step further and included complaints of illness and disease brought to the *maulavi* of Nagina, Rajasthan, famous for giving successful charms, in the category of justice seeking.[36] For understanding the functioning of this forum we have to understand the religious beliefs of the people concerning God's justice.

'God's Court' and its Functioning

The fear of God, as the Great Judge not only on the day of judgement but also in this life, controls the actions and behaviour of the individuals to some extent. There are innumerable stories and cases which are interpreted as a punishment by God. 'Tahir's buffalo died because he had refused the money of Aslam'. 'The children of Niamat do not treat him properly because he had not treated his mother well'. 'Sadique has five daughters and no son because his mother has given him a *baddu'ah* (curse)'. The disease and death of animals, human beings, and other misfortunes are explained as a punishment of God because of the ill feelings, curses and *baddu'ahs* of the weak, poor and the holy persons. These examples are considered the decisions of God for punishing an individual for his actions. Curses by the poor are feared as having greater potency. It is said 'beware of *mazloom's* (oppressed) *baddu'ah*, it shakes the heavens'. The reflection of this fear could also be concluded from the local sayings such as: 'God's club makes no noise'; 'There is certainly delay but no injustice with God'; 'the hands of those who are strong and the tongues of those who are poor are effective'; and that 'God gives sufficient chance before punishing'.

God is not only known for fear and punishments but also for His rewards. The birth of male children, good crops or other chance gains and benefits, and narrow escape from an accident are all explained as the rewards of God against some injustice done by somebody. But this side is far less stressed, perhaps because of the lack of the element of revenge.

A difference is made between the rights of God (*haquq-ullah*) and the rights of human beings (*haquq-ul-ibad*). If one ignores the rights of God, it is between him and God but if one injures the rights of other human beings, then justice will be done between them.[37] The are two angels sitting on the shoulders of every human being, keeping record of what man does. The one on the right shoulder keeps the record of good deeds and the one on the left shoulder is responsible for noting down the evil acts. God is the Judge between human beings, He knows everything but He is *beniaz* (Master of His own will) because He punishes some in this world and others in the next.

The general imagination of the villagers about the world and its functioning is: God has created the world with one word *kun* (be) in all its beauty and variety. Above the seven heavens lies *arsh*; i.e. His own abode is unapproachable by any human or non-human being but still He lives not only within a human being, but nearer than any thing or being. The world view is dominated by the existence, presence, unimaginable and unlimited powers of God. Ambiguities and ambivalences are the most prominent part of this. The occurrence of an earthquake could be, on the one hand, because of the evil doings of the community[38] but it could, on the other hand, be a test from God because He tests His beloved ones. Enough examples of the prophets of God in which they were put to tests are quoted from the Holy Quran. Similarly, examples of the punishment of the communities to which the prophets belonged are also given. The general response in such cases of test or punishment is to give alms (*sadqah, khairat*), for individuals or the whole community as the case may be.

In short, we may say that the fear of God is to a certain extent a sort of control on the behaviour of the people towards others. But this does not mean that because of the fear of God people always and totally control their behaviour. Mostly, people do not bother about whether their actions are in accordance with Islam or not and act under the circumstances and the pressures of the society. Hoebel reports an interesting case from Pakistan:

> The police arrested one of our household servants two or three years ago for complicity in murder. His brother had been charged, and also four others.

I went to X as a 'character witness' on his behalf. They were all acquitted.

A couple of months later my servant introduced me to a cousin who is a corporal in the army. He said he was the actual killer; he had killed because a man in the other family had killed his brother three years previously. He thanked me profusely, took my hands, etc.

I asked him why he did this sort of thing when it is contrary to Islam, forbidden expressly by the Koran. He said he had not thought about the Koran. 'The women make us. 'Are you a man?' they taunt us', he said. I told him he would go to hell, that Allah would punish him for what he had done. Then he was terribly frightened. (...). The prospect of Hell was disturbing.[39]

The forum of God is open to both the complainant and the defendant and every one can pray to and request God for help.

Saints as Agents, Lawyers, and Judges

The holy men seem to function mostly like lawyers or agents, but in some cases also as judges. The usual argument given is that ordinary human beings cannot reach God as easily as holy persons, so they are used as *sifarish* (intercession) to God. One cannot reach the roof top of a house without a ladder. The saints and holy persons are considered ladders to God. To determine the role the saintly people play in this forum two aspects need to be looked at: First, who are these holy persons and secondly, what sort of people go to them and what types of cases (problems) are brought to them for adjudication?

Different types of persons may be identified as those who help people seeking justice like, *maulavi*,[40] *hafiz*,[41] *pir*, and *shah* or *syed*,[42] etc. In addition there is a person called *baba mast* in the village, who is apparently a lunatic or mentally deranged, but his prayers are considered very successful. Similarly there are two shrines of holy persons in the village which are quite frequently visited by the villagers. People also visit holy persons and holy shrines in villages and towns in the neighbourhood and beyond for *mannats* (wishes) which include complaints of in-justice. People also go to get charms or items like pieces of bread or other eatables, a piece of cloth, or even a little amount of earth from these shrines and holy persons. These are to be consumed or used in prescribed manners.

The range of problems and the types of complainants who visit these shrines vary from case to case. There are women who cannot conceive children or only female children; women who have problems with their husbands or mothers-in-law; people coming before going to the official courts, or those who cannot pay the court fee and do not have enough influence in the *panchayat*, people who think their animals or houses have lost *barkat*, or have been influenced by the evil eye. Also there are patients who come to have their diseases healed. Generalizing, we may say:

(i)   There are complaints of the weak and poor against the rich and strong whether it is a dispute over land, quarrel about debt, a cruel husband, or one pursuing other women. These are complaints from people seeking justice against a strong opponent. They can not go to the police courts or *panchayats*, one being too expensive and the other because of the lack of influence. People come to this forum when the aggressor or opponent is not known or a claim is not possible in the courts or *panchayats* (the influence of the evil eye, or magic [charms for harming]).

(ii) There are complaints of illness from patients who are poor and/or weak—mostly women. How could the complaints of the patients, of illness, be treated as problems of justice? There are different explanations for treating illness as an injustice and a part of this forum. We can consider illness a result of social injustice. In the words of Moore: 'This is not to say that the phyiscal complaints were necessarily disconnected from social ills.'[43] She gives the example of women possessed by spirits from Rajasthan India (not uncommon in the village of present study) and comes to the conclusion that this is the result of:

Their low status in their husband's families and their heavy work load which leads to stress and collapse. (...) the active use of the maulavi in dispute processing and the extensive treatment of women for spirit possession and gender-specific ills call attention to female repression and the exclusion of women, as well as other weak members of society, from legal arena of courts and *panchayats*. When men petition the maulavi they can discuss their social conflicts in a legal discourse. Women, more often, must mask their complaints against the patriarchy in a medical discourse. They somatise the complaints.[44]

Still another explanation is that illness is also seen as punishment or trial by God; by going to 'God's forum' people pray for justice; complaining directly to God. This is reflected in how people express self-pity: 'Oh God why this injustice to me: I am poor, my crops have been bad, my animals have died, my wife gives birth only to daughters, and now I am ill, I have no one to take care of me', and so on, in a variety of expressions. Or they even go to the holy person and tell and ask him the same and instead of addressing 'Oh God', they say 'Oh *baba* (...)', why this oppression on me, I have done nothing wrong'.

Thus it is mainly a forum of the have-nots, poor, depressed, patients, who have no other way out except to go to this 'forum of God'. As those who are poor cannot go to the official courts and *panchayats*, they also cannot pay for the medicine and fees of the doctors. The medicine of the doctors sometimes does not help, or people think that the doctors and medicine cannot treat their ailments which are due to the evil eyes and charms. Moore justifies the reason for treating physical illness and social injustice together: 'Justice and health are different names for the same aim: harmony, peace, and order.'[45]

NOTES

1. Darling, 1934, pp. 138–9.
2. Hoebel, 1965, p. 44.
3. Cohn, 1965, p. 83.

4. Moore, 1985, p. 21
5. Refusing marriage in spite of earlier engagement is a great insult to the father and the family of the girl and, therefore, leads to serious conflicts. The family itself could take action against the boy refusing such a marriage.
6. Slocum, 1960, p. 30.
7. Moore, 1985, p. 31.
8. Cohn, 1965, pp. 83–4; Berreman, 1963, pp. 280–81.
9. Baxi, 1982, p. 335.
10. Baxi, 1982, p. 336.
11. One of the case studies in the fourth chapter.
12. Baxi, 1982, p. 336.
13. Moore, 1985, p. 29.
14. 1981 District Census Report of Faisalabad, p. 106.
15. The justice provided by the *panchayats* is 'relative' justice, according to the status and position of the disputants within the community. A deed permissable to a farmer or a son of a farmer may be forbidden to a *kammi* or his son.
16. Similar punishments have also been reported from India. Baxi wrote about the punishment methods of the *jati panchayats* in India: 'The *jati* and village *panchayats* have a repertoire of sanctions—which include fine, public censure, civil boycott, ostracism, and varied public opinion pressures by village notables and sometimes by predominant groups in the area. The *jati panchayats*, additionally, have the very potent sanction of 'outcasting and excommunication', (...)' Baxi, 1982, p. 338. According to Cohn, punishments include: 'Sanctions that caste councils can apply are: fining, ritual expiation, public shaming, beatings, and outcasting. This last sanction can be the most potent as it means the person, and in some instances those in his immediate family, cannot get marriage partners.' Cohn, 1965, p. 99.
17. 'No fines are imposed and in extreme cases *huqqa* and water are banned.' Darling, 1934, p. 140.
18. Moore, 1985, pp. 97, 102.
19. 'A study of the history of the extent and nature of crime in the Indo-Pakistan subcontinent leaves one with the conclusion that creating awe in the neighbourhood has been one of the favourite means of maintaining authority by the landlords and even *rajas* and other chieftains. One of the most effective measures for creating awe was the harbouring and protection of criminals. It is a well known fact that these measures are still employed in varying degrees particularly by those landed gentlemen (...)' Ahmad, M.T.: 'Offences in Rural and Urban Areas'. Unpublished, p. 41.
20. For further details of 'little kingdom', see Cohn, 1976, pp. 139–42.

21. Cohn, 1965, p. 96.
22. Law Commission Report 1967–70, pp. 58–9.
23. Cohn mentioned: 'In Mughal times, in addition to payment of land revenue, the lineage was also responsible for the provision of troops.' Cohn 1967, p. 140.
24. Baxi, 1982, p. 296.
25. M.A. Khan, 1959, pp. 24–5.
26. Law Reform Commission, 1967–70, p. 167.
27. Ahmad, 1972, p. 100.
28. Ahmad, 1972, p. 99.
29. Ahmad, M.T., 'Social Problems in the Developing Economy of Pakistan'. Unpublished, p. 27.
30. For further details see the decision of the High Court, West Pakistan 1959, p. 593 in the case of Balquis Sureya vs. Najm-ul-Ikram Quereshi. The other example is Rashida Begum vs. Shahab Din and others, decided 21 July 1960 (High Court of West Pakistan 1960). Both cases have been quoted and explained by Hoebel, 1965, pp. 48–52.
31. Some details about their forms and function are given in the next chapter on Official Justice System.
32. Constitution of Pakistan, 1990, p. 157.
33. Constitution of Pakistan, 1990, p. 159.
34. For further details of the introduction of Islamic laws in Pakistan see Haider, S.M. ed., *Shariah and Legal Profession*, Lahore, 1985.
35. Many marriages take place against the wishes of boys and girls. It is well-known that the fathers or mothers or other relatives move the head of the girl to indicate her consent at the time of the Nikah (marriage).
36. 'I observed a wide variety of complaints that came to the maulavi. The patients complained of stomach aches; possessions; depressions; babies that cried, did not nurse, had fevers, or passed bloody stools; infertility or the conception of girls only; children who would not go to school, would not study, or were frightened at night; husbands who had a 'wandering eye' or beat their wives; businesses that failed; or even livestock that fell ill. (...) the active use of the maulavi in dispute processing and the extensive treatment of women for spirit possession and gender-specific ills call attention to female repression and the exclusion of women, as well as other weak members of society, from legal arena of courts and panchayats. Justice and health are different names for the same aim: harmony, peace, and order.' (Moore, 1993, pp. 534–5).
37. Gluckman mentions in one of his lectures:
    'The beliefs argue by implication that if the moral situation of the individual in relationship with his fellows were satisfactory, all would go well. If he suffers misfortune, it is because he himself has committed some wrong', Gluckman, 1972a, p. 4.

38. Similar ideas of community punishments were also recorded by Gluckman in Africa: 'In major, widespread disasters—there is something wrong in the moral state of the society as a whole'. Gluckman, M., 'Moral crises: magical and secular solutions', 1972a, p 4.
39. Hoebel, 1965, pp. 44–5.
40. The one who leads the prayers in the mosque.
41. The one who knows the Quran by heart.
42. Descendants of the family of the Holy Prophet [PBUH]
43. Moore, 1993, p. 535.
44. Moore, 1993, pp. 538–9.
45. Moore, 1993, p. 524.

CHAPTER 4

THE OFFICIAL JUSTICE SYSTEM

The official justice system in Pakistan functions through the police and courts. Courts are divided into civil and criminal parts. The police is responsible for the maintenance of law and order and for the administration of the criminal justice. For understanding the functioning of official system it is important to understand and look at the administrative divisions of the country and the structure of the courts.

The Administrative Division of Courts in Pakistan

The whole country is administratively divided into provinces and each province is subdivided into divisions. A division has districts subdivided into *tehsils*. Each *tehsil* is divided into *qanungo* circles, a *qanungo* circle into *patwar* circles and a *patwar* circle, into *mauzas* (revenue estates).[1] At the *tehsil* level comes the *thana* (police station) and each *thana* covers many villages. The *thana* is the lowest unit of the official system of justice administration; for example, the Naglan *thana*, which is responsible for the area of the present village under study, covers 52 villages. And so upwards, several *thanas* make one *tehsil*, four to five *tehsils* make one District, the same number of Districts makes one Division and the Divisions together make one Province. Pakistan comprises four provinces, the Federal Capital, the Federally Administrated Tribal Areas, (FATA, also called the Agencies), Azad Kashmir and the Northern Areas of

Pakistan. Diagram no. 4 illustrates the processes linking the lowest unit of the *thana* to the highest supreme court level of the judicial system.

The Hierarchy of the Courts

At the lowest level the courts are divided into Civil and Criminal Courts. A Magistrate is a judge in Criminal Courts but at the same time is a part of the police administration. Both these types of courts are situated at *tehsil* level. There are no courts or other institutions for providing justice at *thana* (police station) and village levels except the Union Councils which are more a part of the traditional system. Next to *tehsil* courts are Sessions and District Courts. Some *tehsils* have more than one headquarters, depending upon the size of the population and the area.[2] Correspondingly, one permanent or sometimes one more Additional Sessions judge sits once or twice a week in these *tehsil* headquarters. The Sessions and District Courts serve, as appeal courts for the Civil and Criminal Courts and also as courts of first instance, since the powers of the lower courts are limited. Sessions Courts are authorized to deal with any kind of case and can give any punishment permissible under the law.

High courts, one in each province, are the appellate courts having the power to review the decisions of the Sessions and District Courts. According to the constitution of Pakistan, the decisions of the High Courts[3] are binding to subordinate courts and the High Courts supervise subordinate courts.[4]

The Supreme Court is at the top of the hierarchy of the judiciary in Pakistan. The functions of the Supreme Court, according to the Constitution of Pakistan, include hearing and determining appeals of judgements, decrees, final orders or sentences of a High Court, and of serving the President as an advisory body. The Supreme Court has the power to transfer the cases from one court to the other. The decisions of the Supreme Court are binding for all other courts.[5]

Diagram No. 4 showing the structure of the courts and the administrative divisions of Pakistan.

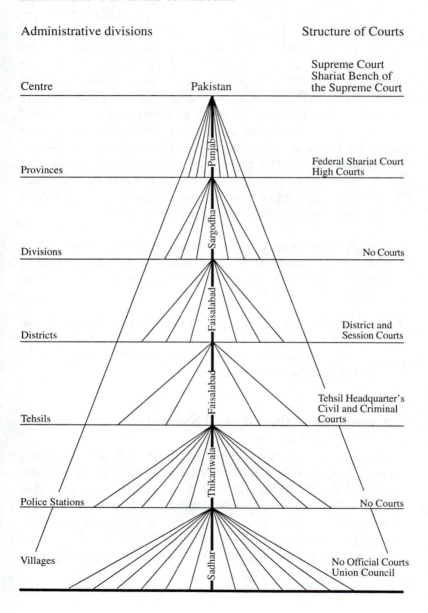

Administrative divisions

Structure of Courts

Centre — Pakistan — Supreme Court / Shariat Bench of the Supreme Court

Provinces — Punjab — Federal Shariat Court / High Courts

Divisions — Sargodha — No Courts

Districts — Faisalabad — District and Session Courts

Tehsils — Faisalabad — Tehsil Headquarter's Civil and Criminal Courts

Police Stations — Thikariwala — No Courts

Villages — Sadhar — No Official Courts / Union Council

There is no other division of courts based on special functions or problems like family, land. The only special provision is that family cases like divorce, maintenance, rehabilitation etc. are dealt with by the Civil judge, class one.

The Federal Shariat Court needs also be mentioned here. Its uniqueness lies in the constitution of the Shariat Bench: 'not more than four shall be persons each one of whom is, or has been, or is qualified to be, a judge of a High Court and not more than three shall be Ulema who are well-versed in Islamic law.'[6]

At the lower level, the same judges of the Sessions Court deal with the cases of the Shariat Court such as cases of *Hudood* and *Qisas-o-Diyat*. The appeals are then brought to the Federal Shariat Court. The principle seat of the Court is in Islamabad. The Federal Shariat Court has a status similar to the High Courts but its decisions are binding on the High Courts:

> (203GG. Subject to Articles 203D and 203F, any decision of the Court in the exercise of its jurisdiction under this chapter shall be binding on a High Court and on all courts subordinate to a High Court.).[7]

For an appeal against the decision of the Federal Shariat Court:

> (...) there shall be constituted in the Supreme Court a Bench to be called the Shariat Appellate Bench.[8]

Formalities of the Official System

The official justice system does not function as it theoretically should. There is a lot of difference between the 'Formal National Law' and the 'Real National Law',[9] i.e. the law in theory and in practice. This is not only so in Pakistan, but even in the most developed countries of the world we find gaps between the theory and practice of law in society.[10] In Pakistan, however, that gap is very wide. A look at the court procedure will help in understanding why this gulf exists.

Court Procedure

The procedure followed in the Criminal Courts is based on the Code of Criminal Procedure and and that of the Civil Courts is drawn from the Civil Procedure Code. In the Criminal Courts cases like murder, theft, and adultery, etc., where police intervention is required, also known as *faujdari* cases are dealt with. In criminal cases the police or the State are a party on behalf of the complainant.

Civil cases that include marital problems like divorce, return of the dowry, maintenance allowance, guardianship, inheritance, land and property are brought to the courts by the plaintiffs themselves through their counsels.

The other difference between Criminal and Civil Courts' procedure is that the Criminal Courts are manned by magistrates of first, second and third class, having varying powers to impose fines and award imprisonment. The Civil Courts have Civil judges also ranked as first class, second class and third class Civil judges. As stated in the Law Reform Commission Report:

> The civil judges, First Class have unlimited pecuniary jurisdiction, while the civil judges, Second class and Third class have pecuniary jurisdiction up to fifteen thousand Rupees and five thousand Rupees respectively.[11]

The Procedure of the Criminal Courts

A criminal case has three stages: investigation, inquiry, and trial. After the occurence of an event (fighting, murder, theft, adultery, etc.):

> In cognizable cases, the machinery of the law is put into motion through a report under section 173 of the Code of Criminal Procedure,[12]

The police writes down an FIR (First Information Report) and, if required, arrests the accused. The police has the right to keep the suspect in custody for twenty-four hours and after presenting the case before the magistrate, might get an extention for the so-called physical remand, of up to fifteen days. Afterwards, if still required, a judicial remand could be acquired. In the judicial lock-up the police has to present the accused after fifteen days at the latest and could again get a remand, for a further two weeks, if the magistrate finds it essential.

The police presents a report including all the small details involved in the investigation like, in case of a murder or injury, the FIR, the Medical Forensic Report, if needed, a map of the location, statements of the witnesses, objects recovered like weapons, blood-stained clothes, and chemical reports, report on the body and the judicial remand depending upon the nature of the case and other documents and material helpful for the trial and investigation.[13] Before the *challan* (report of the police investigations) is presented to the magistrate, it is processed by the prosecution section also working under the police, and is examined whether the case is fit to be presented before the magistrate. The prosecution branch helps in the legal investigation of the case.

Inquiry is the pre-trial proceeding conducted by the magistrate to determine if, how and where the case is to be tried. There are three parts to the trial procedure; sessions procedures, warrant procedures and summons procedures. After the *challan* is completed and scrutinized by the Prosecution Agency, it is presented before the Magistrates for recording evidence. The proceedings are then conducted by the Sessions Judge. The difference between the two is that:

> In cases punishable with not more than six months' rigorous imprisonment, the summons-case procedure is applied, and, for more serious offences, the warrant-case procedure has been laid down. Under the first procedure, the trial starts with the accusation being put, the accused questioned and the defence evidence, if any, recorded. Under the latter procedure, first there is a preliminary

enquiry to determine whether the facts would justify the framing of a charge. If a charge is framed, the accused is asked to state whether he pleads guilty or not. If he pleads not guilty and the trial proceeds, the accused has the right to recall any of the prosecution witnesses examined before the charge, for further examination. On the conclusion of the prosecution evidence, the statement of the accused is taken and then the defence evidence is recorded.[14]

The Procedure of the Civil Courts

The difference between the procedure of the Civil Courts and that of the Criminal Courts is marked by the absence of the police involvement. The petitioner's lawyer,[15] prepares a *daawa* (pleading) based on all documents relevant to the case, together with the *wakalat nama* (power of attorney), enclosed in an envelope called *lifaf-e-dastaawizaat* and is put in the petition box meant for the court of the Senior Civil Judge. This box is attended daily at nine in the morning and at twelve noon. After the pleadings are checked and found to be correct,[16] the Senior Civil Judge allocates these suits to different Civil judges according to their jurisdiction and work load. The summons are issued which are brought to the defendants by the *piadas* (notice-servers, who earlier went on foot, hence the name!) who then appear through their counsels who file a written statement on behalf of the petitioner. After the examination of the parties and the comparison of the documents, the issues are framed. Where essential, a special commission for local examination and investigation might be set up. Finally the witnesses are summoned. Then evidences are recorded, followed by the arguments of the lawyers on which the decision can be announced.[17]

Official System in Practice

In actual practice there are other steps which are perhaps more important for even initiating a case in the court, or to turn it into a successful case. Before going into the details of how in actual practice an FIR (First Information Report) is registered, what the forensic medicine and the Medical Reports are meant to do, and what the role of lawyers, judges or employees of the courts is intended to be, it is important to mention here that we are not going to treat the Criminal and Civil Courts separately. There is an overlapping or at least an uncertainty in some cases as to what comes under criminal law and Criminal Courts and what should be treated in the Civil Courts. Most of the criminal cases have their roots in civil cases. These cases are either not brought before the Civil Courts or the hopeless situation prevailing in the Civil Court on account of delays, corruption, etc., does not help them. So people are left with the only alternative of using direct physical force to solve their conflicts and, as a result some become criminal cases. In the words of Ahmad:

> The classification of crime into congnizable and non-cognizable by police was presumably based on the argument that the State should not interfere in private disputes, family life and minor cases, but we find in practice that many serious offences have their roots in some apparently minor incidents. A survey of F.I.R.s in four districts in the former province of the Punjab has shown that the percentage of non-cognizable ones ranges from ten per cent to as far as fifty per cent. The absence of a mechanism for nipping the evil in the bud goes a long way to sow the seeds of frustration in the villagers.[18]

Some examples are cited for elaboration:

(i) The question what one could do if there is a doubt about the location of the boundary of a house, a field, or a street. This is a very common problem since these boundaries are not properly marked, and one knows them approximately. If the official law is approached it might take months if not years before a decision is taken and it will cost a lot of money. If one wants to reconstruct the fallen boundary wall of one's house, there is a disagreement with the neighbour about its location and one does not have the money for paying the Boundary Commission. One does not want to wait (being without a boundary wall is like sitting on the street in the village because the daily activities are undertaken in the courtyard and not in rooms) until the courts or the Boundary Commission decide about the location of the boundary. Not the least, one does not want to be labelled a coward. In such situations one tries to solve these problems directly through negotiations or more often by physical force, without going to the Civil Courts. This leads to serious fights and, ultimately, the case comes to the police and then to the Criminal Courts.

(ii) In every village there is land which does not belong to anybody. It could be called the common property of the whole village but it is neither clearly marked with boundaries nor clear as to who should control it and how it should be used. There is the example of the village *raries* (the place for playing, public toilets, ponds, *charagah* [meadows for grazing], etc.) which have already been, at least most parts of them, occupied by those who needed them and usually by those who were clever, fast and powerful. There are continuous conflicts about the occupation and reoccupation of these places. There are no proper records of these places for which the Revenue Department of the government is responsible. Further problems arose when the successive government distributed such areas among the poor or landless, and then suddenly owners of these surfaced claiming the same lands. Those already occupying such places were said to have been given the legal rights. There are either no written records as to which place belongs to whom, or there is exploitation by the *patvaries*. Very often, the same piece of land is claimed by more than one party, one may be occupying it, while another may have the papers of legal rights. Some of the civil suits are started as complementary suits in addition to the criminal cases, to exert pressure and bring about the early surrender of the opponents, and is a very common practice.

Similarly, the procedures followed in the two courts are actually very closely related, as are the rights and conflicts. The problems enumerated in the procedures are very similar, especially the use of fake documents, the bribing of the personnel concerned with the courts, delaying tactics, etc. Therefore, the two types of courts are very closely related and interconnected. We shall mainly be concerned with a study of the Criminal Courts, yet bearing in mind its close similarity with the Civil side.

The operation of the justice system, or the process of arriving at a just decision, is influenced by two factors:

1. The personnel directly or indirectly involved in and influencing the functioning of the courts, like lawyers, judges, witnesses, court employees, etc.
2. The documents presented before a judge, like the police investigation report (FIR, challan), the medical report, statements of the witnesses, and other documents.

In the next part, we shall examine the role mechanism the court machinery plays in the manipulation of the system and how different documents are fabricated. This would help us understand the alienation of the villagers to the official system of justice.

Courts[19] in Practice: Personnel

It is common knowledge that the people who are directly or indirectly concerned with the lower courts are generally corrupt. Those who are not are exceptions to the rule. A summary of literature available on the subject bears this out:

> Below the level of the High Courts all is corruption. Neither the facts nor the law in the case have any real bearing on the outcome. It all depends on who you know, who has influence and where you put your money.[20]

Lawyers and other people corroborate these views about the official justice system: 'Our courts are academies of corruption'; 'the Magistrates are totally corrupt and Civil judges are mostly corrupt'; 'parties are weighed and the one whose side of the scale contains more money wins. The best would be to give the justice system on contract. Every year there should be an auction'. 'Once you start a court case you will lose everything down to the last straw of your hut'. 'May God save even the worst of the enemies from an illness and a court case'.

These are the kind of observations one hears when one asks about the courts. Public disappointment about the courts is echoed even in the two Law Reform Commissions (1967-70), which have noted:

> It has been represented to us that corruption among the subordinate court officials and process-serving staff as well as investigating staff is rampant with the result that no action is taken by them unless the parties involved approach them and tender some extra-legal consideration. One of the main criticisms levelled is that papers in a case move only when these officials are approached by the parties.[21]

In the Law Commission Report of (1958-59) it was observed that:

> There are widespread complaints that subordinate Court officials who have to deal with the public, extort illegal gratification from the litigants before condescending to give them any relevant information or to take any steps which are necessary in the progress of a case in Court. Several duties of a subsidiary nature fall to be performed by these Court officials. Petitions and other papers are not put up to presiding officers, unless these people are propitiated by the tender of some monetary consideration. It is said that papers move only on golden or silver wheels.[22]

We shall now examine, one after the other, the role of the above-mentioned personnel in this corruption: who takes money and how; and how does it affect the litigation and litigants in the courts.

The Judge[23]

'A judge is a king of the courts or even the god of his small world called courts. He has enormous powers but it is obvious that if he lived on his salary he would be the poorest creature in this world of his own. A third class lawyer of his world, a *munshi* of the lawyer, his reader (clerk), even the orderly (who calls the names of the parties in a case) would earn more than him.

Enormous wealth moves within the courts. The Sessions Judges or Additional Sessions Judges have almost the power of life and death of an accused. People come with lakhs and lakhs of rupees and try to give these through all possible ways. Only an angel could refuse these offers perhaps the first time, the second time, the third time, but then (...). This does not mean that there are no judges who do not accept bribes, otherwise what little hope exists would be finished. But in our lower courts such angels are seldom to be found.

A judge does not simply accept bribes from one party and makes the decision in their favour. What he does is sell his 'discretionary power'. Take an extreme example, say a man kills his wife or sister, or and also the man he suspected her of having an illicit relationship with. He then pleads that he was driven by extreme emotions and thus not responsible for his action. Now, say that at the time of sentencing the judge has the power to imprison this man from one to ten years. He sells this discretionary power. In another example, as may be a case of bail, he can sell his power of discretion whether to release somebody on bail or not. Similarly, the manner in which often a judge examines the witnesses and the arguments of a lawyer or the *challan* could also be manipulated. Often they totally reverse the situation. They also have the power to cause a case to linger by adjournments or other methods giving one party the benefit.

The judges of High Courts and the Supreme Court, are to our belief very fair. There is no corruption there, but who should pay the fee of their lawyers ranging from thirty thousand, fifty thousand, to a hundred thousand rupees and more. In addition, there are touts and *thags* (cheats), hundreds of them, around these courts who are masters in plundering the simple villagers.[24]

Helmken quotes a similar situation from India:

> Today an honest judge living in the neighbourhood of a corrupt judicial officer has to live like a beggar by the side of a princely personage and is often contemptuously looked down upon.[25]

The Law Reform Commission reports:

> There is a wide-spread complaint that criminal cases are generally delayed inordinately by some Magistrates with a view to extracting illegal gratification. There are also instances wherein delays in the disposal of criminal cases have compelled the parties to approach the Magistrates concerned and, finding them unresponsive they begin to tempt them by subtle means not only to expedite the disposal of the case but also to make favourable orders. It is being said that 'oiling of the wheels' is necessary to make even the judicial machinery run smoothly and with speed at this level.[26]

There are three methods reported as to how the judges receive this money: (i) through their subordinate staff like the reader, clerk or orderly and this is easiest method of extorting a bribe; (ii) through the advocate, but this is not very popular, since in that case, the advocate might misuse his knowledge. The advocates employed for such purposes must be very reliable and must have good connections; (iii) the safest way, usually preferred by the judges, is through acquaintances and so-called friends. Such business acquaintances are visited by the judge in the evenings for chatting, telephoning, taking tea, etc. The two parties find out about these places for greasing the palms of the judges, through the subordinate staff of the judge, by bribing them. These contact persons of the judge with this staff also have their links. This practice is not only limited to Civil judges and magistrates, but police officers are also known to have this type of connections. According to the statement of a lawyer 'the clever judges never show their faces directly to the parties'. There are some direct deals though these are very rare. The relatives of the judges are also sometimes used for these purposes.

Judges, being the heads of the courts, are the major factor responsible for the delays in the courts. According to a lawyer 'the judges are themselves *kanee* (blind of one eye),[203] how could they correct others'. Only so it can be understood that so many adjournments are given. The Law Reform Commission observed:

> During our visit to a particular District Court, we were surprised to find that service of a senior lawyer practicing mainly in that court could not be effected for about a year on the plea that he was not available even though he was attending the court almost every day and appearing in cases occasionally even before the judge-in-charge of the Nazarat.[28]

The same Law Reform Commission wrote at another place:

> (…) in one police-case relating to Sargodha Division the prosecution was given 54 adjournments for production of its witnesses.[29]

Some pages later the Commission wrote:

> (...) in some cases as many as 29 adjournments were occasioned by the non-appearance or non-production of the accused.[30]

In order to control such negligence and to improve the efficiency of the judges and at the same time to eliminate the delay in the cases a control mechanism was introduced according to which every judge has to make certain units[31] every day and to write a monthly report to the higher authority on his performance. The number of units to a case depends upon its type. According to the lawyers this leads to the practice that many judges spend more time on cases for which they can easily make units.

The Lawyer

'We buy the worries of our clients',[32] was the claim of a laywer in the courts. An advocate is an important part of the Official Justice System. He is, supposed to help the judge in the interpretation of law through the process of fact-finding and at the same time to win the case for his client. For the layman he is both a great help in this unknown world of the courts, and a cheater. The only thing which makes a lawyer creditable is his ability to win a case. Most of the lawyers do not specialize in any branch of law. Towards the end of their professional career, when they become 'seniors', as they are called then, attracting enough clients, they choose some special branch of law. Otherwise, the majority of them take all sorts of cases which happen to come their away. The only specialization among the lawyers, if at all, is Civil law or the Criminal law.

The foremost problem of a lawyer is to solicit a large number of clients. The number of clients a lawyer has depends upon many factors, and different strategies are adopted. The success of a lawyer does not only depend on his knowledge of law, his capabilities and success, but the village or area he comes from, his touts and friends, relatives, and the *biradari* he belongs to. That is one of the reasons that lawyers write down their *qoum* or *biradari*, especially if they belong to an important one in the area, on their sign-boards and visiting cards like; Rana Abdur Rashid, Chaudhary Karim Ahmad, Mian Muhammad Khan, Iqbal Bhatti, Nisar Bajwa, etc. Cohn describes similar ways the lawyers attract clients in North India:

> The few lawyers I have interviewed in Junapur, heaquarters of the district in which Senapur is located, all stated they drew most of their cases from the part of the district from which they came. At the train and bus station some lawyers keep touts to bring clients to them.[33]

In the words of a lawyer from the Faisalabad District Court, for a successful practice as an advocate, a lawyer requires: 'an efficient team. In this team you have to have people in the villages, relatives, friends, acquaintances, a strong and rather big *biradari*. The other part of your team must be active in the courts, having connections and access to the police. A member of the team is to be from amongst the court employees like a reader, a clerk, legal inspector or so and you must have friends among the judges. You must have personal *guts* for being able to arrange all that. A lawyer must also have enough resources to live on, at least in the early years of service. If they all work together, then his practice is successful. Most of the good lawyers have all or some of these things.' The *munshi* (clerk) of the lawyer also contributes by bringing the clients.

The goal of the lawyers is to win at every cost. Lawyers are those who know the law and they are, therefore, also those who exploit it. They are the ones who teach the witnesses to give false statements on the lines of arguments which would help them win the case. They try their best to confuse the judges. Frank Khanna reports similar role of a lawyer in India:

> (...) the lawyer aims at winning in the fight, not at aiding the court to discover the facts. He does not want the trial court to reach a sound educated guess if it is likely to be contrary to his client's interests. Our present trial method is thus the equivalent of throwing pepper in the eyes of a surgeon when he is performing an operation.[34]

The courts present an atmosphere of a *Juma Bazar* (Friday Market): a huge area, with 'shops' of lawyers, brimming over with people in their best clothes. Everything is on sale for the right price. Every lawyer has his agent who does many jobs: indulging in propaganda (spreading rumours like: the judge is the relative of the lawyer or his own relative etc.) to attract customers. This agent, called *munshi*, has to execute all the official functions like: bringing a case application to the court of the judge, settling appointments, and waiting till the call comes, reporting the presence or the absence of the lawyers etc. He is also in contact with the staff of the judges for causing a certain case to be given priority; when necessary, he gives the court employees their share of the bribe etc.

There are no satisfactory arrangements for the training of an advocate. There is one Law College in Lahore and Private Law Colleges in Faisalabad, which are neither properly provided with libraries nor with full-time staff. The Law Reform Commission writes on the standard of these Private Law Colleges which are nearly all evening colleges:

> Private Law Colleges should not be allowed to degenerate into mere machines for producing legal practitioners. (...) At present most of these private Law Colleges are evening institutions run in borrowed or hired buildings, by a band of lawyers who teach on a part-time basis. There are hardly any library facilities available for the students and there can obviously be no corporate life in such institutions.[35]

Many of those who choose to study law are those who cannot get into institutions to study medicine, engineering, and other such subjects either because of insufficient marks in their Higher Secondary examination or because they cannot afford to study full-time in a regular institution. After at least three years of education there is an examination which in reality tests a candidate's ability to learn by rote. The Law Reform Commission reported:

> Experience shows that by and large the students put in a spurt of activity on the eve of the annual university examinations and do not study their courses throughout the year.[36]

We know of similar law education from India, as observed by Helmken:

> The examination of law schools checks only the memory of a candidate. Learning by heart is the success.[37]

Every Law graduate has to work under a 'senior' lawyer having at least ten years of experience in court. This apprenticeship is seldom taken seriously. There are rumours that one can get the certificate of apprenticeship without really having gone through it. Most Lawyers do not have an adequate number of law books, law bulletins, and periodicals in their chambers. No proper library is available for consultation and study in the courts. The chambers are small and very often shared by more than one advocate having no private space for preparing the cases. As a result, many of the lawyers come to the courts unprepared and hence do not properly represent the cause of their clients. Lawyers starting their careers or those not having the support of a 'team' have to fight tenaciously for their survival. There are very many new lawyers coming to the courts every year. This is also evident from the increasing numbers of chambers and their deteriorating standard.

The above is not true about all advocates or the whole legal profession. There are lawyers who are famous in their fields and they charge high fees. They very often employ a 'junior' advocate to keep up with their appointments. These juniors represent them when their presence is not important at a certain stage, or simply for getting an adjournment on the pretext that the senior lawyer is busy in another case in another court. They represent their clients in other courts, too, and also have cases in the High Court. They 'sell their names' as the other lawyers say. It is said that even the judges respect and fear such lawyers. As the Law Reform Commission writes:

> During our visit to a particular District Court, we were surprised to find that service of a senior lawyer practicing mainly in that court could not be effected for about a year on the plea that he was not available even though he was attending the court almost every day and appearing in cases occasionally even before the judge-in-charge of the Nazarat.[38]

The fee of a lawyer is not fixed; it varies from client to client and from case to case. It is, however, the major part of the expenditures on a suit. The price might vary for a similar case for the same lawyer between 500 and 2000 Rupees, depending upon what a client can pay and to the extent he can be exploited. It depends upon things like: a villager coming to the courts for the first time, coming alone or with a tout, having knowledge of the courts or not. If the client has already been to another lawyer who has demanded a low fees he might be asked to pay even less, but then there are other methods of getting the money. Some clients who know the courts a little go 'lawyer shopping'.

The lawyers play a significant role in delaying the proceedings of the courts as also in promoting corruption. There are different possibilities of delaying a case like, as already noted above, by remaining absent; by keeping the client absent; by keeping the witnesses absent; by making unneccessary lengthy cross-examinations of the witnesses, and other similar methods. Similarly, they play their role in the promotion of corruption. Some lawyers are known to the touts of judges. In the same way, lawyers are mainly responsible for corrupting the lower staff of the courts. Instead of going through the lengthy process, filling in forms, and waiting for their turn they pay the money in order to get things done immediately. The money comes from the pockets of the clients anyway. At the expense of the clients they make contacts with the employees for getting some illegal job done.

The Munshi: Lawyer's Clerk

Every 'good' senior lawyer has at least one *munshi*. The job of a *munshi* is to keep the record of cases, to bring new clients, to prepare the papers for the petition, to inform the lawyer about the times and courts of the cases, to represent the lawyer before the court in his absence, to get information and copies of the documents from the court, etc.

A *munshi* is said to have a direct access to the pocket of the client. The lawyer's fee is paid in the beginning all at once, but a *munshi* takes money every day. He needs it for photocopies, for papers, court fees, he needs it to pay to the court employees, he gets it for the documents from the courts, and so on. This money, according to the lawyers, the clients are not willing to pay. There is also a sort of status difference; a lawyer would not ask for small amounts every day and would always fear the refusal of the client. As against this, the *munshi* does not mind these refusals and also has small arguments if necessary for getting the required amount. His own small share is always included in these daily amounts. It is these daily small amounts which make the burden of expense of a legal suit the most unbearable.

The most important job of the *munshi* is to serve as contact between the courts and the judge, on the one side, and the lawyer and the litigant on the other side. Lawyers doing the jobs of the *munshi* are not liked and respected by the lower staff of the court and also laughed at by their own colleagues. The lawyers themselves find it below their status to act as the *munshi*, in paying small amounts of bribes to the lower staff of the courts whereas the lower staff themselves are uneasy when demanding such amounts from the lawyers.

Most of the *munshies* are barely educated, but what is important for their job is their experience in the courts and perhaps the *biradari* they belong to for bringing in clients. There is a loose arrangement between the lawyer and his *munshi* and most of them do not get a fixed salary. They mostly get a percentage of the fee of the lawyer, from the client.

The Tout

A very special thing about the tout is that he is found in all the branches and fields of justice. There are touts among the public, the police; some lawyers act as touts; court employees and the clerks of the lawyers are touts. The Law Reform Commission noted:

> Besides the professional touts, we understand that some subordinate police officials, lawyer's clerks and petition-writers also contribute their quota to the rank of touts.[39]

In the villages, there are people who, because of their experience with the police and courts, become experts in law, in the practical sense and in tricks of exploiting each and every situation. This means that they know whom to bribe, how and where to get the 'right' or 'wrong' documents so much needed in the courts. They do not know the sections of law, i.e. which law applies to which problem, but they know the addresses and relatives of the judges, their clerks and other officials like *patvaris*, *tehsildars*, etc. and use them if and when the need arises. There are several people in the village of our study like Naeem, Yasin, Taida, Mehbub, called 'sea lawyers' by Cohn: 'Today one meets villagers, people who become expert 'sea lawyers'.[40] These people become acquainted with law because of different reasons. For example, Yasin knows the law through his land conflicts and pursuing his cases in different courts. Naeem is a political figure in the village. He goes to the courts with the people and is involved in several conflicts himself. Mehbub is a retired army officer and has also gained experience in the courts. Taida is the leader of his *biradari*, a big landowner with similar involvement. Most of these 'sea lawyers' are involved in the disputes and have cases going on in the courts themselves. In a new case they go along with the parties to save their own expenditures on transport and food etc; and at the same time to get a commission from their lawyers bringing new clients.

The methods of the touts vary in different circumstances. The policeman who is the tout of a higher officer, has ways and possibilities which are different as compared to a villager who has connections with the police. Similarly, court employees who act as touts of the judges, or lawyers acting for judges, or a layman who works for a lawyer all have their own ways of going about. The first and the most important factor which allows such decadence is the ignorance of law on the part of the people and then the existence of corruption in job. The possibility and the desire of getting things done fast by the use of such methods which would have been impossible under the law also encourages such practices.

The Staff Subordinate to the Judge and the Other Employees of the Courts

This category includes all employees of the courts other than the judges and magistrates. Their jobs are varied and of administrative nature like registering petitions, keeping records of the cases, giving dates for the proceedings, writing down the orders of the judges. Broadly speaking, these employees can be divided into two categories, i.e. the staff of individual judges and the general court staff. Every judge has a reader, a stenotypist, a record clerk, and a peon with multiple duties.

According to the nature of their duties, all these employees play their part on the speed with which a case is disposed of. They have nothing to do directly with the decision making process. But if they are not given their share of the money they may cause problems and impede the process and, in case of a corrupt judge, they can even influence the decision of a case. In the words of a lawyer from District Courts, Faisalabad:

> Suppose we have taken all the preliminary steps and are told to come on a certain date early in the morning, but that day the judge is not present, we need a new date. It costs anything between 20 to 100 Rupees depending upon the date you want to have, early or late. Of course, the opposing parties may be pressuring for an earlier date. A clever reader takes money from both sides and gives a date somewhere in the middle.
>
> The other possibility is that you come a little late so that your name has already been announced. The orderly calling out the case numbers of the people would demand say 20 Rupees for calling it again. Likewise, if the *munshi* of the lawyer needs a copy of the claim of the opponent party for which the client, through the *munshi*, pays 20 Rupees to the record clerk of the court. The summons are to be sent, the *piada* (process-server) wants some *kharcha pani* (literally means, bribe money). We, the lawyers, are also responsible for this corruption. There is a proper procedure for doing all that but it takes an unnecessarily long time. If we follow it we will also make the subordinate staff angry. We have to deal with them every day and it is not always the legal jobs we want from them. The

other thing is that the parties want us to do everything immediately, otherwise we are not considered good lawyers. For example, there is a case of bail and suppose the bail application is accepted. The Magistrates have given the powers of controlling the *muchalka* (a note of bond; recognizance of criminals) to their *almads* (record clerks). Until and unless you give this clerk some money he will not pass your *muchalka* on. He would either find faults in it or use other delaying tactics like asking you on several occasions to come back again and again. On the other side, our party or client would not simply wait till we get it done through legal means. He would be even disappointed and could say that I am not a competent lawyer, but our client would find no fault with paying 50 Rupees. This is how things are. It is not one party but the system as a whole.[41]

The Law Reform Commission 1969-70 wrote the following about the corruption of the court employees:

The integrity of the ministerial and process-serving staff of the civil courts is equally doubtful. It is said that papers and petitions are not put up to the presiding officers unless the *Sheristadar*, the *Peshkar* (Bench Clerk) or the Reader of the court is well looked after. The process-servers also extract money from parties for service of processes. The copying section also does not move until the silver-tonic is applied. It is generally complained that the process-servers do not move out from the court-premises unless their tips are paid in advance to them or settled by the parties. If they are not approached by any party, the process-servers are apt to file false service returns.[42]

The court employees serve as a sort of connection between the judges and the lawyers as also the *munshies*. *Munshies* and readers have fixed prices for different jobs which are higher if the party goes directly to the court employees. Whereas not all judges are corrupt; the same cannot be said about the subordinate staff.

The process of corruption starts right with the filing of the petitions (in civil cases) since these are directly addressed to the Senior Civil Judge; the people want to influence the decision by determining which judge they want their complaint to be sent to. After the Senior Civil Judge has allocated the case to a judge it must be registered, and brought to the court of the concerned judge. Even here it is only after the clerk has been paid his share that the file moves directly to the concerned court.

The bribe paid to the court employees is in a sense different from that paid to the police, judges, medical doctors in that it does not directly affect the decision of the case. Helmken calls it 'speed money'. Parties want to get things done very fast and if the money is not paid, the court employees would want to do things deliberately slow. If we divide bribery into 'safe' and 'unsafe' bribes as Helmken[43] did, most of the bribes accepted by the court employees fall into the category of 'safe' bribes. In fact most of the bribes in the courts fall into this category. But, as a general principle, the safer the bribe, the lesser one has to pay, and the more 'unsafe' the purpose of paying the bribe, the higher the cost. The 'safe' bribe is difficult to locate and take action on. The police officers taking money for writing an FIR, the medical doctor accepting money for writing a Medical Certificate, the legal inspector charging money for forwarding the case, the court employees getting money to speed up the process, are all taking 'safe' bribes.

The question that most often comes to mind is that if everyone knows that the readers, process-servers, and other lower staff are charging money, is it not also known to the judge, and if it is then why cannot they check their immediate staff? Helmken got an interesting answer for this question from the judges:

> I may protect the litigants against staff corruption, but who protects me? Any minute I could put my bench clerk in jail, but the case will fail, because the staff will depose against me. They will take revenge by telling, that I always took bribe (...) I may be dismissed or not promoted (...) In this country you never know, what connections a man has, including your own clerk.[44]

Public Prosecutor or Legal Inspector

After the police has prepared the *challan*, which includes all the documents, starting with the FIR, the Medical Report, the statements of the witnesses, the Remand Report, the Chemical Report, the weapon and other documentary material seized, it is brought to the prosecution section or the Public Prosecutor, depending upon whether the case is for the Magistrate Court or Sessions Judge respectively. The case does not move any further till the concerned parties pay the desired bribe.

Courts in Practice: Documents

In this part of 'Courts in Practice' we would concentrate on the documents like the FIR, Medical Report, Chemical Report, etc. which play an important role in the making of a decision. The main objective remains to present how these important documents are, in practice, made and acquired. To give an idea of what kinds of documents are required the list of documents from the index of a file of a criminal case are reproduced:[45]

Date of the registration of the case: 4.1.91.
Date of decision: 8.7.93.

State through Karim versus Accused 1. Mehndi Khan, 2. Muhammad Shabir, 3. Faryad, and 4. Riaz

Crime under section 307/34 of Pakistan Penal Code.

S.	Sort of paper	No. of pages
1.	This index	1
2.	Case diary	5
3.	First Information Report	1
4.	Road Certificate police	1
5.	Challan police	1
6.	Medical report	1

7.	Custody report	1
8.	Sketch map showing the place of occurrence	1
9.	Custody reports	2
10.	Report of the Search Warrant	2
11.	Remand police station	2
12.	Judicial Remand jail	2
13.	Statement of the witnesses	3
14.	Statement of the victim	1
15.	Statement of the witnesses	4
16.	Copy of the FIR (First Information Report)	1
17.	Police Remand	2
18.	Interrogation of the accused Faryad	1
19.	Interrogation of the accused Shabir	1
20.	Statement of prosecution witness no. 1	1
21.	Statement of prosecution witness no. 2	1
22.	Statement of prosecution witness no. 3	1
23.	Statement of prosecution witness no. 4	1
24.	Statement of prosecution witness no. 5	1
25.	Statement of prosecution witness no. 6	1
26.	Medical Legal Report	1
27.	Statements of prosecution witnesses nos. 7, 8	1
28.	Statement of prosecution witness no. 9	1
29.	Orders of release on bail of the accused	1
3o.	Notice of the court to the Public Prosecutor	1
31.	Security bonds of the accused	2
32.	Orders of the release of the accused	1
33.	Application of the lawyer	1
34.	Application of the Defence lawyers	1
35.	Statements of the accused	1
36.	Statement of the prosecution witness	1
37.	Statement of the prosecution witness	1
38.	Interrogation of the accused	2
39.	Warrants	3
40.	Summons	2
41.	Statement of the Defence witness	1
42.	Supplementary Statement of the accused	1

43. Decision of the court   9
—   Total number of the pages are   70

Different documents mentioned in the above list are examined to see what they are about and how they are collected and prepared. Not all documents mentioned in the above list are individually important, there are many repetitions and some exist only for the sake of formality.

The method followed is: A single document from the above-mentioned list is taken and a summary of the contents of the document given in case file is reproduced. (This may be considered as the formal or official part of the the document.) This is followed by the detail of how in practice these different documents are made and achieved. The whole part concerning documents is described in the form of a story which should provide an idea of the what goes on behind each case, which these documents represent.

FIR (First Information Report) and the Police[46]

Date of reporting: 4.1.91.

The report was written by Zaffarullah Khan, the Head Constable and *muharer* [the one responsible for writing jobs in the Police Station], at the police station in Naglan. The case comes under Pakistan Penal Code 307/34. Reported by Karim s/o Ahmad Bakhsh *Qoum·Araeen.*

> I am an inhabitant of Misalpur and own a bakery. I was alloted plot No 288 in Jinnah Abadi Scheme by the Junejo Govt. This plot is in my possession. One day, at about four o'clock, I was told that Mehndi Khan and his sons, inhabitants of Misalpur, had occupied my plot and were filling it with earth. I, along with Muhammad Akram, my son, and Muhammad Jamal and Muhammad Salim went to Jinnah Abadi Scheme area. Akram was a bit faster, arrived there and told them to stop; Mehndi made a *lalkara* (challenge) and told

his sons to kill Akram. Faryad, Mehndi's son, attacked him with a
knife and hit him in the belly. Shabbir, his brother, also attacked
him with a knife and hit him on the left side. Akram fell to the
ground and Riaz attacked him with a stick. We were afraid and did
not take part in the fight. Afterwards, the accused left the place.
M. Jamal and Allah Ditta Salim saw the incidence with their own
eyes (...)

Police Action: The verbal report of Mr. Karim, inhabitant of
Misalpur, was written down word for word. The report was read to
him and after having found it correct he signed it in my presence
which I herewith certify. The crime comes under section 307/34 of
the Pakistan Penal Code. Zaffarullah (muharer).[47]

The FIR in Practice

FIRs are generally denied, delayed, exaggerated, and falsely
constructed. Without *kharcha pani, chah pani* or such
commissions (different names for palm greasing) or/and *sifarish*
(normally translated as recommendation) nothing happens. Both
the police and the people are responsible for this. The procedure
for filing an FIR is as follows:

An FIR is the word for word report of the complainant written
by the *muharer* in a police station under section 173 of the
Code of Criminal Procedure and is signed by the reporter or
complainant after it has been read to him by the scribe. This,
theoretically, is the right of every citizen but in practice an FIR
is only written on the order of the SHO (Station House Officer)
in charge of the police station. This report is followed by a
small commentary by the scribe or the person in charge of the
case and includes information as to who reported the case, and
under which section of the Code of Criminal Procedure the case
comes.

Since an FIR is the basis of any criminal case, there is a lot
of exaggeration in it. In all the cases recorded and heard about,
no true FIR was recorded. Elopements become abductions,
beating by one turns into a beating by four and FIRs are written
against innocent people just to annoy and harm them. One party

wants the FIR written and the other party wants to obstruct it; sometimes one party even makes an FIR with fabricated reasons. As a normal practice, both parties come to a police station after a fight.

Ashraf's party, of case study reported in the Appendix, did not only report that their *haveli* had been captured but that 50 bags of cement, 10 bags of fertilizer, chicken and agricultural implements, etc. had also been taken away. The pattern in other case studies involving FIRs is similar. The complainant tries to make the case as strong as possible to have the opponent punished and to make it an example for others and to earn honour therein. The other reason for making grossly exaggerated FIRs is that no 'true' FIRs are written. People think, not without reason, that by reporting a true situation they would not get justice.

Not only are the FIRs exaggerated but that it is a very difficult job to get one written. What should be the right of every citizen (being able to report a complaint to the police when something happens) is made so difficult that not every man can afford it. Without money or the *sifarish* of an influential person or both, no FIR is written. We have seen in our case studies that in Ashraf's case it was the *sifarish* of a high ranking Senior Police Officer, but even then 500 Rupees had to be paid; in the case of Dildar it was 3,000 Rupees. The FIR of Akram's murder was written on the *sifarish* of the most important political figure in the village two weeks after the incident, and the other side is said to have paid an enormous amount of money to obstruct it.

The Law Reform Commission in its findings on FIRs wrote:

> The police-station is the main centre of corrupt activities because of the vast powers given by law to officers-in-charge of police-stations or Station House Officers. A case is not registered or an F.I.R. is not accepted nor is sufficient interest shown in the investigation unless the complainant gives a handsome gratification to the O.C. or the S.H.O. If the accused party is more generous the scales are invariably tipped in its favour. Both the parties are often kept equally satisfied by a clever Investigating Officer who sends

the cases up to the Court of the Magistrate with such lacunae therein that the accused may make capital out of them.[48]

The FIR of a murder case was delayed for nearly four weeks. Moreover if the complainant is a poor man and his opponent is a rich and influential person action might even be taken against the former. The police has no lack of excuses for doing so. As Aslam (in one of our case studies) went to the police a second time to report the abduction of his daughter by someone from his own *biradari* who had the support of a rich tout of the village, he had to spend five days in the police station. The FIR was registered only when he arranged a visiting card with remarks 'to help' from Ansari, at that time an MNA (Member of the National Assembly from Aslam's *biradari*). In another case, the FIR was written after the *sifarish* of the DSP. The Law Reform Commission wrote on this aspect:

> It is common knowledge, and some of the witnesses, who appeared before us, have made no secret of the fact, that in a vast majority of important cases like murders, the First Information Report is not recorded till after the investigating officer has visited the scene of occurrence. Right from the inception of the case, delay creeps in, and with this delay corruption also creeps in, involving the possibility of roping in innocent persons along with the culprits, or of letting the guilty escape altogether. This initial setback adversely affects the prospects of collection of evidence and immediate arrest of criminals (...) the reluctance of subordinate police officials to take action at the instance of poor and illiterate complainants, unless they are backed by an influential person of the locality or are otherwise able to induce the police to act.[49]

Not a single job, however small, is done by the police without a certain fee—even for attesting the character certificates, necessary for a job or a passport. Some people injure themselves, or sometimes the poor servants are made the victims for getting a strong FIR written. According to a lawyer: 'the police charges one side for including the innocent people in an FIR and charges the other side for again declaring them innocent. If the FIR would be true and the opposite party would accept it, it would not be in the interest of the police, because then they cannot get a bribe'.[50]

Only a small fraction of the total cases which come to the police station are filed as FIRs. According to the estimate of an advocate, 'FIRs form less than 30 per cent of the total cases coming to be reported and the rest end up in a so-called compromise'. There are many reasons for refusing to write an FIR such as: there is a competition between the police stations to have the minimum number of crimes reported. This shows the efficiency of the officer-in-charge of a police station[51] in controlling crime. This does not mean that the police is interested in preventing crimes, conflicts, and fights in the community; actually it is the other way round. Every new conflict coming to the police, every criminal or so-called criminal falling into the hands of the police is like a lucky draw for them. That is what, as it is said, keeps the motor running.

Another reason for not wanting to write an FIR is that every new FIR means more work. The police very often takes up the role of a mediator—one who is paid. As an institution of conciliation and compromise, having the powers and resources necessary, the police do play an important role though the outcome could be called 'relative justice', i.e. at the cost of the poor. In our case study, the *haveli* of Ashraf, the police played this role twice and both times both parties had to pay *kharcha pani*, the question is how and why both sides paid it.

Ashraf's party was disappointed at the slow functioning of the courts and were even doubtful if they would be able to get back their *haveli*. Again they went to the police, through a tout, to effect a compromise. *Kharcha pani* was paid and the police pressed the other party; an agreement was made in which Ashraf got the major part of his *haveli* back. The other party paid since they were, in any case, illegal occupants and only due to the favour of the police they could retain a part of the occupied *haveli*. These acts of the police seem to be indirectly designed to keep away the cases from the courts. This 'argument' is also sometimes used as an excuse for the slow speed of the courts: if these are slow, corrupt and expensive it encourages a compromise out of court or in the traditional way.

The normal procedure is that if one goes to the police one has to submit an application written on plain paper written by an expert (applications written by ordinary people are not accepted in Naglan police station. The expert is a retired police SHO living in the neighbourhood of the police station). The opposing party is then called to the police station, if they are not there already; both may be threatened, money taken and a compromise may be forced upon them.

In every village there are police touts, who not only inform the police when something happens but also serve the villagers as a sort of connection with the police. They function as agents stating the demands of the police as to how much money the complainants would have to pay if they want to get a case registered. There are also rich villagers who pay a monthly amount to the police and others who are politically influential and do favours for them like promotions or transfers to the areas of their wishes. The police also have relatives and friends whose jobs they must do. At the same time, there are one or two policemen in the station who act as touts for the one in charge of the police station.

The police is one of the most important constituents of the official justice system, especially in criminal cases, and plays an important role in the delay of criminal court proceedings. The system of the police functions in such a way that bribe has become an inherent part of the system. The one who would not take a bribe or is not a master in the techniques of getting bribes would be addressed with expressions like *khusto spahi* or *dhella spahi*, etc. by his colleagues. In some police stations the bribe money collected is divided hierarchically among the members. Of course, very little flows to the junior staff, who, therefore, have devised their own methods and sources. There are certain norms that are followed : if one makes a deal outside the police station, the profit or bribe is all one's own but a fixed monthly amount has to be paid to the police station. If the deal is made in the police station it is to be divided. There is a great deal of corruption within the institution of the police. Decisions like who is chosen to police the traffic or and who is made responsible for jobs like *muharer* are highly important, as are those concerning the area one is sent to on duty. There are 'good areas' with high incomes through bribe, and there are 'bad areas' which are less lucrative. It is important whether a policeman is posted in a police station (especially one in a village, or in a city, the kind of village, the part of the city, etc.) or in a so-called line office. Line office duties have little to do with the public; less money is expected, and is therefore, not a sought-after job.

Since we are mainly concerned with justice in practice and the role of the police therein, we will not go much deeper into the details of the problems of jobs, education and training of the police which are many but some of these will be mentioned. There is nearly no minimum educational requirement for employment as a police constable, apart from perhaps being able to read and write, but in some cases 'the constables even today remain illiterate and ill-paid'.[52]

The working hours of the police are not defined and housing facilities are poor. Food is equally bad if served from the mess. The job is full of risks and the promotion chances, of the lower staff, are minimal and the salary is inadequate. The training of the police recruits is such that it turns them into abusive sadistic individuals; a far cry from the ideal policeman one reads about in books. Similar conditions of the Indian police led Baxi to call them 'A Subhuman Species'.[53]

In spite of their problems the policemen are expected to perform miracles as beautifully expressed by August Volmer:

> (...) the wisdom of Solomon, the courage of David, the strength of Samson, the patience of Job, the leadership of Moses, the kindness of the Good Samaritan, the strategical training of Alexander, the faith of Daniel, the diplomacy of Lincoln, the tolerance of the carpenter of Nazareth, and an intimate knowledge of every branch of the natural, biological and social science.[54]

It also needs to be mentioned that the police is misused by the politicians and the bureaucrats for their own ends. The police is also invested with more power in comparison to their training and ability.

Medical Report[55] in Practice

> Akram, son of Karim, inhabitant of Misalpur, male, age 35 years. Nature of the wound: [the wounds are shown on a drawing of a human body and are numbered from one to four]. Injury nos. one and two are caused by blunt weapon and are simple. Injury nos. three and four are caused by a sharp edge weapon and are grievous in motive.[56]

These few words of the medical doctor are such an important piece of evidence that it can become the dividing line between guilt and innocence. There is hardly any possibility of control over the concerned medical officer. The most important aspect of the Medical Reports is the corruption it represents.

In every Tehsil and District Headquarters, there are medical officers known as C.M.O. (Casualty Medical Officer) who are responsible for issuing Medical Reports in the case of crimes, involving murder or assault. This report must include all necessary details like, the severity of the wound, the time of death, the analysis of the blood and urine, etc. On the basis of this information the nature of the crime and the criminal is identified. This requires integrity as also the necessary knowledge of forensic medicine. The lack of facilities contributes to the apathy but what is even worse, is that these C.M.Os. are very corrupt. The usual pattern is that if there is a clash in a village and someone is wounded he does not come to the hospital alone, as he will probably not even find the right ward. He goes to some *Chaudhary* or *Rana* and asks them to accompany him. These 'big men' not only know where to go but also have connections with the Medical Officers and their subordinate staff. The rivals also might tell the doctor or his touts: 'it does not matter how much it costs but we want such a report that the opponent party should not come out of jail or else (...).'

It is not only the doctors who can change a report showing a grievous injury as a simple one or vice versa; there are other methods of making the case strong. After a fight in which somebody is wounded, the rivals immediately contact the hospital to get the injury report in. The arena, now is the hospital. To win the case or at least to make it strong people injure themselves at home, and others have it done in the hospital. In the village, there are enough people known as 'brave' who are known to have their enemies or opponents punished by wounding themselves, their sons or servants.

Torture and Confession: Custody Reports and the Statements of the Accused

In the presence of the following witnesses, M. Shabir son of Mehndi Khan *qoum Rajput*, inhabitant of Misalpur, accused, on body remand, disclosed during interrogation the location of the knife used in the fight. Accompanied and under the arrest of the police, the accused, walking ahead of the police took out the knife from under the clothes in the northwestern corner of the *baithak* [usually translated men's house]. The blade which is of 5" and has a wooden handle and has three nails in it which go through. On the blade, is written in English 'stainless steel'.[57]

Witness No. 1. Muhammad Rafiq son of Karim [a relative of Karim, the complainant]. Witness No. 2. Abdul Sharif son of Ahmad Bakhsh [brother of the complainant].[58]

It is perhaps sufficient to quote the Law Reform Commission which admits the existence of the methods of torture used by the police:

Even today the object of the thana officers, more often than not, is the achievement of results regardless of the means adopted.

Extortion of confessions, padding, frequent use of stock witnesses are practices commonly resorted to.[59]

After the police has written an FIR and obtained the Medical Report, if required, the next step would be to arrest the accused. The police has the right to detain him for twenty-four hours. This can be extended for further investigation upto fifteen days through the magistrate.

The police is known and feared for using 'third degree' methods for getting confessions. There is a common saying that even the dead speak out of fear of the police thrashing. The confessions are either statements admitting a certain crime or lead to the recovery of items used in the crime. It is common knowledge that in the police stations and jails, because of contact with the criminals and due to the behaviour of the police, simple and innocent people turn into criminals. The cruel techniques of remand such as beating the hips with dry shoes, tying a cup of water to the testicles have been reported. There are other cruel methods of securing a confession. Walsh wrote about the methods used by the police:

> The forms of torture alleged are: beating with stinging nettles; tying a pot containing wasps to some naked part of the body; allowing water to drip slowly on to the body for hours; keeping awake all night by making hideous noises; and burning cayenne pepper, or causing it to be inhaled; (...).[60]

The reasons for using torture as a means of securing information or confessions is that[61] the accused or the criminal is the best informant and torture is the easiest way of getting the information. There is a lack of investigation staff, and of modern equipment for carrying it out. There is also pressure from the other party who want the information quickly, especially those who are directly affected by the incident. A most commonly used practice is that if the accused is arrested and the opposite party has influence and resources, they go to the police station and make a deal with the police that each time the accused is beaten with a shoe the policeman will get ten rupees. Still another reason for the use of methods of torture is the intervention of politicians and their opponents.

This does not mean that the information thus obtained is always totally invented, but still quite a number of cases are known in which the police fabricated cases against innocent persons. Whether the confession was the result of torture, cruelty, fear or promise of granting pardon or independent choice, it is usually denied as having been done after the accused takes a lawyer.

Evidence: Statements of the Witnesses

> I was working on my power-looms when Karim, Akram, and Jamal came and asked me to go with them to the Jinnah Abadi Scheme where the plot of Karim and Akram was reported to be occupied by Mehndi and his sons. We went together to the house of Salim who accompanied us too. We all went together to Jinnah Abadi. Akram, the son of Karim, was going ahead of us. As he reached there and told Mehndi and his sons not to occupy their place Mehndi made a *lalkara* [challenge]. Faryad and Shabbir attacked him with a knife while Riaz hit him with a *sota* [stick]. Akram fell to the ground before our eyes. (...)

Witnesses in Practice

If the FIR and the police are the means of access to the Criminal Courts, the witnesses are the foundations on the basis of which a criminal case is built. Testimony is not given for the love of truth or fairness but because of the love for the relatives, for the sake of reciprocity or because one of the party is one's enemy. Giving evidence against a strong party is making the other party one's enemy. The testimonies are fabricated according to the requirements of the case.

Coming to the case studies: The witnesses for Ashraf, in case study one, were his own brothers. In the beginning, when he needed witnesses, he asked different people including his *biradari* but no one except his brothers was ready to testify against Goora and his sons. One reason was that there was no reciprocity to be returned since the family of Ashraf had, for the most part, moved to a town, and kept themselves aloof from politics; and the other reason was that no one wanted the enmity of the *Ambalvi biradari*. The situation changed somewhat when Goora's *biradari* became divided. Those opposing Goora came to Ashraf and offered themselves as witnesses which was refused due to the fact that they could change their mind again at some point. Similarly, Dildar's witnesses were also his uncles and relatives. The same is the case with the witnesses of Akram's murder. No one except his father and the opponent party was present at the time of his murder but the police needed eye-witnesses other than his father.

According to the view expressed by a lawyer 'more than 99 per cent of the evidences are wrong'. Most of those who become eye-witnesses were probably not present at the time of occurrence. There are even professional witnesses, to be found in courts, who charge money and are ready to give any kind of testimony. The problem of false evidence is one of the gravest and has not improved since the introduction of the official courts of justice by the British. Moon wrote:

> Greenlane and myriads of Indian magistrates daily spent hours in their Courts solemnly recording word for word the evidence of illiterate peasants, knowing fully well that 90 per cent of it was false. Even if the events described had actually occurred, the alleged eye-witnesses had not seen them.[62]

There are numerous cases and stories recorded by the English magistrates, judges and those concerned with the administration of justice which are as true as ever. We quote here one case in which because of a false evidence, though the real case was known in the village, an innocent life was sacrificed. The Magistrate, though himself sure of the innocence of the victim, was helpless. Here is a summary of the case as reported by Moon:

A young man of twenty-two named Karam, was murdered in broad daylight as he was driving his cattle from the village pond. (...) Meanwhile the police have been busy investigating and have arrested two men named Raja and Jahana. (...)

The motive for the murder is also plain. The dead man had been making love to Jahana's wife, who was also Raja's sister. (...)

Although during the whole afternoon he (Greenlane, the magistrate of the area) had never stepped outside his tent, inside it he had received a number of visitors; and from some of these, notably the local Zaildar, (The leading man of a 'zail or group of villages. He receives a small emolument in return for services rendered to Government officials and enjoys considerable local prestige), an excellent young man of his own age who belonged to this very village, he had learnt a good deal about the murder. (...)

The murder was the work of one man, not two. Raja, the brother, was responsible; Jahana, the husband, had no hand in it. It had been witnessed by none of the alleged eye-witnesses; it had been witnessed in fact by no one save a single timorous shopkeeper, who had not the courage to give evidence or to make a statement to the police. (...)

Karam's white-bearded grandfather was ready to give any evidence that might be required of him. But a solitary eye-witness, and he a near relative of the deceased, clearly would not satisfy the courts. More eye-witnesses, unconnected by blood or marriage with Karam's family, were essential. Two men were available, who were willing to pose as eye-witnesses; but they demanded a price— Jahana's blood. One of them simply bore Jahana a grudge; he thought that Jahana's influence had prevented his son's betrothal to Jahana's niece. The other hoped that some land belonging to a distant relative would eventually come to him, if Jahana was out of the way. Both felt that this convenient opportunity of removing Jahana was too good to be missed; and the relatives of Karam, provided they got Raja, were quite willing to have Jahana thrown in as well.

All, therefore, was arranged accordingly, and the three eye-witnesses were carefully instructed in their parts before anyone was sent off to the police station to call in the police. (...) All three told exactly the same story; all three were unshaken in cross-examination; indeed cross-examination was necessarily ineffective; the story they told was so brief and so simple (...) He himself could arrive at the truth, because he was in constant touch with the people of the countryside and knew which of them were good men and true, whom he could trust to tell him honestly all the relevant facts, concealing nothing, and adding nothing. But the Sessions Judge, sitting seventy-five miles away in Derajat, knew none of these people; and why should he believe the hearsay report of Greenlane, a quite junior officer whom he had only met once? Why indeed should he listen to him at all?

So Greenlane did nothing; and Jahana was hanged along with Raja.[63]

This story is an excellent example of the many problems of the official justice system in the village and though recorded in the first half of this century still represents a lot of day-to-day happenings in the village. There are many similarities with our case studies, like the witnesses being either relatives or those having their 'own axes to grind'. The witnesses are arranged before one goes to the police and courts. It is mostly the lawyer who instructs the witnesses about what to say and how to say it. For example if we compare the statements of the witness quoted above and the FIR reported by Karim we find them very similar. The same was the case with the other witness.

The problem of the witnesses could perhaps be understood like this: A party has not only to find witnesses but to find such witnesses who are trustworthy and would not change their loyalty. The problem of changing loyalties is not uncommon. Sometimes parties wait and try all possibilities to change the loyalty of the other's witnesses. The Law Reform Commission noted:

(...) the parties try to win over the witnesses and on this behalf no effort is spared. If influence fails, money is tried, and in some cases not without success. In cases triable by the Sessions court, if a party fails to win over the witnesses at the stage of enquiry preparatory to commitment it does not lose hope and in a number of cases succeeds in making the witnesses agree to admit some points in cross-examination during trial.[64]

For securing witnesses a party can take a relative or non-relative as witness. Standing witness against another is one of the many reasons of disputes and quarrels. Also there is considerable wastage of time. The practice in the courts is such that the evidence is not recorded in one session. There are several adjournments, sometimes due to the negligence of the clerks inviting more parties than possible to attend one sitting, sometimes because of the laziness of the judges or magistrates who do not finish their job and simply tell the parties to come back the next time. But the most frequent reason, especially if one party is rich and influential, is that it has a better 'senior' lawyer and is interested in prolonging the case till eternity to make the other party bankrupt.

The Law Reform Commission records in its report about these inconveniences for the witnesses:

> It is a matter of common knowledge that the people who are summoned to appear as witnesses in courts have to face a lot of inconvenience. First of all, they have to wait for long hours outside the court before the case in which their evidence is to be recorded is called. Secondly, there is no proper seating arrangement for them both in the court-room and outside. Thirdly, the witnesses are generally treated with lack of courtesy and sometimes even with rudeness. The right of cross-examination is also sometimes misused by the counsel of the opposing party because all sorts of personal and embarassing questions are put to the witnesses in cross-examination. (...) The Commission has found that there is a common practice in the courts to adjourn cases and send away witnesses in attendance without recording their evidence. The Commission was informed by the D.I.G. of Police, Karachi that in one year alone as many as 8,000 witnesses were sent away by the courts without recording their statements.[65]

Helmken does not agree with the view that the above-mentioned factor affects somebody's decision of becoming a witness and says it might be true about the people of the city but not of the people of the village. In his view:

The prospects of a cost free visit to the District Headquarters and the possibility of food at the cost of the party, as also curiosity about the state of affairs of the case together with the normally given duty of loyalty as a witness to the party (kinship, dependence, factional ties, neighbourhood) are so strong reasons that the inconveniences like oppressive atmosphere of the court room for a short while for answering some uncomfortable questions does not count much.[66]

His argument is of course only valid where the witnesses are already obliged to give evidence. These above-mentioned factors could be taken as additional motivation. As a rule if it is left to the parties alone, it is mostly the relatives or people of the *biradari* or close friends who are brought as witnesses so that it can be ensured that the witnesses say exactly what the lawyers conduct them to.

The Decision

I have compared the statements of the prosecution and defence witnesses and have studied the file with care, likewise have also looked into the discussions of the prosecution and defence lawyers. Besides the wounded four, other eye-witnesses have made statements as eye-witnesses (...) Karim has reported the FIR. According to his statement he came immediately to the police station for reporting the FIR. But from the FIR it turns out that it was reported at 4 o'clock, whereas the medical report shows that the medical check up of the wounded was done at 1.45 p.m. This shows that ASI, M. Nawaz, had taken the statement of the wounded in the presence of the medical officer before writing the FIR and that the wounded was in his senses. In this report he has mentioned three accused and has also us told that he had recognized them. The action of the police and the statement of SHO Mr. Jhang show that the police did not register the FIR immediately after having received the information, but the SHO sent the ASI for investigation first to the hospital where he recorded the statement of the wounded and then on his return the *muharer* wrote the FIR. This is wrong according to the rule of procedure. (...)

This shows that the police failed in investigation. (...) Therefore the prosecution has failed to prove the crime under section 307/34 Pakistan Penal Code.

It is therefore ordered that: The accused, in the absence of the proof of crime under section 307/34 of Pakistan Penal Code, are honourably set on liberty.

The decision of the court depends on the documents, the FIR and investigation of the police, the Medical Report, the statements of the witnesses and the arguments of the lawyers. All these, as has already been mentioned above in detail, are usually false. Describing a similar situation Moon quotes Metcalfe:

(The judge) sits on a bench in the midst of a general conspiracy. (...) Everyone is labouring to deceive him and to thwart his desire for justice. The pleaders have no regard for truth.[67]

The desire for revenge is exacerbated if the decision of the court is against the expectations of one party. Such stories of seeking vengeance are not uncommon. M. T. Ahmad wrote about such a case in Malakpur, a Pakistani Punjabi village:

He congratulated the murderers of his brother (who were acquitted by the court on the benefit of doubt) and said to them, 'I am glad you are back home and it is good that no one else usurped my right to avenge the death of my brother'. (...) One night when the marriage celebrations were in progress in B's house (the murderers' family) a hail of bullets killed four persons on the spot. (...)[68]

The Execution of Decrees and Orders

The problem does not end with achieving a decision but often starts after it has been announced. In the words of the Law Reform Commission 1967-70:

The difficulties of a litigant in India (before partition) begin when he has obtained a decree. (...) The things have not changed very much since then and what was said almost a century ago holds good.[69]

In the case study of 'Ashraf's *haveli*' we have seen that after the decision was made in Ashraf's favour, Goora's sons had to vacate the part they had. This was the decision of the court which was put into action but after two hours of the police leaving the village the opponents captured it again. The whole conflict started anew. This ineffectiveness of court decisions in many cases discourages people from going to the courts.

Wealth and Power *vis-à-vis* the Official System

Money plays an important role in the courts at every stage like for starting a court case, court fees, payment of bus fares, food, copies of the documents from the court records, lawyer's fees, the commission of his *munshi* and that of the tout, as also for greasing the palm of the different agents of the processes—like the police, the medical doctors, the court employees and even the judge himself.

The element of *sifarish*, political and bureaucratic power, also plays a very important role in the functioning of the official justice system. The *parchi* or visiting card one brings and what is written on it may become decisive. *Parchies* are accepted like bank cheques which are sometimes cashed back, of course depending upon who gave it—a senior officer, a friend, or a politician in power. Telephone messages also can be effective.

These expenditures could be divided into categories followed by Helmken in the case of the Civil Courts in Dhanbad District in India:

a) Costs required by the law (e.g. court fee)
b) Costs arising from the court procedure itself or related costs (e.g. travel costs, lawyers' fees). The latter may again be subdivided into:

aa) Legal costs, intended or tolerated by the system (e.g. clerk costs)

bb) Illegal costs, prohibited by the system but not prevented effectively (e.g. payment of bribes to the court employees).[70]

The other possibility would be to divide them into the costs for starting a case, for maintaining and speeding it up and for making it successful. This division is important from the point of view of the consumers of the legal system (disputants) since they do not divide them into legal and illegal; they divided them into avoidable and unavoidable; as also between that to be paid now or latter.

These expenditures hinder the dispensation of justice. It is very difficult, rather impossible, to give the real amounts paid in figures. They differ from case to case depending upon its nature and the parties involved. It becomes even more difficult to provide estimates about the expenditures of categories (aa) and (bb), following Helmken, i.e. the fee of the lawyer, the charges of the lawyer's clerk and the bribe paid to the court employees. The amounts paid by different people for different and equal jobs to the police, in the courts, to medical officers, as court fees, the fees paid to the lawyers, and so on has been provided in the last chapter.

The illegal costs are a much bigger part of the expenditures than the legal and allowed costs. Generally, according to lawyers, the legal costs in the Criminal Courts are less than in the Civil Courts but that the illegal costs in the case of Criminal Courts are comparatively higher; in other words the Criminal Courts are more corrupt.[71]

According to the Law Commission Report of 1958-59, the justice administration does not only meet its expenses from what it earns but also makes a profit thereof:

Figures of relevant receipts and expenditure, have been supplied to us by the two Provincial Governments (...). These figures may not give a true picture of the situation as all the relevant factors may not have been acounted for while working out the net profit and loss (...). After considering these statistics, our feeling is that the

State may be actually making a profit, both on the criminal as well as on the civil side of the administration of justice.[72]

The litigants or disputants could be divided into two categories:
1) The plaintiffs, who could be further subdivided into (a) legitimate and (b) illegitimate or ill-willed complainants.
2) Similarly, defendants could also be divided into (a) those who are innocent and (b) criminals.

This is a very simple classification but not unrealistic for the present purpose. According to the statement of a lawyer: 'It is better to let 99 per cent criminals go unpunished than punishing one innocent'.[73]

Every or at least 99 per cent of the complaints are considered false by the court system. This is why the formalities of law necessary for initiating a suit are so expensive, i.e. how the court fee, the lengthy and costly procedure of the summons are to be legitimized. In the words of the Law Commission:

> (...) the thinking was that the levy of court-fee was desirable because it would reduce litigation.[74]

Not only are the costs very high but are mostly only paid by the plaintiff or the complainant. There is some credence to the view that many people start bogus cases against their opponents to drive them into bankruptcy, to satisfy their insulted pride, to harass them or to maintain local political dominance, but the result is that since the whole machinery of justice seems to adopt a strategy to stop this misuse, it ends up doing exactly the opposite. The complainant finds himself to be a criminal until he has proved his innocence. In the words of the same lawyer quoted above, the result of this policy is that: 'Not only 99 per cent of the criminals go unpunished but that one per cent innocent are also punished'.[75] According to another source:

> (...) according to an estimate about seventy per cent of the actual murderers have gone unpunished in a certain district.[76]

It is therefore absurd to suppose that court-fees or other expenditures and formalities necessary for a complaint would reduce the number of false complainants. It discourages the poor and rightful complainants from coming to the courts, and on the contrary encourages the rich in false complaints, to bring to courts to assert their political dominance.

Similar ideas were expressed by Lord Macaulay on the introduction of the court fees:

> The real way to prevent unjust suits is to take care that there shall be just decision. No man goes to law except in the hope of succeeding. No man hopes to succeed in a bad cause unless he has reason to believe that it will be determined according to bad laws or by bad Judges. Dishonest suits will never be common unless the public entertains an unfavourable opinion of the administration of justice. And the public will never long entertain such without good reasons (...) [The imposition of court fees] neither makes the pleadings clearer nor the law plainer, nor the corrupt judge purer, nor the stupid judge wiser. It will no doubt drive away dishonest plaintiffs who cannot pay the fee. But it will also drive away the honest plaintiffs who are in the same situation.[77]

There is also the question of the poor and rich complainants. In the words of Helmken:

> (...) experienced litigants engage a cheap lawyer (mostly a junior) in the preparation period while at the later stage of the process i.e. the oral hearing they give the case into the hands of an experienced but expensive (senior) lawyer.[78]

The lawyers and their *munshies* charge more money from inexperienced clients on various pretext as the court-fee, for bribing the court employees, or for other formalities and sometimes even in the name of bribing the judge for winning the case. Helmken reports an interesting story of manipulation by two lawyers from Dhanbad, India, from the interview of a District Judge; such stories are not unknown in Faisalabad:

He was directed by the High Court to keep an eye on the activities of two lawyers of the criminal side inconspicuously. The two had developed the following method of earning profit: In police cases they tried to be engaged as lawyers, one from both parties. Shortly before the decision they demanded from their respective parties bribe money for the judge. After the decision the lawyer of the losing party gave the money back with the remark that the other party had given more. The rest of the money was then divided between the two.[79]

Although the courts are theoretically supposed to treat the disputants as equal, in practice money and power influence its functioning to a very large extent. As a result the decision of the courts can also be seen as relative justice.

The Question of Colonial Nature and Background of the Official System

The question of the colonial nature and background of the official system, in South Asia, is disputed between anthropologists and jurists. The anthropologists[80] seem to hold the colonial background responsible for the alien nature and for all the problems of the official system of justice. Cohn's description is a representation of this point of view:

> The way a people settles disputes is part of its social structure and value system. In attempting to introduce British procedural law into their Indian courts, the British confronted the Indians with a situation in which there was a direct clash of the values of the two societies; and the Indians in response thought only of manipulating the new situation and did not use the courts to settle disputes but only to further them.[81]

The disparity in society could be because of two reasons: (a) The opposing interests (economic and socio-political) of the rulers (colonialists) and those being ruled; and (b) the anomaly, since the system was developed and meant for a different type of society. Here again the first does not apply to the present situation because colonial rule does not exist any more. The clash of values could only be based on the different social structure of the society and the system of justice.

The main focus of criticism, according to the anthropologists, in this clash of values seems to be that the society is based on the idea of inequality of the individuals whereas the justice system takes them as equal. In the words of Cohn:

> The Chamar knows he is not equal to the Thakar. He may want to be equal but he knows he is not. The Thakar cannot be convinced in any way that the Chamar is his equal.[82]

The mistake of the courts is that they act 'as if the parties to the dispute were equal'.[83]

Moore writes:

> The British system, as it has developed in India (and America), examines one distinct dispute under 'laboratory conditions'. The courtroom is seen as a vacuum into which only carefully circumscribed testimony and evidence are presented and manipulated by professionals. In theory the disputants lose their social status and are viewed as equals before the law.[84]

If this is the basic difference of values between the society and the official system of justice, then one might ask: Should the aim of the justice system be to provide justice according to the social status of the individuals—perhaps a raised place for a *Thakar* and a lower one for a *Chamar*. And, should the traditional system be adopted because it provides justice according to the social status of the disputants?

The jurists[85] trained in the official justice system represent the other extreme and do not believe that the problems of the official justice system lie in its colonial background and alien nature. Their viewpoint is best represented in the report of the Law Reform Commission:

It is hardly correct to say that the present judicial system is a foreign transplant on Indian soil, or that it is based on alien concepts unintelligible to our people. (...) The present day complications and delays in disposal of cases are not so much on account of technical and cumbersome nature of our legal system as they are due to other factors operating in and outside the courts.[86]

The problems of the judiciary do not only lie in the shortage of resources and facilities as thought by the juristis. The official system is, in many cases, alien to the customs and values of the society. This estrangement and alienation should not only be located in its colonial nature as done by the anthropologists, but also because of other factors, called by the Law Reform Commission as 'factors operating in and outside the courts'.

NOTES

1. *1981 Census Report of Punjab Province*. Population Census Organization Statistics Division, Government of Pakistan, Islamabad, December 1984.
2. For further details see, *1981 Census Report of Punjab Province*, Population Census Organization Statistics Division, Government of Pakistan, Islamabad, December 1984.
3. Theoretically these courts are also open and approachable by any and every citizen but getting a case registered and being in a position to pay the expenses of a lawyer etc. almost exclusively rescue them for a certain class and sort of people.
4. Constitution of Pakistan, 1990.
5. Constitution of Pakistan, 1990.
6. Constitution of Pakistan, 1990, p. 131
7. Constitution of Pakistan, 1990, p. 139.
8. Constitution of Pakistan, 1990, p. 138.
   For further details about the Shariat Courts see Constitution of Pakistan. For further detail and to comprehend the hierarchy of the courts see diagram no. 9
   Note: It is important to mention that in spite of making reference to Supreme Court, High Courts and Shariat Courts here and there we shall be concerned with the lower courts, or the courts of the first instance in this study.
9. Both these terms have been borrowed from Hoebel (1965, p. 44) and some detail has been already given in the Introduction.

10. In the words of Berry:
    'It is not uncommon to find areas in the law which do not reflect distinctive human conduct. Even in the most sophisticated legal systems are found segments of legal propositions which do not lend themselves to demonstration through empirical study.

    There is often a sizeable gap between the refinements of the lawyer's law on the one hand and popular notions of legality on the other.' Berry, Willard, 1966, p. 3.

11. The Report of the Law Reform Commission, 1967-70, p. 388.

12. The Report of the Law Reform Commission, 1967-70, p. 268.

13. See for further details of the police Challan, as it is called, our case study in 'courts in practice'.

14. Law Reform Commission, 1958-59, p. 38.

15. A layman may theoretically approach the courts directly but it is almost impossible that his pleading would be accepted.

16. The correctness of the pleadings is not self-evident. According to the Law Reform Commission:
    'Pleadings in this country are usually unsatisfactory in many respects.' See for further details: Law Reform Commission Report, 1967-70, pp. 36–7. The mistakes in the pleadings are a proof, among others, of the standard of education of the advocates to which we shall come later on.

17. Besides personal observations and experiences of the formalities of the court, most of the information for the formal part of the study is drawn from the Law Reform Commissions reports, especially Mr Justice Hamoodur Rahman Commission's Report of 1967-70 and the Report of Mr. Justice S.A. Rahman's Commission, 1958-59. There was another Law Reform Commission headed by Mr. Justice S. Yasinul Haq in 1978, and finally, the Law Reform Commission was made permanent in 1979.

18. M.T. Ahmad, 'Offences in Rural and Urban Areas'. Unpublished, p. 41.

19. Misalpur, is about fifteen kilometers from the District and Tehsil Headquarters, Faisalabad, i.e. the administrative centre of the district. Tehsil Headquarters, besides being an administrative unit, serves as the lowest rung on the ladder of the Judiciary. The District Headquarters include the District and Sessions courts, a step above the Tehsil, but lower than the High Courts. This indicates a favourable location of Misalpur with respect to the official courts vis-a-vis many other especially remote villages of the district.

    The most interesting place is where the old building of the lower courts,—both Civil and Criminal—are situated. There are normally two approaches to this part of the courts, one for those with cars and the other side for those on foot, or riding motorcycles and bicycles. The offices of the judges, on the side of the car entrance, are in a row at the end of which is normally the office of the highest police officer of the District called the SSP (Senior Superintendent of Police) Between the row of the judges' offices and the boundary wall there are parking places and patches of grass and trees. The private entrances to the judges' offices are also on this side of the offices, including the 'retiring room' for the judges, where they sit when not in the court room. This side of the courts is not only more clean and better taken care of (the lower parts of the treetrunks are white-washed with a red rim) but also presents a peaceful atmosphere.

On the inner side of the same building there is a veranda (terrace) followed by the courtrooms. When the court is in session, the veranda as well as the courtroom is full of people. The architecture of the courts presents a mixture of colonial style with a blend of post-independence construction, as is the law itself.

Immediately adjacent to the pedestrian entrance are the lawyers' chambers. These chambers are, as a rule, small and narrow. In front of most of these chambers sit the *arzi nawees* (typists who types out applications), *munshies* (the clerks of the lawyers), Oath commissioner's agents, the photostat machine operators and the newspaper sellers. The shoe-shine boy, fruit sellers, cold drinks vendors, and the *chai walas* (tea servers) crowd the very small lanes, where there is space left over by parked scooters, bicycles and motorcycles. Often two lawyers share one small chamber which are normally full of people, some of whom may not be clients. The presence of the mosque is only felt at the time of *Azan* (call for the prayer). Similarly, there is a judicial jail on the premises where those prisoners are lodged who are to be presented in the court and who wait for transport to the jail respectively. Such places are overcrowded with relatives and friends who want a glimpse of their relatives before they are boarded for the final jail. If the responsible police officer is bribed, the loading might start well before time and proceed slowly that prisoners and their relatives have enough time to meet.

There is a bar council building, the meeting point of the lawyers for chatting, taking tea, and especially for a shoe-shine, which is required if you walk in the chamber area of the courts. It is famous for its quality. There are also some restaurants located close to the chambers of the lawyers.

20. Verbal communication quoted by Hoebel, 1965, p. 45.
21. Law Reform Commission, 1967-70, p. 414
22. Law Reform Commission, 1958-59, p. 101.
23. The material on the judges comes from the interviews of lawyers, those people confronted with courts, i.e. the laymen, the *munshies* of lawyers and personal experiences. Judges were not interviewed because of their unwillingness to talk.

24. Conversation with a lawyer in the District Court, Faisalabad.
25. Helmken, 1976, p. 244.
26. Law Reform Commission, 1967-70, p. 414.
27. *Kanne*: defective fruits; blind of one eye: known for being corrupt, in most of the cases to the lawyers and subordinate staff, or themselves allow such tricks.
28. Law Reform Commission Report, 1967-70, p. 415.
29. Law Reform Commission Report, 1967-70, p. 186.
30. Law Reform Commission Report, 1967-70, p. 188. There are so many other examples, for details see the Law Reform Commission Report, 1967-70.
31. Every type of case has been alloted a number of units depending upon the time expected for the hearing.
32. Interview with Tariq Mehmood, Advocate, District Court, Faisalabad.
33. Cohn, 1965, p. 107.
34. Khanna, *Judiciary in India and Judicial Process*, 1985, p. 51.
35. Law Reform Commission Report, 1958-59, p. 119.
36. Law Reform Commission Report, 1958-59, p. 117.
37. Helmken, 1976, p. 122.
38. Law Reform Commission, 1967-70, p. 415.
39. Law Reform Commision, Report, 1967-70.
40. Cohn, 1965, p. 106.
41. An interview with an advocate of the District Court, Faisalabad.
42. Law Reform Commission Report, 1969-70, p. 415.
43. Helmken, 1976, pp. 224-5.
44. Helmken, 1976, p. 225.
45. This official file of record belongs to one of our case studies. The original names of persons and places have been replaced on the request of the court clerk, who allowed us to photocopy the file. It is the same case which, together with the details of some cases, form the basis of our fictitious case study, the details of which are given in the text.
46. Here are some observations about Naglan police station responsible for the village of Misalpur: Naglan is the main police station in this area. It lies about five kilometers to the west of Misalpur on the same main road linking Faisalabad with Jhang. Its approach is marked by a speed breaker and the barrier signpost as the red and blue checkpost. Its premises comprise a tiny room serving as a prison, which is, more often than not, full of prisoners, who sit and sleep, if they can, on the ground. There is a big courtyard. The most important place in the building is the room of the *muharer* (the person who is supposed to write the records), considered a very important post in the police station next only to the officer in-charge of the police station usually called SHO (Station House Officer). The room of the *muharer* is the real activity room. He makes note of the *amad* (arrival) and *rukhsati* (departure) of policemen to and from duty.

He performs the formalities necessary for the Traffic Challans and deals with those whose *garies* vehicles, (car, bus, wagon, etc.) which are to be *band karni* (confiscated). He is the one to write an FIR (First Information Report) of any case coming to the police station on the orders of the SHO.

In this room an observer might meet a traffic violator or a murderer side by side. Somebody provides *dudhpatti* (milk with tea leaves, so loved here by the police), another has to bring along stationery (papers, pens or pencils, stamp-pads), and still others must arrange for lunch, etc. The SHO is mostly absent, either on official tours or 'taking a rest', which is the most common excuse. His house is in the vicinity.

Naglan police station covers an area of more than fifty-two villages which are more or less the size of Misalpur. There is only one vehicle in the police station which is solely for the use of the SHO. Everyone wanting to register a complaint or to take the police to far-away villages must arrange for a car himself. There are, in all, eighteen constables, three Assistant Sub-Inspectors, two Sub-Inspectors and one SHO.

The open courtyard, outside the building but inside the boundary of the police station, is the most interesting place. It provides sunshine in winter and the shadow of the big banyan tree brings some shades of coolness in the hot summer afternoons. Under this tree the SHO, if present, sits at his convenience. If the SHO is not available, those who come to lodge complaints sometimes sit and wait for days. The routine answer is: the SHO is not there; he is a taking rest; he is busy; and in the end, a complainant might be told that his claim is not correct. These are only a few of the countless possible answers which the complainant might get. A retired SHO is also important, having his hut not far away from the police station, writing applications and providing good suggestions.

The SHO has a constable assigned to him who works as his tout. Talking about giving and taking money to policemen other than SHO is not taboo. It is generally known that if an opponent is in the police custody (at the police station) and he is to be thrashed, the rate is normally ten Rupees for one beating with a shoe (10 *rupai jutti*).

47. This section has been taken from our case study.
     Note: The FIR was written four weeks after the incident. The police wanted to write down the names of two as the accused, as many other people in the village also said the case was, but the complainants wanted to involve all male members of the family, as was then done.

48. Law Reform Commission, 1967-70, p. 414.

49. Law Reform Commission, 1969-70, p. 268.

50. Ahmad writes similarly:
     'Many Investigating Officers unknowingly, or sometimes knowingly, include the name of some innocent persons along with the guilty ones in

the chalans.' Ahmad: 'Offences in Rural and Urban Areas'. Unpublished, p. 41.

51. 'It has been pointed out by Mr. N.A. Razvi in his article on Burking in the last issue of the Sentinel, that many S.H.Os decline to register cases for the fear of a bad name.' Ahmad, 'Offences in Rural and Urban Areas' (unpublished), p. 41.

52. Law Reform Commission Report, 1967-70, p. 269.

53. Baxi, 1982, p. 88.

54. Baxi, 1982, p. 90.

55. The last two items i.e. nos. 4 and 5 in our list are again formality items:

    4. Road certificate: This road certificate is again a formality laying down that the four accused, Mehndi, Shabir, Faryad and Riaz with two knives, one shirt of brown colour with blood stains, and one green undershirt also with blood stains were sent to the court (...)

    5. Challan of the police: This is to say the investigation report of the police on the basis of which the case is then followed. In this challan, besides the names of thirteen witnesses and the list of items recovered, is also the report of the investigations of the police officer deputed for the job. In the investigation of the said case, on the basis of the statements of the eye-witnesses and others, Mehndi, Shabir, Faryad and Riaz were proved guilty.

    This investigation report or *challan* as is also known was supported by fifteen other documents (which are also included in our list).

56. The Medical Report from our case study.

57. The other confession is also very similar except that the knife is a little bigger and the witnesses are others and that the kife is found and confession made on the next day. The place is the same *baithak* and the clothes are lying on beds and the method is similar. The witnesses here are the same as those in the FIR. The other point to mention is that documents nos. 7–12 and 17–19 (list of documents provided in the beginning) could be, more or less, summarized under confessions, recovery and torture.

58. This is again a quotation from our case study.

59. Law Reform Commission, 1967-70, p. 269.

60. Walsh, 1929, p. 30.

61. M. Foucault wrote about the arguments which were used as the legitimization of torture in Europe of the Middle Ages:'Ist der Angeklagte schuldig, so sind die Schmerzen der Folter nicht ungerecht: im Fall seiner Unschuld aber sind sie die Zeichen seiner Rechtfertigung. Schmerz, Kampf und Wahrheit sind in der Folter miteinander verbunden: gemeinsam bearbeiten sie den Koerper des 'Patienten'. Die Wahrheitssuche durch die Folter soll gewiss ein Indiz zum Vorschein bringen, das schwerwiegendste aller Indizien - das Bekenntnis des Schuldigen.' (...) 'Die Schuld begann nicht erst nach der Vereinigung aller

Beweisstoecke; sie wurde von jedem Element konstituiert, das einen Schuldigen erkennen liess. So liess ein Halb-Beweis dem Verdaechtigen nicht seine Unschuld, sofern er nicht vervollstaendigt wurde: er machte aus ihm einen Halb-Schuldigen. Das leichte Indiz eines schweren Verbrechens machte jemanden 'ein bisschen' kriminell. Die Beweisfuehrung bei Gericht gehorchte also nicht dem dualistischen System wahr/falsch, sondern einem Prinzip der stetigen Abstufung; eine bestimmte Stufe der Beweisfuehrung bildete bereits eine Schuldstufe und hatte darum eine bestimmte Strafstufe zur Folge. Der Verdaechtige als solcher verdiente immer eine bestimmte Zuechtigung; man konnte nicht unschuldigerweise Gegenstand eines Verdachts sein. Der Verdacht bildete fuer den Richter ein Beweiselement, fuer den Angeklagten das Zeichen einer bestimmten Schuld und verlangte deswegen auch nach einer bestimmten Strafe. Ein Verdaechtiger, der verdaechtig blieb, wurde damit nicht fuer unschuldig erklaert, sondern in eingeschraenktem Masse bestraft. War man also zu einem bestimmten Grad des Verdachts gelangt, so konnte man legitimerweise eine Praxis anwenden, mit der zweierlei erreicht werden sollte: eine erste Bestrafung angesichts der bereits gesammelten Indizien und mittels dieses Anfangs die Erpressung der noch ausstehenden Wahrheit.'

62. Moon, 1930, p. 51.
63. Moon, 1930, pp. 44–51.
64. Law Reform Commission, Report, 1967-70, p. 407.
65. Law Reform Commission, 1967-70, p. 187.
66. Helmken, 1976, pp. 174–5. [trsl. by the present author]
67. Moon, 1930, p. 52.
68. Ahmad, 1972, p. 100.
69. Law Reform Commission, 1967-70, p. 375.
70. Helmken, 1976, p. 69 [trsl. by the present author].
71. We have already quoted the lawyer who said 'the judges (lower courts) are mostly corrupt and the magistrates are totally corrupt'.
72. Law Reform Commission Report, 1958-59, p. 74.
73. Verbal communication with a lawyer in the courts of the District Headquarter, Faisalabad.
74. Law Reform Commission Report, 1967-70, p. 401.
75. Verbal information given by an advocate of the District Court, Faisalabad.
76. Ahmad, M.T. 'Offences in Rural and Urban Areas', unpublished, p. 41.
77. Baxi, 1982, p. 54.
78. Helmken, 1976, p. 127.
79. Helmken, 1976, pp. 140–41.
80. By 'anthropologists', as was already mentioned in the Introduction, we mean here those who did research on the Indian and Pakistani legal systems (Cohn, Moore, Hoebel).

81. Cohn, 1967, p. 155.
82. Cohn, 1967, p. 155.
83. Cohn, 1967, p. 155.
84. Moore, 1985, p. 6.
85. By 'jurists' we mean mainly the members of the two Law Reform Commissions whose reports served us as a sort of basic material.
86. Law Reform Commission, 1967-70, p. 102.

CHAPTER 5

CONCLUSION

Traditional methods of solving conflicts provide 'relative justice'. The conflicts in the village have their origin in *zan, zar,* and *zamin.* Once started, they grow and intensify. In many cases, the conflicts begin because of *izzat* and *ghairat.* Through conflicts, *izzat* is gained by winning and lost by losing or maintained by continuing or intensifying the conflicts. The amount of *izzat* and *ghairat* depends upon many subjective and objective factors, such as: the amount of wealth and political power one has, the group or *biradari* one belongs to, one's behaviour towards others, social activities, honesty, the behaviour of the women of the family, etc. Every villager is accorded a certain quantem of *izzat-o-ghairat* in the eyes of his fellow villagers.

In a village council, according to the traditional justice system, a conflict, which is, aimed at increasing/maintaining the *izzat,* and the *ghairat,* is resolved keeping in view this accepted *izzat* and *ghairat* of the disputants thus: 'In the village council, a dispute is seen as part of the environment from which it grew. The individuals, their families, the community, the histories that led to the discord are on trial'.[1]

Influential people, those having more *izzat* because of power and resources, become members of the *panchayats,* Reconciliation Councils or Union Councils. This perpetuates the societal status quo of hierarchy. This is why we called it 'relative justice', since the status of a disputant is taken into account at the time of making a decision or compromise. It may be concluded that the traditional system of justice functions in relative terms and these then are accepted as the values of the society.

In the chapter on the official system the difference between how the system should theoretically function—'formalities necessary for starting a court case'—and the way these formalities are fulfilled in practice—we called it 'courts in practice' were analysed. The personnel concerned with the courts like judges, subordinate staff of the judges, lawyers, etc., do accept bribes. The documents necessary for a court case like police reports, medical certificates, etc. are faked through bribery, political power and other methods. There is some difference of values between the courts and the society. The courts are corrupt, money is paid as bribe; *sifarish* and *parchi* are used. They are expensive and the practice is that the complainant must bear most of the expenses (as a rule the weaker side is the plaintiff, as has been explained before). The court decisions are delayed and there are difficulties in the executing of the decrees of the courts, especially against strong opponents. In other words, the courts fail in achieving their goals—'equal justice for all'. The problems of the courts are complicated and manifold. The courts are not supposed to take into account the positions and status of the disputants at the time of making a decision. 'In theory the disputants lose their social status and are viewed as equals before law'.[2]

The result (decision) of the courts is comparable to the justice of the traditional system, i.e. 'relative justice'. Those who are rich and have more power (political and bureaucratic offices), usually those belonging to the higher status *biradaries*, can pay and thus influence the court decisions. We may say, the procedure and methods adopted in the two systems are different, but the results are similar. This was also the view of Baxi, as has already been quoted, who compared the traditional and the official justice systems of India. He writes:

The lesson to draw from these ongoing explorations is not that there are no differences between the NSLS (Non-State Legal

System) and the SLS (State Legal System) but that these differences
are of degree rather than of kind.[3]

As to the suitability of one of the two systems raised in the
introduction: both the traditional and the official justice systems
provide 'relative justice'. If the thesis of the legal anthropologist
is followed that the traditional justice system functions according
to the values of the society it may also be concluded that the
official system, too, functions according to the values of the
society. If contrary view of the legal anthropologists is taken
into account that the official system does not function according
to the values of the society and conclude that both the traditional
and the official systems of justice do not function according to
the values of the society. In any case, the thesis of the legal
anthropologists is refuted that the values of the official and the
traditional systems of justice are different.

The two systems function according to the same criterion as
both complement one another. All those conflicts and quarrels
which are brought before the *panchayat* (the formal part of the
traditional system) are, at the same time, brought to the police
and courts (see also the case studies). A decision or compromise
is arrived at with the cooperation of the two systems. It may be
said that they are two parts of one system. Theoretically, they
may function independently, but in actual practice they work
together.

This could lead to the conclusion that Pakistani society is
corrupt by nature and that its people do not believe in equality
of justice, that the values of the society are based on inequality.[4]
If both the traditional and the official systems of justice function
according to these values, then why are the people dissatisfied
with both?

Another premise could be that: both systems do not function
according to the values of the society. The only difference
between them is that at least the objectives of the official system
are nearer to the ideal values of the justice in society. The
values of the society, as 'collective values', are, ideally, based
on equality before the law. This ideal in Pakistan is based on

Islam[5] the religion of more than 97 per cent of the population. But in practical life, everyone tries to use his position and resources for winning a conflict or suit.

Summarizing, 'the collective ideal values' of the society and the goals of the official system of justice are similar, if not the same. Similarly, 'the values in practice' of the society and the official system in practice are also the same. The function of the official system of justice is to eliminate or at least to reduce the difference between collective ideal values and values in practice. If the official system is effective then the ideal collective values may become practical values. For example we suppose that stopping at a red traffic light is an ideal collective value. Some people violate the traffic signal, it is the practical value. The function of the official system is to eliminate the violation and therefore, it introduces automatic video-cameras, hidden in the traffic lights and fines the violators. If the official system is successful then the ideal collective values could become practical values. Drivers would stop at the red light without the presence of a camera. On the other hand the official system has also to adopt the new and changing values of the society.

The problems of the official system of justice or the dissatisfaction of the people with the system is due to its failure in achieving its goals, because of technical deficiencies and the alien system.

It is not only that society influences and manipulates the official justice system and that it has totally failed in achieving its goal. The fact is that in spite of the corruption and malfunctioning of the official system it has affected society, especially the functioning of the traditional system, to a very large extent. The mere presence of the official system and the improving access to the courts etc., means that the poor villagers are not left to the mercy of the village 'big men'. The most common way of arriving at a solution is by the interaction of both systems. As the process of reconciliation in the traditional *panchayats* continues, the position of a case in the courts affects and plays a decisive role in arriving at a compromise in the village councils.

In the opinion of the legal anthropologist, the problem of the official system is its colonial nature—'the British confronted the Indians with a situation in which there was a direct clash of the values of the two societies'.[6] The jurists on the other hand attach no importance to the differences of values of the system and the society. 'It is hardly correct to say that the present judicial system is a foreign transplant on Indian soil, or that it is based on alien concepts unintelligible to our people'.[7]

The difference of values leading to the estrangment has mainly three aspects: There are rituals and customs which are not taken seriously when used in the official system (the difference between oath-taking in the courts and in village). There is a difference of opinion about certain laws between society and the courts; e.g. the concept of what constitutes a crime, or the share of a daughter in the property of her father etc. There are some aspects of life which are important for the village society but they are not taken into account by the courts; for example, *izzat* so important in the village life has little significance in the courts. The reason of these differences is mainly the lack of anthropological and sociological research into the law of the society and the courts.

The technical problems could be enumerated as follows:
- an insufficient system
- legal pluralism
- lack of legal awareness among the people
- non-effective control mechanisms

Propositions

On the basis of the preliminary findings the following suggestions could be considered:

The problems of dispensing justice could be divided into those requiring preventive and remedial measures as well as short and long term measures.

Such measures are mainly to prevent the emergence of the conflicts and to make the system foolproof and thus indirectly reduce the chances of manipulation. Many conflicts in the village arise from unclear and ambiguous rules and laws and ineffective methods of putting these laws into action. For example, the boundaries of agricultural fields, houses, and common village and government lands are vaguely marked and the methods of ascertaining them are also very expensive. The boundaries of the fields as well as of houses, streets, and other lands must be marked clearly and categorically. This would reduce the conflicts in the villages to a large extent.

Similarly, rules pertaining to the right of passage into the fields, and the passage of irrigation water, if made clear, simple, effective and made public through radio, television, and other methods of communication available in the villages, it could reduce to a large extent the number of serious conflicts. The methods of clearing ambiguities and misunderstandings when they arise, must be streamlined. The rules of the division of property between relatives must be made clearer, simpler, more self-regulating (at the death of a relative it should be automatically transferred to the heirs). The share of every daughter/sister in the property of her parents should be given to her, and all fraudulent means of depriving her of her share must be eliminated (sister or daughter declaring, in writing, in the courts that they do not want to claim what comes as their share etc.). Agricultural land and related problems are the reasons why there are more crimes in villages than in urban areas.[8]

Legal pluralism also plays a considerable role in creating these ambiguities about a certain law or custom. The example of a daughter's share in her father's property is a case in point. The official law gives it to her and the traditional system does not. Those daughters who claim their shares against the wishes of their brothers are excommunicated from the family.

The frustrations in the forums very often give rise to the feeling that the only dependable alternative is the use of direct physical force. Ruediger Schott describes the situation as follows:

It is not without a certain cynicism that some anthropologists are of
the opinion that in such a situation of 'legal pluralism' people may
choose between different legal systems; this might be true of
individual cases. Very often, however, an illiterate person has no
access to the courts; if, however, the traditional institutions for
solving a conflict do no longer function, the only way would be
through self-help by sheer force.[9]

One aspect is that the individuals have problems selecting
from the multiple system, the governments of such countries
who have inherited this legal pluralism themselves face the
dilemma of choice whether they should turn to the traditional
system, as was tried by Ayub Khan in Pakistan in 1962, or not.
His actions to introduce the Frontier Crimes Regulation known
under the name FCR, in a changed form under the name of
Jirga System in 1962-63, was viewed by some as efforts at
'repairing the damage done to the national character in the years
of subjection' by finding the 'nation's true roots'[10] and by others
as: 'by throwing the honor of the nation at the mercy of the
'Jirga system' the Government is inviting a bloody revolution.'[10]
This debate is far from over and, at present, there is a sort of
mixture of the two system. Schott also mentions this problem:

> The governments of the countries granted independence, too, are
> undecided whether to codify traditional, unwritten 'common law',
> i.e. to turn it into written law—thus preventing it to become subject
> to changes—or to enact laws irrespective of hereditary traditions
> (...).[12]

For an effective functioning of the official legal system its
unitary character is very important and it is the ambition of
every state to depluralize the legal system. The Pakistani state
has been very slow in this. It is a very complicated process even
when properly done. It is therefore, recommended that the
ambiguities created by legal pluralism should be cleared by
finding out, through research, the rules acceptable to the
common people and making them as the only law.

The remedial measures concern the efficient solution of the conflicts and problems. Due to development, modernization and through improved methods of communication, the social and political structure of the village population has changed and continues to do so. The access to the courts and knowledge about the rights is also improving. Due to all these developments, the effectiveness and the area of influence of the traditional system is decreasing. The effective functioning of the traditional system presupposes the existence of a functioning and clearly hierarchical system (details have already been given in the chapter on the traditional system). The problem is not only that official courts are not increasing according to the increase in the demand but a certain gap seems to be a part of the policy. By making the courts more expensive, intentionally, by higher fees and, indirectly, through corruption, the demand for more courts is reduced. This is also one of the factors that leads to the 'relative justice' of the courts. The first and most important suggestion which is not only the result of the findings of the study but can also be found in the recommendations of any of the many Law Reform Commision reports is to provide a 'full system', i.e. a system to meet the entire justice requirements of the society. As has been said, the solution to a bad democracy is more democracy, the solution to a bad justice system is a more comprehensive system. The major problems of the official justice system and its corruption are the lack of resources, personnel[13] (judges, magistrates, court employees, etc.), facilities (waiting rooms, transport, toilets, etc.) and infrastructure, (not enough courtrooms, furniture and other necessary and basic items, typing machines etc). They are located at far away places; the lowest courts are found at the *tehsil* level having limited powers (for detail see 'the administrative divisions of Pakistan' and the 'hierarchy of the courts'), leading to the problem of transport. The delay about which it is said that 'justice delayed is justice denied' is mostly due to the above-mentioned factors.

According to the report of the Law Reform Commission 1958-59:

We consider that the State should not make a profit out of the administration of justice. (...). After considering these statistics (supplied by the Provincial Government), our feeling is that the State may be actually making a profit, both on the criminal as well as on the civil side of the administration of justice.[14]

It may be recommended that the number of courts and its facilities should be increased to meet the demands of justice. It would be ideal if every village community gets, at least, one lower court, with the mandate of 'free and fast justice for all'. The policy should not be to increase the price of justice (court fee) which actually comes to reduce the demand of justice (the poor cannot afford going to the courts); it should be: to set up a sufficient and cheap system that all can benefit from and to improve the quality of justice so that those who are ill-willed should not hope to win. These are the recommendations which could produce immediate results.

On the question of the quality of justice a difficult and important point regarding the administration of justice is to be considered. In the post-colonial era to improve the quality of justice, it is important to bring forward a group of young and energetic people who do not accept the feudalistic and capitalistic inheritance and whose concept of honour and prestige does not lie in the traditional affiliation to a *biradari*, but in compassion and humanity. Education, training and the respect for the profession has to be made the mark of self-pride. Education is the most important requirement for improving the quality of justice.

In conclusion, the present study proposes a research project with the aim to reduce the gap between the values of the society and the law. The project should conduct field studies in each province. At least two studies in each province on the rural urban basis will be necessary. The number of these studies should be further extended to ethnic groups and types of populations within the provinces. These micro-level studies should be conducted by anthropologists. The jurists, by the very nature of their profession and training, are interested in the details and explanations of laws and paragraphs, i.e. from the point of view of the law givers (makers). Anthropologists, by their training, are concerned with the study of people and are by virtue of their research methods,—among others, participant observation— able to see the problems of justice faced by the people, i.e. the receivers of law from a much closer angle. This could help provide a much-needed perspective.

The results of these studies should be collected and analysed by one central executive body, consisting of jurists and anthropologists, to enact national laws. They should not be used to reduce the scope and variety of law but to make it representative for the whole country. The recommendations based on the findings of this project—reasons and types of conflicts, and the problems in the functioning of the justice system—should be used by the jurists in making and improving laws. The anthropologists should again be involved, in the process of law making, representing the people they studied.

NOTES

1. Moore, 1985, p. 6.
2. Moore, 1985, p. 6.
3. Baxi, 1982, p. 347.
4. The point may be raised that both Cohn and Moore did their fieldwork in India. Moore did her fieldwork in Rajasthan—more than 55 per cent Muslims and situated adjacent to the Pakistani border. Cohn was engaged in research in North India and the description of the population is not much different from that of Pakistani Punjab. We may also ask if the difficulties of the Indian official justice system are due to the values of inequality found in caste system, why the Pakistani official system has similar difficulties, seeing as the inequality is not based on religious values. In any case, the conclusions of Baxi's research, an Indian jurist, show astonishingly similar results, as has already been quoted in the text, to the present study. When we accept that in the case of India it is true, how should one explain this inequality in the case of Pakistan?
5. 'In the name of Allah, The Beneficent, The Merciful. O ye who believe! Stand out firmly For justice, as witnesses To God, even as against Yourselves, or your parents, Or your kin, and whether It be (against) rich or poor: For God can best protect both. Follow not the lusts (Of

your hearts), lest ye Distort (justice) or decline To do justice, verily God is well-acquainted With all that ye do'. (Quran, Sura IV:135).

6. Cohn, 1967, p. 155
7. Law Reform Commission Report, 1967-70, p. 102.
8. As Ahmad wrote: 'the hypothesis, viz., that the crime rate in the rural areas in Multan (a district in Punjab) is lower than that of the urban area, has not been upheld (...). We find that excepting in the cases of suicide and cheating the rural areas show a higher crime rate. Of particular interest is the fact that the proportion of the incidence of murder in the urban and the rural area is one to ten. Crime against property is also higher in the rural areas.' Ahmad, M.T., 'Offences in Rural and Urban Areas', p. 40. Not published.
9. Schott, 1983, p. 200 [trsl. by the present author].
10. Berry, 1966, p. v.
11. Berry, 1966, p. 98.
12. Schott, 1983, p. 200 [trsl. by the present author].
13. We reproduce here the recommendations of the Law Reform Commission Report 1967-70 concerning the 'Investigation of offences by the police and prosecution in Courts':

1. The terms and conditions of service of the Police Department should be improved so as to attract educated men to the police force.

2. Shortage of the lower subordinate staff should be made good as early as possible.

3. At each police-station, the investigation branch of the police should be separate from the watch and ward branch (...).

4. There should be separate Medical Officers especially in large towns to attend to the medico-legal cases.

5. Transport and communications facilities should be provided to the police at most of the police-stations.

6. Crimes Branch of the police should be expanded and strengthened in both the Provinces (...)

7. Criminal Intelligence Section on the pattern of London Metropolitan Police should be set up at each of the aforementioned zonal headquarters.

8. Forensic Science Laboratories should be set up at each zonal headqurter of the Crimes Branch.

9. The number of Police Prosecutors should be increased so that there is one prosecutor for each whole-time First Class Magistrate's court.

10. The status and emoluments of a Public Prosecutor should be equated with those of a District and Sessions Judge.

11. The appointment of Public Prosecutors on short-term contracts should be discontinued and they should be appointed on permanent basis like other Government servants.

These recommendations are reproduced here, as an example, to give an idea about one of the important branches of law. The position in the other areas of law is not better.

14. The Report of the Law Reform Commission, 1958-59, p. 74.

CASE STUDIES

Introduction

There were several points which were considered in the selection of these case studies such as: to give an idea as to what kind of conflicts arose, between which types of groups, and what were the causes and their origins. These case studies also give an idea about, in Gluckman's words, an 'apt illustration' of the situation regarding the functioning of the justice system, i.e. the conflict resolution.The conflicts are either solved locally, i.e. through traditional methods or are brought to the official courts or, what is even more common, that they are brought to the official courts and at the same time tried in the *panchayat*.

The types of conflicts and the choice of forum chosen are closely related to each other. The sequence adopted in the presentation of the cases, in this study, is keeping in view the local types of conflicts—conflicts of land followed by conflicts on the issue of women and those relating to money. However, in the selection of the case studies preference has been given to the procedure followed for their solution—traditional or official as also to present a maximum of possible types of solutions and the details of the process.

The first two case studies, which provide us a fair amount of detail about the functioning of the justice system are over a piece of land the status of which is not clear—government land, private land, who is its real owner, etc. The conflict in one case involved murder and in the other a long process, ending in a compromise without direct retaliations. The next is the case study of an elopement. Here, we can again see both the formal court process and the traditional methods being adopted. Then

comes the third type arising out of abuse, money lending, etc.
The last case study is the conflict biography of Ashraf's family.
This gives us a general picture of a normal family life in the
village, which reflects the majority of such family-based disputes
between brothers, sisters, and close relatives.

1. Dispute over Ashraf's *Haveli*—Animal-house

One morning as Ashraf was working in his fields, his wife
Maryam came and told him that Goora's[1] sons had occupied
their *haveli* and had driven out the animals. Though there had
been some unpleasant exchanges over the boundary of his *haveli*
for some time, Ashraf had not expected this. The controversy
began when the four sons of Goora and Jabbar (younger brother
of Goora), both from the *Ambalvi biradari*, with the active
support of some members of their *biradari* and friends started
filling the pond near the boundary wall of Ashraf. They began
by filling at a distance from the wall and meeting no resistence
gradually advanced towards the front of Ashraf's *haveli*. Then
one day they buried some of Ashraf's belongings, like fire-
wood, animal fodder, etc., lying near the boundary. There was
still no strong reaction from Ashraf since he wanted to avoid a
fight to which the sons of Goora fully inclined.

Maryam, Ashraf's wife, went to Khana, (a respectable villager
also belonging to *Jat biradari* like Ashraf. He is a distant relative
of Ashraf), and told him the whole story. Two of Goora's sons
were working on the power-looms belonging to Khana, who
then arranged a compromise, which entailed giving away some
land belonging to Ashraf and construction of a temporary wall
(on the pond side of the *haveli* there had been no boundary wall
before that) thus dividing the place. This was a humiliating
compromise for Ashraf. He had not even participated in the
negotiation for compromise and gave Khana the *ikhtiar*
(authority) for a settlement.

The brothers of Ashraf came to him and they decided to file
a case against Goora and his sons. When they did so the police,

perhaps already contacted by the other side, told them to bring written proof, called *fard*, from the *patvari* (one of the lowest rank employee in the Revenue Department, responsible for keeping the record of land, crops, houses, etc., and the first to be approached for any record of house or property), stating that the place which was filled by Goora's sons actually belonged to them. Ashraf and his brothers went to the *patvari*, who are known among the villagers for being the most corrupt functionaries of the Revenue Department. The *patvari* denied any kind of record of Ashraf's *haveli* although Ashraf had occupied this place since 1947. On the contrary he said that the area inhabited after 1947 was illegally occupied. After weeks of running after the *patvari* and waiting outside his office and seeking the support of the latter's friends and relatives the *patvari* finally demanded five thousand rupees as bribe for providing the official document (*fard*) that Ashraf and his brothers were the legal[2] occupants of this place. He also assured them that the other side, too, was after the case and that he could not give them a *fard*.

The situation changed completely when the sons of Goora forcibly occupied Ashraf's entire *haveli*, throwing his belongings and cattle out. The police was again contacted to register an FIR against the occupation but they refused to take the report and said that the place belonged to the government and none of the parties had any right to it. Actually, the police never paid any attention to them. The *muharer* said that he could only write the report when ordered by the SHO. The SHO was, in the first instance, absent most of the time, reportedly on official tours. Even when present, he was said to be busy with important meetings and whenever contacted he ignored the situation. They were repeatedly told to come again. Each time the SHO would not be there. The other side had already contacted the police through a 'big man'—an influential of the village (Naeem) who was known to be a police tout, a rich man, and at that time the chairman of the village council. It was believed he paid a monthly 'hush' money to the police. A policeman of a lower rank on duty with the SHO, unofficially told Naseer (the elder brother of Ashraf, also their spokesman) that it would cost ten thousand rupees if they wanted to register the case or get their *haveli* back.

Ashraf then hired a lawyer and in the meantime, Qasim, one of Ashraf's brothers who was a Professor at a university in Islamabad, arranged for a *sifarish* from a high official from Islamabad, through one of his students. With a recommendatory letter from a retired SSP (Senior Superintendent of Police) officer, Ashraf then went to the DIG (Deputy Inspector General of Police) who, on his part directed an ASP (Assistant Superintendent of Police) to look after the case. Ashraf was now given the choice either to get back the *haveli* without court procedures or to have the FIR registered. It was a difficult decision for Ashraf and his brothers to make. It then became a question of not only the recovery of the *haveli*, but also one of the damage done to the status and honour of their family in the village, with an entire history of the conflict and the emotions it involved, as well as the known circumstances which led to the dispute in the first place. Still another reason was that Goora was not ready to vacate the place they had occupied in front of their *haveli*. Therefore, the mere return of the *haveli* would not end the dispute. Ashraf was also somewhat encouraged by the changed attitude of the police who now seemed to be under some pressure and therefore, chose to register an FIR. Once that happened, the case became a written record.

Prehistory of the Conflict

Ashraf's family had migrated from India to Pakistan in August 1947 and settled in this village. As refugees they occupied the houses abandoned by former residents both Sikhs and Hindus. Ashraf and his brothers took possession of one of these houses which by chance was not big enough for the large family. They made an animal-house (*haveli*) near the pond where there was some free space and also filled a small part of the pond. Some people in the village tried to stop them from doing so but

Ashraf's family persisted since they were five young, strong, and united brothers and occupied the place of the present *haveli*.

Ashraf and his brothers got married and started their separate households. There were quarrels among them and so they divided their house and *haveli*. One brother got a job in a town far away while sons of the others also got jobs away from the village. Only three, by now much older, brothers remained in the village and even they were not united as they were at the time of independence. Meanwhile, the pond lost its earlier importance since every household now had water taps and water-pumps.

The *haveli* of Ashraf's family which once lay in the outskirts of the village was slowly surrounded by other houses. The land around the village, once cheap and plentiful, became scarce and precious. The *haveli* had the advantage of being situated on the boundary of this pond, which was out of use then. They could fill it with earth and garbage and thus create new and additional land. There was general dissatisfaction and grumbling about this encroachment in the village.

In 1975, Ashraf who got the share on the street side, rebuilt one of his fallen rooms and included some ground from the street to make the room square. A *maulavi* by the name of Mian Ditta of the mosque, which lay on the other side of the street, came and told Ashraf not to encroach but Ashraf had already put in the foundation and thus he countinued to build. The following day, some people of the village came together, representing different *biradaries*, and destroyed the boundary wall of Ashraf's *haveli*. Ashraf's family offered no resistance and the construction of the room was postponed. After a while, Ashraf contacted some respectables of the village, like Khushi Muhammad, and with their intervention the wall was allowed to be reconstructed where it stood earlier.

This incident proved to be, among other things, a test of power and strength of Ashraf's family and relatives. Neither his brothers nor *biradari* came to help him. He had five sons and one daughter. All his children were going to schools and colleges at various levels and two of the older ones were not even living in the village. Being students and living far away, his children, and other members of the whole family, did not involve themselves in village politics. They did not take part in any dispute, nor did they side with any party in several other conflicts in the village and tried to remain neutral. There was a general jealousy in the *biradari* and village about his sons getting educated, and there was no relationship of reciprocity. No one wanted to be a witness before the police or in the court. One morning, he called the immediate members of his *biradari* (those in the village who were not only *Jats* but had also migrated from Chanman/Hoshiarpur in India, the same village he himself had come from) and asked them if anyone could be a witness—a normal practice in the village. They all made excuses and he perforce had to give the names of his brothers as witnesses.

As the boundary wall was reconstructed in 1975, Ashraf was told not to do any construction work along the disputed wall. Ashraf thought that the people must have forgotten and other houses around the pond were being expanded by the dwellers. So he constructed two shops, but not on the forbidden side, which he used as the entrance. This was not an actual violation, but there was a growing dissatisfaction about the general encroachment upon the pond by a few families. The family of Ashraf was chosen as a sort of scapegoat.

Goora belonged to the *Ambalvi biradari*, which though not the biggest and strongest, yet was comparatively more united than other *biradaries*. They had one very rich man, Taidah, as their leader who had good connections with the police and courts. This man had died but the tradition of cooperation still continued. The members of this *biradari* had several disputes among themselves which were often, though not always, solved within the *biradari panchayats*. Goora's family did not have much land for agriculture and had a small house which was not big enough for the extended family and also had no animal-house. They did not have the money to buy land for the new house or the animal-house. Goora's sons did not go to school and had grown up in an atmosphere in which they had lots of time and kept the company of people habitually involved in conflicts.

This prehistory had no direct connection to the present conflict; it was in the knowledge of both the parties who reacted accordingly. For example, Goora's party benefitted from the general dissatisfaction prevailing about the encroachment by Ashraf's family, who thus could not seek much help from their fellow villagers.

On the advice of Yasin, Hanif Shah, both inhabitants of the same village, was engaged as a lawyer by Ashraf. The FIR was written after more than three weeks of the incident . Since the *safarish* letter, of a higher officer was already arranged for, no further gratification was demanded but still Hanif Shah told Ashraf to give five hundred rupees as a gesture of good-will because the final report, which was very important, was still to be prepared by the police. It turned out later on that this was done because Hanif Shah wanted to gain the favour of the *muharer* whom he could ask for help, which he so often required. Hanif Shah advised them to start several cases at the same time to harass Goora's party. Two of Ashraf's close relatives who had experience in the affairs of the police and courts also came to stay in the village and help him.

The whole group went to the courts every day, sat by Hanif Shah, waited, or discussed different aspects of the case with him, and Hanif Shah, on his part, always encouraged them. The bus fares and expenses for food for these peoples, was paid for by Ashraf. Hanif Shah charged five thousand rupees in advance as his fee for attending the case in the court. Every new application, as was explained to Ashraf, had to be written by the *arzi nawees* (application writer), who must be paid for. There were many such applications, which were all to be paid for. The application had to be written on an affidavit paper, which also had to be bought. The inventory charges, *kharcha pani* (*bakhshish*), of the court clerk, photocopies of the court orders and documents, etc. were all to be paid for completing the prerequirements of the suits. Similarly, *bakhshish* and fees were to be paid for sending the summons, obtaining the photocopies, the attestments, and so on and so forth. This was the daily routine of Hanif Shah's *munshi*. One day, within one month of the start of the case, Hanif Shah also presented his list of expenditure and Ashraf was astonished to find that five thousand rupees had already been spent on items like car rents, *bakhshish* and his fee etc., whereas Ashraf himself had never travelled in a car. Ashraf's family was in general dissatisfied with the performance of this lawyer. They had the feeling that if they did not come to the court, nothing moved, and that Hanif Shah had so many other cases to think of and deal with and could not give his case proper attention. Ashraf started to look for another lawyer and after some searching he met one of his old acquaintances in the court. On his advice the services of a lawyer whom the acquaintance had engaged in his cases, were hired. It seemed as though this would lead to reduced expenditure, but this was not to be.

Nothing seemed to move forward without Ashraf's presence, and thus the initial enthusiasm began to diminish. Weeks and months passed and there was no movement and progress. Goora and his sons had the *haveli* and were working and walking free in the village, even terrorizing Ashraf and his family. It was believed that there was some law that if Goora would remain in the *haveli* for a certain time it would be impossible to get it vacated again, and also that Ashraf and his family had in any case no sure proof that the *haveli* belonged to them. They came to be known as cowards in the village. Those few who had, in the beginning, supported them also became silent. One of Ashraf's son was engaged to be married, and there were rumours that the bride's relatives had said that they were not willing to give their daughter to a family of cowards. If a family was unable to defend their house, how would they defend their women if the need arose? The women of their own house taunted them and asked if they were men at all. The people in the village including the relatives started saying that the only way to get the *haveli* back was by sheer force.

Yaseen, another member of the *Jat biradari*, himself involved in many disputes and known for being reckless, made an offer to get the *haveli* vacated on payment of ten thousand rupees through some toughies at gun point. The pressure on Ashraf's family, both financial, and psychological, was such that his wife became seriously ill. She feared that her sons and husband would get into fights and she feared the loss of the bright future which she had worked and dreamed for. The pressure in the village was building up for a direct physical intervention.

During one of the hearings, the judge decided to send a commission to study the situation on the spot. However, the head of the commission was contacted by Ashraf through his *munshi* and two thousand rupees were paid to obtain the required results. Meanwhile in the Civil Court all four cases which had been filed took, from Ashraf's point of view half an eternity till the first summons were issued. Goora's party had also hired a lawyer who had advised them to use delaying tactics. Summons after summons were sent, every time filled and paid for by the lawyer of the complainant. This created a sense of hopelessness for Ashraf.

Under the circumstances differences cropped up between Ashraf and his brothers about what should be done. One brother wanted to take the *haveli* by force and he had the required information with the help of mercenaries. Others disappointed with the slow court procedures, wanted to make peace even under humiliating conditions. Yet another wanted to continue pursuing the cases in the courts. Goora and his sons were encouraged by this situation of family differences and wanted no compromise or *sulah* (reconciliation).

The group which was disappointed with the court system joined the group which wanted to use sheer force, including, among others, Ashraf and his two relatives who came to his help from their own villages, since they feared that Ashraf could lose his *haveli*, contacted the police through another police officer, an acquaintance from another area, and asked about means of settling the dispute. The police charged two thousand rupees as *chah pani* (*bakhshish*) for making the agreement according to which Ashraf was to get his *haveli* back, but on the terms and conditions set forth by Goora's party. A part of his own *haveli* and also a part of his brother's was to be given away. Disagreements arose over this compromise between Ashraf and his brothers on the terms and conditions of the agreement.

Goora and his sons became even more arrogant, proud and highhanded. They taunted one of Ashraf's brothers calling the family cowardly. Since two of the brothers were dissatisfied with the agreement anyway, they started the court cases all over again, which had still not been withdrawn. After two years, Ashraf finally won the case in the court which declared him the rightful owner of the *haveli*. The police came and the rooms built by Goora's sons were vacated and Goora's sons had to leave the place. But as soon as the police left the village, Goora and his sons recaptured the place and the dispute erupted all over again. Ashraf was so disappointed by the whole affair that he decided to sell his place even at a very low price and to leave the village. The problems between the brothers worsened. Ashraf's other brothers did not want to be called cowards for selling the *haveli* and leaving the village, also they could not sell their parts of the *haveli* even if they wanted to because of financial complications connected with migration. In fact, they even bought back Ashraf's portion from the new owner, still worsening the already bitter relations among the brothers.

Goora and his sons had also spent a lot of money in court and on the police. They also suffered financially from not having been able to work for some time. In the beginning, one rich man of their *biradari* (Razaq), a neighbour who often accompanied them to the police and courts, lent them some money. As the loan increased beyond a certain limit which he thought they could not repay, he started demanding that they sell their land to him. Under this pressure, and due to some other circumstances, Goora and his sons came in contact with drug traffickers. This was the quickest way of making money, they became known for their new business in the village. Goora's *biradari* became divided. One day Ashraf's party arranged a 'frame up' by reporting where Goora's son had hidden the heroin to the police. Jamal, Ashraf's nephew, hired a car and brought the police with him to catch Goora's sons red-handed, who despite their contacts with the police, were taken by surprise and opened fire. During the search, the police found some heroin. Goora's sons were arrested and the police gave them a terrible beating, especially because one of their members had been injured. Goora's sons knew that the whole affair had been arranged by Ashraf's party so they now contacted Naeem, Chairman of the Union Council at that time, and other influential people of the village and requested a settlement. The police was also one of the initiatiors of these peace talks. Ashraf's party was fed up with the ongoing situation and wanted an opportunity to settle it once for all. It was decided that Goora's sons should be allowed to keep the place they filled themselves and that they must beg forgiveness from Ashraf's party which was given.

2. The Murder of Akram Araeen

The government of Prime Minister Junejo (1988-89) had announced the distribution of five *Marla*[3] of residential plots among the landless and poor farmers. Karim a resident of Misalpur, belonging to the *Araeen biradari*, had also occupied such a plot in the Charagah, the place declared for the said allotment. The final allotment of the plots, through the *patvari* for preparing the records of ownership of the plots was not made as yet because of party politics. One day, somebody told Karim that Anwar and his sons, also a resident of this village, from the *Rajput biradari*, had forcibly occupied his place.

The villagers of Misalpur are divided into the two political parties: the Pakistan Muslim League and Pakistan People's Party. The *Araeen biradari*, which is one of the largest and politically the most organized in the village, supports the Muslim League, and a majority of the *Rajputs* support the People's Party. The *Rajputs*, in this village, are in any case of two origins—those who came at the time of Partition from Ambala also called *Ambalvi Rajputs*; and those who lived here before Partition. It is said that, the second group, came to be called

Rajput for the money which they had acquired and so the other section does not recognize them as true rajputs.

Anwar had allegedly occupied Karim's place on the instigation of the *Rajputs* belonging to the People's Party. It will perhaps not be out of place to mention that the *Araeens* are known in the village as vegetable growers, educated, business-men. In contrast, the *Rajputs* are known for being brave, ignorant, owning much land.

When Akram and his father Karim reached Charagah they found Anwar and his sons busy constructing walls around their land. Karim showed them the allotment papers as proof of ownership of that place but Anwar who was about seventy years of age threatened (*lalkarna*) Akram and his sons attacked him with knives and sticks and killed him on the spot. Karim came back to the village and, together with his relatives and the people of his *biradari*, planned how and what should be written in the FIR at the police station.

The police came and the dead body was taken for post-mortem. At the time of writing an FIR, Karim and his *biradari* wanted to involve Anwar and three of his sons as accomplices. They accordingly instructed the witnesses, who were their own relatives and the members of their *biradari* and the exact statements for the witnesses were prepared by Karim's lawyers which were short but precise and to the point. The three sons and the father were charged for the murder of Akram.

Anwar's party had already contacted the police and, according to Karim, had paid them forty thousand rupees as bribe. The police, therefore, did not want to include the names of all four of them but only one as the murderer. Naeem, the Chairman of the Union Council, also of the *Araeen biradari*, who was help-ing Karim, went to the DSP (Deputy Superintendent of Police) and asked him to write the FIR, threatening that otherwise he would contact the higher authority. Being an important member of the Muslim League, who were then in power, Naeem had useful contacts with the Punjab government at that time.

There was a tough struggle on the part of both sides to get the FIR written in their favour and both sides used their

influences, connections and resources to the maximum. This
competition between the rivals continued for more than two
weeks before the FIR was eventually written in which all four
persons, mentioned above, were included as murderers. This
was clearly success for Karim and his *Araeen biradari*. It is
important to mention that Anwar's *biradari* (old resident *Rajputs*
of Misalpur) are small in number and not very united. Moreover
the sympathies of many villagers were with Karim because his
son had been murdered.

All four of the accused were arrested and put behind the bars.
In the next one and a half years the case did not make much
progress except only that old Anwar was released from the
prison on bail. This was another success for the *Araeens* and
also a signal to the *Rajputs* that the former's case was very
strong. Karim's party had hired Aslam Shah, a well-known
lawyer. During one and a half years, Aslam Shah appeared in
the courts only twice, on the days of hearing of the bail
applications; otherwise, his junior lawyer always attended the
proceedings on his behalf.

Both parties having experienced the dealings with the police
and the courts, felt the lethargy with which the trial proceeded,as
also the burdensome expenditures of the courts in pursuing the
case. The absolute defeat of Anwar in the previous two events—
the lodging of the FIR and bail application—convinced him that
he would lose the case. Hence Anwar's party was all for an out-
of-court settlement. Daneyan Walee, an influential family of the
Rajputs and also distant relatives of Anwar, contacted Naeem
and requested to arrange an unconditional compromise. He
contacted Ditta, who was a relative of Karim's and had great
influence with his family but Karim's *biradari* was not very
willing to accept the compromise.

Meanwhile, certain influential members of a section of the
Rajput biradari and some of Karim's *biradari* entered into a
dialogue and arrived at an agreement, according to which Anwar
and his sons paid five *lakh* (five hundred thousand) rupees to
Karim and only Anwar, was allowed to live in the village and

all the other members of the family would have to migrate to some other village or area.

Karim told the author that he spent more than thirty-five thousand rupees on the case, in spite of the influential people of the *biradari* being on his side. The other party is said to have sold all their property to pay for the court procedure, including the compromise money. Anwar, the only person of the family living in the village, is so disheartened by the situation that he does not talk about this issue with anyone.

According to Karim, one of the reasons why they made peace with their enemy was that the two eye-witnesses, his close relatives, Jamal and Allah Ditta, whom he presented to the police, were not actually present at the time of the murder. This was essential to fulfill the requirements of the courts. They had to swear on the Holy Quran in the court as eye-witnesses to have seen the occurrence, before giving their statements. The eye-witnesses were Karim himself and some other people who did not want to get involved. Karim, being a religious man, did not want his relatives to swear falsely on the Holy Quran. The people of the village, other than those of his *biradari*, gave another explanation for the compromise that this is a behaviour typical of the *Araeens*, they go for money instead of blood revenge. The arguments from Anwar's side, as also the common members of the *panchayat*, were: 'Akram is dead and by killing or hanging to death anyone we cannot return Akram, let us therefore find a solution among ourselves'.

3. The Elopement of Aslam Ali's Daughter

Aslam and Sharif Wahabi lived in the same *mohalla* (quarter of the village) and both belonged to the *Malik biradari*. Aslam had a thirteen year old daughter (Jamila), Sharif had a son (Akram) who was twenty years old. Aslam and his family used to make *ghaliche* (rugs) and other people, including Akram, came to work on wages. Aslam and his wife were very often away from their house in the mornings to fetch grass and fodder for their animals. Jamila and Akram, who worked together, fell in love with each other and decided to elope and get married. Akram arranged a forged *nikah nama* (certificate of marriage) and one day he disappeared with Jamila.

Babu, another villager, was suspected by the parents of Jamila, of having helped the two in the arrangement of the *nikah nama* and also to have arranged a place for their refuge after elopement. He was a *Malik* like Aslam, lived in the same street and was known to indulge in such activities for money. He had been earlier involved in a similar case in another neighbouring village. Babu was asked to appear in the *paryah* (another word for *panchayat*); before that he was asked by Shah Muhammad, a neighbour of Aslam, why he had helped the two to elope. He totally denied the charge and wanted to know who had blamed him for the elopement. Shah Muhammad told him that it was Sufi Yasin, an acquaintance from Chack No. 40, who had told him about it. It was decided that if Yasin would tell the same in *panchayat* in the presence of Babu, then he must be considered responsible for such an action. According to Shah Muhammad, Yasin had told him that some time ago Babu had come to him with a boy and a girl and all three of them stayed overnight at his place because he had wanted to arrange a *nikah* between them. When Yasin had refused to cooperate with him in arranging the *nikah nama*, they left.

The *panchayat* was convened and Yasin was requested to come. Babu brought Yasin to his house and put him up for the night before the meeting of the *panchayat* and took him along to the meeting the next day. Babu persuaded him during his stay at the house to change his statement which he did by giving in his statement a description of the boy and the girl differing from that of the couple in question.

Among those who attended the meeting were Akhtar, a respectable man from the *Jat biradari*. All the others were *Maliks*, except Yasin. There was a fierce discussion, but in the end Babu succeeded in exonerating himself. Since his name was included in the police report and nothing could be proven against him by the *panchayat* he sued Aslam, Jamila's father.

The charge was that his name was intentionally implicated in the case to defame him. Consequently, Aslam had to incur expenditure on police and court amounting to twenty-five thousand rupees and spend a lot of his time and suffer damage to his honour.

Aslam had told the police that his daughter, Jamila, was thirteen years old and could not herself decide to marry and that Sharif's son had abducted her. The police asked for her birth certificate. It took Aslam more than two weeks before he got the birth certificate from the Secretary of the Union Council who evaded him because, according to Aslam, the Chairman had told the Secretary of the Union Council not to issue Aslam a birth certificate. Without one Aslam could not prove his daughter was under age. Akram's parents as well as most of the other influential people of the *biradari* wanted that the marrriage between Jamila and Akram should be accepted but Aslam did not want this, due to the humiliation suffered from the incidence.

Aslam, together with some of the people of his *biradari* continued the search for the two and they were successful in ferreting them out. Munshi Karim, also a *Malik* and a member of the Union Council from this part of the village, arranged a compromise whereby Akram under the threat of being tried under the *zina* (adultery) ordinance divorced Jamila. Thus the case ended, and the report of the police was withdrawn.

However, ten days later, they both ran away once more. Aslam again went to the police and wanted to lodge a report but the police detained him at the police station for ten days instead. After some time the neighbours went to the police and paid *kharch marcha* (another name for the bribe) and brought him home.

Aslam, together with his neighbours, Shah Muhammad and his brother Biro, continued the struggle and finally managed to arrange a *sifarish* by Akram Ansari, a member of the National Assembly, also a *Malik*. With his visiting card, wherein he asked for help, Aslam, together with Shah Muhammad and neighbours, went to the Suprintendent of Police. The other side had also managed through Naeem (the already-mentioned Chairman of the Union Council) to approach the same police officer. When Aslam along with his supporters called on the Superintendent of Police, they found Akram's party already sitting there. The DSP (Deputy Superintendent of Police), after failing to work a compromise, wrote an FIR for adultery.

In spite of the police report, it took more than a year before both of them were found in Chak Chumra and they already had a child. This discovery was made possible because of the elections, as one of the political parties contesting the elections helped Jamila's father to find them. The young couple was sent to jail. Tufail, another member of the Union Council from among the *Maliks*, stood bail for them. Akram and his family celebrated the release with a big function and Akram and Jamila, walked through the streets where Aslam lived to humiliate him. Jamila's mother came out and dragged her into their house as they were passing through the street. Akram wanted to take her away again by force. However, some young men of the street gathered and told him not to step an inch forward, otherwise he himself would be responsible for the consequences.

Jamila's parents then started looking for a husband for her. They needed, among other things, her divorce certificate to be able to marry her to someone else. She was legally already divorced but this had to be attested by the Secretary on a proper form of the Union Council. The Secretary evaded this for eight months. The girl's father pursued the document of divorce and one day he managed to achieve the favour of an influential person, Bulle Shah, belonging to a neighbouring village who helped the girl's father to get this paper from the Council Secretary.

The girl was married off to a person from a village far away and the case is still continuing. Now both parties are planning to end the case with a compromise, since they both fear that according to the present laws, both the girl and the boy would be punishable under the *zina* (adultery) ordinance.

4. The Wounding of Dildar Hussain

This story was told by Karim Shah, the brother of Dildar
Hussain. 'It was 10 a.m. and I had barely reached the office
(Water and Power Development Authority (WAPDA)
Faisalabad), when I was informed on the telephone that my
brother, Dildar Hussain, had been beaten up by Yasin and Umar
Din, both of them belonging to the *Gujar biradari*. He had
received severe injury on the head being hit with a *bala* (a piece
of wood used for roof constructions) and was lying in the
Emergency ward of the Civil Hospital, Faisalabad. On reaching
the hospital, I came to know from the doctor that the injury was
not serious. A friend and a relative of ours, also named Dildar,
who had a car, came to the hospital to help us.

We needed the Medical Report of the injury from the doctor
for registering an FIR with the police. We contacted the doctor
and were told that a Simple Injury Report (as the case was) in
which the intention of murder could be shown in the FIR, would
cost three thousand rupees and if the report should contain
Grevious Injury, we would have to pay five thousand rupees.
We contacted the man working in the Medical Store outside the
Civil Hospital, Faisalabad, and told him the problem, and with
his help, agreed to pay two thousand rupees for the Simple
Injury Report on the production of an X ray.

The next step was to find witnesses for which two of our
close relatives who had come with us, Rafiq Shah, my maternal
uncle, and Mahmud-ul-Hassan, the father of my sister's fiancé,
volunteered. Both of them were not present at the time of the
dispute but we had to name them as eye-witnesses to fulfill the
court requirements and for making our case strong. Those who
were present at the time of the dispute were either not on our
side or not ready to give evidence or were unreliable. We, along
with our relatives, drove to the police station for registering the
FIR.

We reached the police station and told about the quarrel. It is
important to mention here that we also took Ghaffar with us
who had an acquaintance in the police station. We were told to

pay four thousand rupees if we wanted to register an FIR. We were then asked to bring white paper, a ballpoint and arrange for a car for going to the hospital to record my brother's statement for registering the FIR. With a bundle of papers, an expensive ballpoint for the Assistant Sub-Inspector of Police (ASI) we reached the Civil Hospital in the car, where after two hours' discussion, the ASI wrote down a draft of the FIR. Afterwards, since the ASI was hungry, we went to a restaurant where we ate a meal which cost about five hundred rupees.

We came back to the police station at around twelve midnight and the final FIR was written by the *muharer* which took another two hours. It was 3 a.m. already and we were told to come back very early in the morning, the next day, with a car to arrest the accused. We reached the police station the next morning around 6.30 a.m. where the police (one ASI and two Constables) took another hour for preparations.

On our identification, the police arrested the uncle of one of the accused and brought him to the police station. We then went to the house of Yasin Bullah but the police could not find him and then, during the house search, Umar Din was arrested while trying to run away. Yasin got bail before arrest after two days, but Umar Din was put behind bars.

My injured brother Dildar was discharged after two days although he was still not feeling well. For some technical reasons, to avoid cancellation of Yasin's bail application (a court requirement), we needed to keep Dildar in hospital for two weeks. In any case, we had to vacate the room for friends of the doctor. After a long search, we found a distant relative of ours who is a doctor in the Allied Hospital, Faisalabad, who arranged through his acquaintances in the hospital, to have Dildar referred to the Allied Hospital for admission. We managed to keep Dildar in the Hospital till the date fixed for the confirmation of Yasin's bail. The Sessions Judge, responsible for hearing our case, could not attend the court and the hearing was postponed for another three days.

We consulted our lawyer who told us to bring a certificate from the hospital stating that Dildar was still admitted there.

We got this report, before Dildar was discharged from the hospital. As demanded by the Sessions Judge, we got a Medical Report that mentioned the severity of the injury, and the bail was cancelled and Yasin was sent to jail. This was a clear victory for us because getting a bail application cancelled in case of such a small dispute case is unusual.

The other party had the favours of Naeem (the Chairman of the Union Council) and thought that they would win. But Naeem did not support them openly because he did not want to annoy the Shahs (the Syed *biradari*) and thereby lose their votes. To show his neutrality, he even visited Dildar in the hospital to enquire about his health. When it seemed that the Syeds would be successful he came to Karim and asked to make *sulah* (peace). Karim said that he would have to ask his father about it but he did not respond for a month. Naeem again went to Karim's house and said that the other party was ready to pay the expenditures so far incurred. After consultation with his relatives he asked for ten thousand rupees and that they should beg his pardon.

At the end, in the *panchayat*, in which our relatives and the people of our *biradari* and also Naeem took part, it was decided that the *Gujars* had to pay eight thousand rupees. After this, the case was withdrawn from the court.'

5. 'The Lending of Money Needs Courage but Getting it Back Requires Wisdom'

Barkat belongs to the *Jat biradari* and holds shares in a transport business. Karim Hussain who is an office worker is his friend. Two of Karim's brothers and some uncles live and work in England. Barkat knew that Karim had money to invest. So he told Karim fascinating stories of his business and convinced him to invest fifty thousand rupees in a minibus. Karim gave him the money and became a share-holder. For the first few days, Barkat brought him from five hundred to six hundred rupees per day as income from the minibus. According to Karim, Barkat wanted to convince him of how profitable the business was so that he was ready to invest even more money in it. Barkat asked Karim if he could invest in another waggon (minibus) but, luckily, Karim had no more money at hand and therefore refused. Then the daily expenditures on the repair of the minibus started exceeding the income from it. Since Karim had a job, he could not attend to the business personally. He had to believe whatever Barkat reported to him. After a month, he ended up paying more than what he earned.

Karim was just planning to withdraw from the business when one day the minibus came to a stand with its motor out of order. Karim countinuously tried to settle his account with Barkat but he tried to put it off. Karim's weakness was that he had no proof of payment. One day while talking with him he recorded their discussion on a small taperecorder but he was told by a friend working in the courts that their conversation on the taperecorder would not help in recovering the money lent to Barkat.

In the meantime, it turned out that Barkat had no share in the bus at all. Another man from Naglan had paid the other half of the cost of the minibus but this did not help because now the bus was grounded and its repair would cost a lot of money which Karim did not want to spend.

Karim summoned some of his relatives—Rafiq, his uncle, Jamil, his cousin, and Hadait, a friend, and took them all to Barkat. The *panchayat* decided that, now that the minibus was out of order, Karim must also bear the loss. It was decided that Barkat would, therefore, pay him twenty-five thousand rupees one month later. It took Karim several months before he could extract this money from Barkat in several instalments and in different forms like one calf, some wheat and some cash.

6. Conflicts in the Family of Ashraf

'Family', in this case, stands for the brothers and sisters of Ashraf, his wife, Maryam, and his children. The conflicts treated here are only those which relate to marriage and division of property. For details of the relatives included for this case study see diagram no. 5.

Marriage conflicts

The details of the conflicts which arose at the time of marriages of the brothers and sisters of Ashraf and Maryam are deliberately not mentioned. However, some detail, which would help understand a certain situation, regarding which brothers and sisters of Ashraf and Maryam married to whom, especially among the relatives, is given below.

Ashraf (1) is married to the father's brother's daughter, Maryam (2). His two brothers Naseer (40) and Tahir (59) are married to the mother's brother's daughters Karim Bibi (41) and Sureya (60), who are also sisters. The other brother M. Ali (52) is married to Nighat (53), outside the family, but in the *Jat biradari*. His sister Ashraf Bibi (46) was married to the mother's brother's son but was divorced and is now married to Maqbool (47), who is also from another *Jat biradari*. One brother, Yaqoob, is not married.

Maryam has three sisters and one brother. Mandan (9), the eldest sister, is married to Zulfiqar (10), the mother's brother's son. Bashiran (18) is married to Rashid (19) and, in exchange, Sharif (23) is married to Rashidan (24), the sister of Rashid. Zuhran (32), another sister, is married to Yasin (33), outside the family but in the same *biradari*.[4]

We limit ourselves now to the conflicts arising out of the arrangements of the marriages of the children: Looking at it from the point of view of Ashraf and Maryam, all the male and female children of their brothers and sisters could be wedded with each other (see diagram no. 5). The limitations in these

Diagram No. 5 showing the brothers and sister of Ashraf and Maryam with their children.

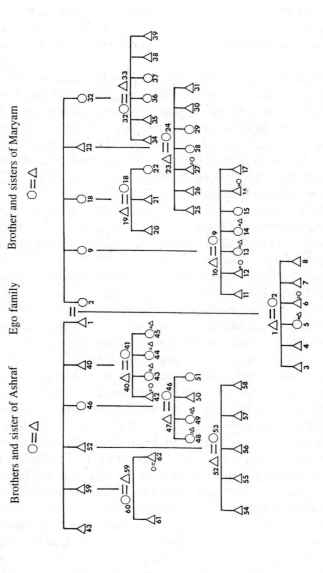

Key: 'Circles' stand for females, 'triangles' for males and 'equal' signs are meant for spouse relationship. Vertical lines are for generations and parallel lines show brothers and sisters.

possibilities are the extreme age differences, the sometimes greatly different socio-economic positions of the families, the dominant role of the mother or father in the family and the nature and availability of marriageable boys and girls among close relatives.

The marriages generally take place in the sequence by age, i.e. the eldest as the first and the youngest as the last but the girls may be married out of turn. Among the daughters, again, the order is the same barring exceptional cases like a good offer for the younger one. If the elder daughter is not very goodlooking or is already too old to be married off, due to the fear that the younger ones might also become too old, the sequence of older first may be broken.

In Ashraf's family, his eldest son (3) has the possibilities of marrying daughters of his wife's eldest sister. But since Mandan (9) has no contact with her side of the family, the reason being the division of property to which we shall come later, no marriage could take place. The next possibility was marrying the daughters of Ashraf's elder brother Naseer, but here again, the conflict over property made this impossible. The next was Ashraf's sister, but Maryam's influence in her family was strong and she did not want to take a girl from the family of her husband's sister. She had quarrelled very often with Ashraf Bibi, who, as a daughter of the family, had very strong influence. Still another reason was that the economic position of Ashraf Bibi's family was not very strong and her daughters were not as educated as Maryam's sons. Zabeen (5), Ashraf's daughter, the third according to age but the first one to be married was given in marriage to Shafiq (26), the son of Maryam's brother. Many conflicts surfaced at the time of her marriage. Maryam had only one daughter and there were many potential husbands like Aslam (34), her sister Zuhran's eldest son, Akram (20) her other sister Bashiran's eldest son, Javaid (25), Sharif, her only brother's eldest son. Similarly on Ashraf's side of the family, Asghar (61) his brother Tahir's eldest son, Dastgir (50), the only son of his sister Ashraf Bibi, and Jamal (42), the eldest and the only son of Naseer who is already engaged. The choice was narrowed to some extent by the fact that Ashraf's side of the family did not offer for Zabeen because of the strong influence of Maryam in the family and the conflicts over the division of the property between the brothers.

Zabeen (5) was first engaged to Aslam (34), Zuhran's (32) eldest son. It is important to mention here that Yasin, the husband of Zuhran, was abroad and had been sending back some money. Sharif (23) and Maryam's mother became angry that Javaid (25), Sharif's eldest son, was not considered in spite of the fact that Sharif had asked for Zabeen. Bashiran (18) was also angry that her son Akram (20) was not considered either, though not openly, because she herself had perpetual problems with Rashid, her husband, and his family. This family was known to be bad because three of Rashid's brothers had run away with girls from their village belonging to different sections of the *kammi biradari* like *Teeli* (oilmen), *Moochi* (shoe makers) and *Julahay* (weavers) and they were also involved in many conflicts and disputes, and, were not even living in their own village. Maryam thought that it should automatically be clear that she would not marry her daughter into such a family. It is said that 'the blood follows blood' (the children follow the father and the uncles of the family) and, above all, the son was not any better (did not attend school and was also quarrelsome) and the economic position of this family and the future of the boy seemed rather gloomy.

Zuhran's two daughters, Karima (36) and Shada (37), were engaged to the older sons of Sharif (23), i.e. Javaid (25) and Shafiq (26). Sharif had borrowed forty thousand rupees from Yasin (33) and Zuhran many years ago to pay for the land he was cultivating. Now Zuhran and Yasin asked for their money back, for which Sharif still did not have the resources. He had thought that he had paid off the major part indirectly through his services, since he had attended Zuhran during illness in the absence of Yasin when he was in Saudi Arabia and also by arranging many welcome parties for Yasin and Zuhran when he returned and visited him. Sharif was forced by his other sisters, relatives (including Daulli, the sister of Yasin married in this village to one of the distant relatives of Sharif) and the *panchayat* of the village elders arranged by Zuhran, to return the money which she had loaned to him. To comply with the decision, Sharif had to sell a part of his land. As a consequence, the relations between Sharif and Zuhran went sour, leading to the breaking of engagement of his two sons.

Even before Zuhran became ill, her son stopped going to school. Zuhran's bad health led to increased expenditure out of the remittances from Saudi Arabia. The financial position of the family slowly deteriorated and Maryam saw the future of her daughter with them in jeopardy. She indicated this several times to Zuhran and finally refused to marry her daughter into this family. The relations between Maryam and Zuhran, and Sharif and Zuhran, became strained. Sharif saw a chance of getting Zabeen for his eldest son, Javaid, and sent his mother, Barkat Bibi, and his sister, Bashiran, to plead his case. Bashiran was promised one of the daughters of Sharif for her son, Akram.

Sharif's son Javaid (25), did not attend school. Ashraf's family decided among themselves to marry Zabeen to Shafiq (26), who was Sharif's second son, and studying in college at that time. Sharif and his family agreed to this and the marriage was finally solemnized.

Zuhran thought that the whole family had betrayed her, although Maryam's refusal to give her daughter to her son was not supported by her mother, Barkat Bibi, her sister, Bashiran, and Sharif, her brother. She was so disgusted that she severed her relations with her brother and sisters.

Sharif had some other plans as well. He wanted to marry his eldest daughter (28) to Ashraf's third son Javaid (6) but Ashraf's family did not agree to an exchange marriage because she was illiterate. When Javaid was married into a family outside the circle of close relatives, Sharif announced the end of relations with them and did not come to attend Javaid's marriage. He even persuaded Bashiran not to attend the marriage.

There were similar conflicts among Ashraf's brothers and his sister. His sister, Ashraf Bibi, first wanted to marry her eldest daughter (48) to Jamal (42), son of his eldest brother Naseer;

this was accepted to some extent but later on the offer was turned down because Karim Bibi, Naseer's (40) wife wanted and finally did marry her son to her brother's daughter, also named Maryam. In the beginning, Maryam, Ashraf's wife, wanted to have Shado (48), the eldest daughter of Ashraf's sister but the latter refused, because at that time Ashraf's sons were very young and the economic prospects of the family did not appear to be bright. When things improved Ashraf's wife changed her mind.

As has already been mentioned, the wives of Naseer and Tahir were sisters and both families had very good relations. Sureya, Tahir's wife, died leaving behind two sons. Karim Bibi, Naseer's wife, wanted to marry her youngest daughter, Naseema (45), to Munir (62), the younger son of Sureya, because the older son had died from a fatal disease. Therefore, Karim Bibi opposed the idea of her brother who wanted to give his daughter in marriage to Munir (62). Later, when Karim Bibi's daughter had a better offer, Munir was rejected. The deterioration of Tahir's economic position over the years also contributed to the factors that led to the refusal.

Naseer's eldest daughter, Sharifan (43), was given in marriage to the son of one the brothers of Karim Bibi who later on refused to marry her, so she was married off in the village. She got divorced after the birth of one girl. Ameen, her husband did not want to divorce her but she did not wish to continue to live with him. Naseer went to court and by order of the court Ameen had to give her a divorce. She married again but outside her close kinship. The other two daughters are also married outside the families.

Ashraf Bibi, after losing her hope from her brothers, married off her eldest daughter, Shado, outside her close relatives, who died after one year during childbirth. The second daughter Nasreen (49), was then married to the widowed husband of Shado, and had three children. Shanaz (51), the youngest, was also married outside the family. She was, however, divorced after a year. One of the reasons people prefer marriages with close relatives in that at least one knows each other beforehand.

There is a saying that: 'even if an *apna* (relative) had to kill you he would at least throw your dead body in the shadow'. That is why close relatives (those allowed) are preferred in marriage.

This has been shown with the help of diagrams but in a very simplified form. Diagram no. 6 shows all the possible chances of marriages of two children of Ashraf and Maryam. These possibilities are indicated by a black triangle. Diagram no. 7 shows the actual offers/requests made. These are again marked with black small triangles. The difference between these two diagrams, i.e. where no request was made and where request was denied, stands for the conflicts, which are mostly based on property. This is also evident from the fact that most of the offers refused or rejected are from the side of Ashraf's brothers who divided the property among themselves. Diagram no. 8 is very simple, showing the marriage of Ashraf's daughter to Sharif's son. The difference between diagram 7 and 8 shows the root of conflicts from refusal of offer/request. Diagram no. 9 shows the strategies adopted to avoid conflicts and hence the breaking down of the relations among brothers and sisters. Maryam gives a daughter to Sharif, Zuhran gives a daughter to Sharif, Sharif gives one of his daughters to Zuhran, and the other daughter to Bashiran. This has been shown in diagram no. 9. If one of them breaks up, all the others are also endangered. These strategies are renewed and adjusted and new problems come to the surface.

Conflicts over the Division of Property

It has already been mentioned that Ashraf has four brothers and one sister and only one brother, Yaqoob, is not married. Maryam has three sisters and one brother. According to the official and Islamic law of inheritance, the sons get one share each and the daughters half a share each. But in practice according to the customs prevailing in the village and for that matter over a large part of the country, the property is divided equally among sons,

Diagram No. 6 showing all possible husbands and wives for number 5 and 6, a daughter and a son of Ashraf and Maryam.

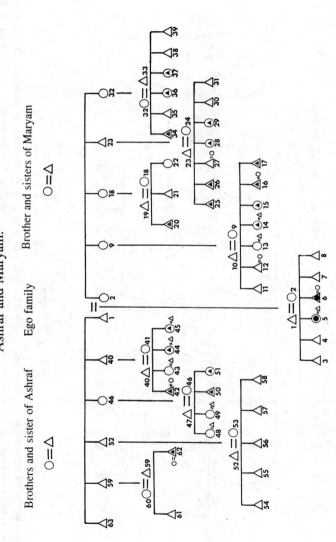

220

Diagram No. 7 showing the real offers/requests for Numbers 5 and 6.

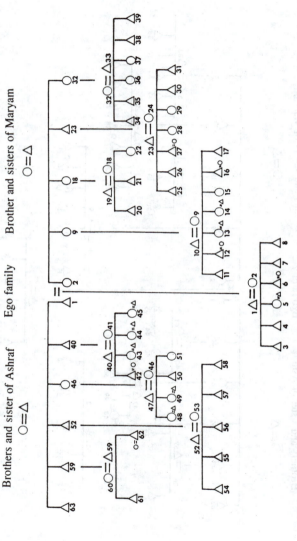

*The difference between diagram 2 and 3 shows those husbands/wives who were possible but were not requested/offered. This is because of the conflicts between the two concerned families, mainly property conflicts. This becomes also clear from the fact that the missing requests are overwhelmingly from Ashraf's side, i.e. the brothers of Ashraf. Property conflicts are mostly between the brothers. This also becomes evident from the request/offer from the sister of Ashraf.

221

Diagram No. 8 showing actual marriage of 5 while 6 is married outside the close relatives.

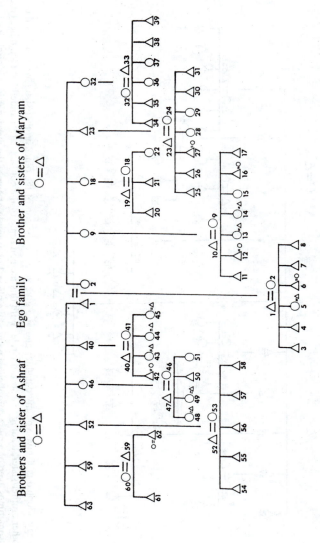

* If we compare this diagram with diagram no. 3 the difference shows those requests/offers which were not accepted. We may suppose that not realizing the requests/offers leads to conflicts and disputes between the brothers and sisters. To avoid these conflicts and disputes, strategies are made which are shown in the next diagram.

Diagram No. 9 showing the strategies adopted to minimize the conflicts.

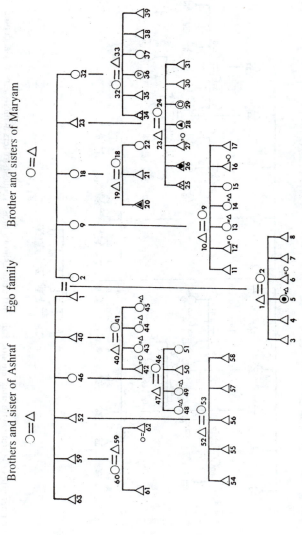

*The strategy adopted is; I give you my daughter and you give yours to the son of the other brother/sister who makes the same with the other brother/sister, leading to a sort of circle. With this method some of the conflicts are avoided but then other types of conflicts, sometimes even of a more complicated nature take place. For example, if one of the marriages in this circle is dissolved the others are at least endangered.

and the daughters do not receive any share from the land and other property.

When Umar Din and his wife, Hussain Bibi, parents of Ashraf, came to settle in Misalpur after migration from Hoshiarpur, a district in the Indian Punjab, they got a relatively big house, an animal-house (*haveli*) and some agricultural land. At that time, none of the sons or the daughter were married. They lived together and formed one household. Naseer (40), the eldest son, got married to the daughter of Hussain Bibi's brother. Some time after the marriage, quarrels began between Hussain Bibi, Ashraf Bibi, sister, and Karim Bibi, the wife of Naseer which led first to the separation of a room for the use of the latter, in one portion of the house, but the land remained united. This meant that Ashraf's wife was given only the necessities of daily life like clothes and cooking ingredients. The marriage of Ashraf to the daughter of Umar Din's brother led to the setting up of another household in another corner of the house to avoid conflicts. The brothers still remained united among themselves and worked together in the fields, and the two wives were provided with clothing and food. The mother and the sister were the persons conducting the activities in the household, while the father managed the farming activities along with his sons. The quarrels were now not only between mother and sister versus the wives but also between the wives.

The situation became worse after the marriage of the third brother with the sister of Naseer's wife. They both formed a united front against not only the mother but also against Ashraf's wife. Ashraf Bibi was married to the son of Hussain Bibi's brother. As a custom, normally the most recently married son and his wife remain with the parents until the next son is married. But, as the quarrels between the mother and Sureya, Tahir's wife, intensified, another set-up had to be established and she got a separate room, too. Therefore, the earlier two separate households now increased to three. The situation was further intensified when Ashraf Bibi returned from her husband's house and decided not to return and ultimately got divorced.

This was a very serious situation. However, it started improving when Ashraf Bibi was married again.

Though the agricultural fields remained undivided, the separate households became more and more independent and strong. The *haveli* was also divided but only to the extent as to who was to use which area. There was hardly a day without a disagreement over the use of the water pump, use and cleaning of the common courtyard or drainage, the distribution of agricultural products and the use of the common courtyard of the *haveli*. It is customary that the younger brothers respect and obey their elder brothers just like their fathers. At the same time, the elder brothers also have a greater share of obligations and responsibilities. The occurrence of quarrels among the women of the household was so frequent, that on more than one occasion the brothers also joined in and once Tahir, who is younger, beat up Ashraf which was totally humilliating. Similarly, on the complaints of the mother about their insulting behaviour, the wives were abused and sometimes even beaten up by their husbands.

The allocated portions of the house and the big courtyard started taking the shape of permanent and independent houses, as was also the case with the *haveli* which was divided into three equal parts. The two younger brothers, Yaqoob, who was not married as well as M. Ali did not claim their shares.

One day, Ashraf demanded the division of land. The question was: into how many shares should it be divided; who should get which fields and how should it be irrigated. The land was divided into four shares, the fourth being for the parents. There was controversy generated on this kind of division because of the fourth part being given to one son for cultivation. Because of the quarrel between Ashraf's mother and his wife, he was declared landless by the parents and for one year he had to cultivate the land of others as a tenant. After one year, he was called back to share the land. Then Naseer's wife and her daughter Sharifan beat up the mother-in-law. It became Naseer's turn to be rendered landless for one year.

The father became old and was not able to work in the fields anymore. The fourth share was again divided among three brothers who were to give some share of the crops to the parents. The family land was adequate for eking out a respectable livelihood for the three brothers. M. Ali, the youngest brother, who had returned from the States and had a good job, decided not to take any share from the land and yet to support the parents financially. The three brothers could finally live exclusively for themselves from this land. Similarly, the *haveli* and the house were also divided with walls. All these divisions of house, *haveli*, land and agricutural tools were done temporarily and unofficially.

Another problem was that the inherited agricultural land was not enough for the subsistence of all the brothers. One was interested in selling it; the other in keeping it for agriculture and yet another wanted to sell it sometime later since its value was increasing very rapidly as it was located in the suburbs of Faisalabad. There were lots of problems involved in the division of this land especially to the part belonging to the unmarried brother Yaqoob, and the share of Ashraf Bibi, the sister.

The division of property among Maryam's brother and sisters was different and in some respects perhaps easier. It has already been said that the sisters, under normal circumstances, do not demand their share and if they do so they lose their contact with the family. Mandan, the eldest sister of Maryam, married a cousin, who lived in the same village; she had quarreled with her brother Sharif and demanded her share of the land. Sharif denied it and she, with her husband, took the matter to court and was finally given her share. Mandan and Sharif live in the same neighbourhood. Since she took her share of land she is considered as their enemy. The other conflict arose at the time of the division of the house between Mandan/Zulfiqar and Sharif along with the sisters and mother. At the time controversy arose about the location of the boundary wall and Zulfiqar wounded Bashiran seriously. Sharif wanted to report the injury to the police, but friends, Shafee and Mandi, intervened and also settled the dispute regarding the construction of the boundary wall.

Sharif asked his other sisters to declare to the court in writing that they wanted to give their share of the land to their brother, which all of them did. One of the reason why Mandan demanded and got her share and the others did not is, that the others were married and living in far-away villages and the share of the land they would get was not very attractive. Demanding her share of the land is the last step a sister would think of taking since girls in rural areas are taught from early years to treat their brothers with veneration. This is one way of showing family unity—an expectation more from the daughters/sisters to give up shares than from males.

Solution of these Conflicts

All the important events of life are divided into those of happiness like marriage, birth, going on a pilgrimage, etc. and those of sorrow such as the death of a person, accidents, and other such extreme events. There is a normal practice that if there is a sorrow like death then the close relatives like brothers and sisters come to attend such occasions by themselves even if they are angry. It was but natural that when Sureya died Nawab and Maryam forgot everything and went to Tahir and other brothers and their wives also came. Similarly, when one of the daughters of Mandan died Sharif and the other sisters took part in the mourning and till the next conflict were on speaking terms with each other.

At times of happiness like marriage the one who celeberats such an occasion would invite the others. He would go to the house of his brother or close relative together with other relatives and friends and bury the hatchet. Very often long discussions are held in which every side narrates their story and the *panchayat* or the group of relatives hear and snub the side which has done wrong, in what is called *char pusch laan taan*. Sometimes, if the disagreement is very serious, it could need several attempts or can even remain unsolved for some time.

But as a rule the relatives coming to make peace on such occasions are not sent away empty-handed.

Conclusion

Legal pluralism was the most common feature in all the case studies. The conflicts were brought to the different legal forums which include, the police, the courts, the village *panchayats*, the *pirs* and the chiefs, alternatively and simultaneously, in different combinations according to the nature of the conflict, the status of the parties and the circumstances. The role played by these institutions, which may be divided into two main categories, the state-run official institutions and the village-level traditional institutions, varies from case to case. These studies also show how police, courts and other institutions of state system are manipulated. The official system of justice is slow functioning, and is expensive and its agents like police, magistrates, judges, and court officials are corrupt. The status and position of the parties to a conflict influence the traditional methods of conflict resolution and they are mostly only accessible to the well-to-do and influential members of the society.

The first case study provides details of the functioning of the justice system both of the official and of the traditional system. It gives an idea of the functioning of family life, relatives, and *biradaries* and co-operation, competition, and reciprocity in conflict between the different groups. It also gives us an idea of the role of the pre-conflict history. An important point about this case study is that the author is a member of Ashraf's family, one of the parties in the conflict.

The second case study is more like a typical village conflict, i.e. the use of direct physical force to solve a dispute or problem—Karim and his son tried to get back their property directly without going to the police, court or *panchayat*. In spite of property being the reason of conflict, it is not representative of such conflicts because most property conflicts in a village concern agricultural land and the problems arising thereof. This conflict provides a good example for explaining how a *biradari* (lineage, clan) may act jointly against another and the role the traditional system plays in solving the conflicts. Besides, it highlights the role of money and *sifarish* in the official system and the influence of wealth, authority and the strength of the *biradaries* in the traditional system. It also shows how the two systems, the official and the traditional, work jointly and how the position of the parties in the courts or *panchayats* influence the process of arriving at a decision/compromise. Who accompanies whom to the courts, or who gives evidence for and against whom, who sides with whom in the *panchayat* is mostly not decided on the facts of the case such as having seen or not seen an incident, but rather on who is related to whom and who has sided with whom in the previous conflicts as also on the basis of authority, interests and resources of the parties involved.

The third case study is in a sense an exception in that most of the conflicts relating to women are not brought to the courts. Usually, the conflicts relating to women are either solved locally i.e. at the lowest possible forum; i.e. *ghar, khandan, sharika, biradari*, at the most at the village *panchayat* or, if the situation so demands, with direct physical force. The remarks of the farmers about this conflict were that 'Dealing with cases like this is typical of the *kammis*, we would have either killed the boy or both or at least, if nothing else would have been possible, then the girl would have been killed'.

The fourth case study shows that very often reasons like an abuse may lead to serious conflicts and that small conflicts could lead to lengthy litigations. These could be called typical *izzat* conflicts. The conflict starts with the so-called injury to the *izzat* or *ghairat* (both could be translated as: honour; thus the winning of the case or punishing the culprit again becomes a question of regaining the lost *izzat*). It gives a good insight into corruption at different levels in the courts, as also in the hospitals responsible for issuing medical certificates. This also shows the collaboration between the *panchayats* and the official system of justice. Once the position of one of the parties is clear in the court, the local *panchayat* becomes active and may be called upon by the party having the weaker position in court to make the agreement.

The fifth case points out to an important aspect of the village life, i.e mutual trust, sharing, exchanging, and living together. These above-mentioned characteristics sometime lead to conflicts and problems. Money is borrowed and lent, business deals are made, crops worth thousands of rupees are bought and sold and such transactions are done without writing. The reason for not writing down such deals is that most of the villagers are illiterate, on the one hand, and asking for a written contract is considered an insult to the borrower who should have to be trusted, on the other hand. The villagers are, as a rule, also quite dependable and trustworthy because being notorious for being not trustworthy would mean that others would hesitate to deal with them. Such misunderstandings do not always lead to quarrels and fights but are also solved with mutual give and take.

The last case study is again from the author's own family. It is different from the other case studies in many respects because it does not represent the solution process of the conflicts but the types of the conflict among the close relatives and the family. At first glance, it might seem to be out of the range of the objectives of the present study because the conflicts are of minor nature and they were not brought to the courts or *panchayats*. These conflicts and disagreements which seem so harmless could at times become very serious. It also gives us an idea of the nature of family life which is a major source of conflicts.

NOTES

1. Goora is another villager, around 55 years old and belongs to the *Rajput biradari*. He has four sons and two daughters. He owns 16 acres of land, one relatively small house for his large family and no animal-house.
2. The word 'illegal occupant' should not create misunderstanding. This paper (*fard*) was only meant to show that they were the original inhabitants of this place, legal or illegal did not play very important role.

    It was not only Nawab and his brothers who were illegal inhabitants but the whole area around.

2. *Marla* is a scale of measurement approximately one meter by nine meters.
3. The first-cousin (parallel and cross) marriages, in spite of still being the most popular, are on the decrease. The conflicts arising from these marriages are correspondingly also not only solved within the framework of the relatives since in the case of marriages outside the close relatives this body of close relatives having influence on both sides does not exist. There is a trend of change in the marriage arrangements and the resulting conflicts and their solutions.

GLOSSARY

aaq karna	to eject or to evict: to declare a son or a daughter disqualified for a share in the father's property
abat	request or invitation for a short period of work, at the end of which fine food is served
amman hawa	grandmother, 'Eve'
apna	own, in the sense of close relatives, like a son, father, mother, the family, etc.
Araeen	the name of a *biradari* (clan, caste), known as vegetable growers
baba	the way of addressing an old man or a holy person
baba Adam	the first man, grandfather Adam
baddu'ah	invocation, or curse; used as an explanation for an accident or bad luck (*baddu'ahs* of poor and holy men are known)
badla	revenge or compensation
badmash	roguish, or of a bad character; see also, *gunda*
baithak	men's room; a room in which men, not belonging to the family, are entertained
barkat	blessing, holiness, good luck
barkatwala	the one who brings *barkat* or good luck
beniaz	the one who need not be afraid of consequences; in this connection, mostly God is meant
biradari	brotherhood, clan, lineage
chamar	*biradari* of craftsmen, mostly sweepers

charpai	a wooden frame cot, strung with rope
Chaudhary	traditionally *jats* (the name of a *biradari*) are addressed as *chaudharys*, but the term is also used for all farmers
chaukidar	watchman; in each village there is a person responsible for various small jobs, like informing about *panchayat* meetings, etc.
darbar	shrine, see also *ziarat*
dera	traditionally, the farm residence, or day centre, of a farmer on his agricultural land, also used as a status symbol for the sitting place of the men
dhom	the *biradari* of musicians
dogar	the name of a *biradari* known for animal breeding
doli	palanquin
eid-gah	a place reserved for the saying of *eid* (the most important religious festival of the Muslims) prayers
fard	a document issued by the Revenue Department as a proof of the ownership of a piece of land
fiqah	Islamic jurisprudence
ghairat	defence of honour, belongings, and the women of the family
ghair	stranger, as opposed to *apna*, meaning a non-relative
ghar	house, in the sense of the nucleus family
goot	sub-clan, also translated as sub-caste; people having the same great-grandparents
gujar	the name of a *biradari* especially connected with animal husbandry, like the *dogars*
gunda	rascal; especially, if somebody is doing dirty jobs for an influential person

haj	pilgrimage to Mecca
hadith	narration of a saying or action of the Holy Prophet [PBUH]
haveli	animal house; also used for the men's house; status symbol
haya	modesty; especially used for the women who observe the rituals of *purdah*
hadud	boundaries; Islamic penal laws
hafiz	the one who knows the Quran by heart
haquq-ul-ibad	duties towards other human beings
haquq-ullah	duties towards God
hukka	water pipe for smoking tobacco
hukka pani band karna	excommunication
hukkeyanwala	the name of a craftsmen's *biradari* making *hukkahs*
hamsaya	neighbour
ikhtiar	authority, power, control
izzat	honour, prestige
Jat	the name of a *biradari* of farmers
jholi	the front part of the long shirt worn both by men and women
julaha	weaver *biradari*
kammi	craftsmen, *biradaris* other than farmers
karamat	miracle
kath	village assembly or gathering
khaddi	hand driven loom for making cloth
khairat	alms
khandan	joint family, including uncles, cousins, and aunts
khandani	belonging to a noble or respectable family
kharcha pani	the term used for a bribe
khata	a small factory in which the power-looms are installed
khoon	blood

laagi	another name for *kammis* but for those who work for a particular farmer, barber, etc.
lohar	blacksmith
mai baap	mother and father, in the sense of protector
malang	those serving and living in/from a shrine, also used for simple lunatics in the village
Malik	the *biradari* of weavers
mang	request for help. See also: *abat*
mast	a village lunatic, or a very simple person considered to be holy; see also: *malang*
maulavi	officiating priest of a mosque
mian	those belonging to the *araeen biradari* are addressed with this honorific title
mazloom	oppressed, being treated tyrannically
mirasi	musician
mochi	shoemaker
mu'tabar	trustworthy, credible
muhalla	street, see also: *patti*
muharer	person responsible for writing reports in the police station
munshi	a lawyer's clerk
nikkah nama	marriage contract
nikal jana	the running away of a woman with a man from the family and village
naee	barber
ober	stranger, non-relatives
panchayat	gathering of the elders and respectables of the village or *biradari*
panchayati	a member of a *panchayat*
pao aqal	a quarter of a kilogramme of wisdom
paryah	the gathering of village respectables; see also *panchayat*
patti	an area similar to a street; see also *mohalla*

patvari	an official of the Revenue Department, responsible for collecting records and revenue from the village
piada	process server
qoum	similar to the term *biradari* but also used in the extended sense of the term nation
qismet	luck
qismetwallah	one who brings happiness
Rajput	the name of a *biradari* known for their bravery
Rana	title of a member of the *rajput biradari*
sadqah	alms of a specific type, especially given at times of danger or after the danger is over
sharam	modesty, especially connected with women, see also: *haya*
sharif	gentleman
sharika	patrilineage; mostly those living in the same village
sifarish	recommendation, intercession
soorman	brave, fearless
sulah safai	peace and agreement
seypi system	work contract; system of payments and work between the farmers (*zamindars*) and craftsmen (*kammi*)
taili	the name of the oilmen caste
talaaq nama	the document of divorce
tarkhan	the name of the carpenter caste
thana	the police station
thara	a platform, such as a raised place near the entrance of a house, used as a meeting and sitting place of men
ulema	religious scholars
wakalat nama	power of attorney
walima	feast given before or after marriage

zahar pir	a holy person or place which has become popular because of a miracle appearance
zan, zar, zamin	woman, gold, land; proverbial reasons of conflicts
zat	caste, *biradari*
zemindar	farmer, landholder/landowner
ziarat	shrine, see also: *darbar*

BIBLIOGRAPHY

Ahmad, Makhdum Tasadduq. 1972. *System of Social Stratification in India and Pakistan.* Lahore: Punjab University Press.

———. *Offences in Rural and Urban Areas.* (Year and place of publication unknown).

———. *Social Problems in the Developing Economy of Pakistan.* (Year and place of publication unknown).

Ahmad, Saghir. 1977. *Class and Power in a Punjabi Village.* New York: Monthly Review Press.

Akhtar, Sardar M. and Arshad A.R. 1960. *Village Life in Lahore District: A Study of Selected Economic Aspects.* Lahore: Punjab University Press.

Ali, Mohammad. 1966. *And then the Pathan Murders.* Peshawar: University Book Agency.

Aminul-Islam, A.K.M. 1974. *A Bangladesh Village: Conflict and Cohesion.* Cambridge: Schenkman Publishing Company.

Arjomand, Said Amir, 1989. 'Constitution-making in Islamic Iran: The Impact of Theocracy on the Legal Order of a Nation-State'. In *History and Power in the Study of Law*, eds. June Starr and Jane F. Collier. Ithaca: Cornell University, pp. 113–30.

Barth, Fredrik. 1970. *Political Leadership among Swat Pathans.* London: Athlone Press. (1st edn. 1959).

Baxi, Upendra. 1982. *The Crisis of the Indian Legal System.* New Delhi: Vikas.

Baxi, Upendra and Gallanter Marc. 1979. 'Panchayat Justice: An Indian Experiment in Legal Access'. In *Access to Justice: Emerging Issues and Perspectives*, ed. by Mauro Cappelletti and Bryant Garth. Milano: Giuffre ed. Vol. 3, pp. 341–86.

Berreman, Gerald D. 1968. 'Is Anthropology Alive? Social Responsibility in Social Anthropology.' In *Current Anthropology* 9.5, 1968, pp. 391–6.

Berry, Willard. 1966. *Aspects of the Frontier Crimes Regulation in Pakistan.* Duke University.

Bohannan, Paul. 1957. *Justice and Judgement among the Tiv*. New York: Oxford University Press.

———— (ed.). 1967. *Law and Warfare: Studies in the Anthropology of Conflict*. New York: Natural History Press.

Cambridge University Asian Expedition. 1962. *The Budhopur Report: A Study of the Forces of Tradition and Change in a Punjabi Village in the Gujranwala District, West Pakistan*. Lahore: University of the Punjab.

Cohn, Bernhard S. 1961. 'From Indian Status to British Contract'. In *Journal of Economic History* 21.45, 1961, pp. 613–28.

————. 1961b. *The Development and Impact of British Administration in India: A Bibliographic Essay*. New Delhi: Indian Institute of Public Administration.

————. 1965. 'Anthropological Notes on Disputes and Law in India'. In *American Anthropologist, Special Publication*. 67.6, 1965, pp. 82–122.

————. 1967. 'Some Notes on Law and Change in North Inida'. In *Law and Warfare: Studies in the anthropology of Conflict*, ed. by Paul Bohannan. New York: Natural History Press. pp. 139–60.

————. 1989. 'Law and the Colonial State of India'. In *History and Power in the Study of Law,* ed. by June Starr and Jane F.Collier. Ithaca: Cornell University. pp. 131–52.

Constitution of Pakistan. 1990. *Constitution of Pakistan*. Islamabad: Federal Shariat Academy.

Curry, John C. 1932. *The Indian Police*. London: Faber and Faber.

Darling, Malcom L. 1934. *Wisdom and Waste in the Punjab Village*. London: Oxford University Press.

————. 1978. *The Punjab Peasant in Prosperity and Debt*. Colombia: South Asia Books. (1st edn. 1925).

Diamond, Stanly. 1974. *In Search of the Primitive: A Critique of Civilization*. New Jersey: Transaction Books.

Dungen, P.H.M. van den. 1972. *The Punjab Tradition Influence and Authority in Nineteenth Century India*. London: Allen and Unwin.

Eglar, Zekiye. 1960. *A Punjabi Village in Pakistan*. New York: Columbia University Press.

Federal Judicial Academy Islamabad. 1990. *The Constitution of the Islamic Republic of Pakistan*. Islamabad: Federal Judicial Academy.

Friedl, Erika. 1989. *Women of Deh Koh, Lives in an Iranian village*. Washington: Smithsonian Institution Press.

Foucault, Michel. 1992. *Bewachen und Strafen: Die Geburt des Geaengnisses*. Frankfurt: Suhrkamp Wissenschaft.

Geertz, Clifford. 1968. *Islam Observed: Religious Development in Morocco and Indonesia*. New Haven and London: Yale University Press.

Gluckman, Max. *The Judicial Process Among the Barotse of Northern Rhodesia*. Manchester: Manchester University Press.

_____. 1961. 'Ethnographic Data in British Social Anthropology'. In *Sociological Review*, 9, pp. 5–17.

_____. 1965. *Politics, Law and Ritual in Tribal Society*. Chicago: Aldine Publishing Company.

_____. 1967. 'The Judicial Process among the Barotse'. In *Law and Warfare: Studies in the Anthropology of Conflict,* ed. Paul Bohannan New York: Natural History Press. pp. 59-92.

_____. 1972. *The Ideas in Barotse Jurisprudence*. Manchester: Manchester University Press. (1st edn. 1965).

_____. 1972a. *The Allocation of Responsibility*. Ed. by Max Gluckman. Manchester: Manchester University Press. pp. ix–xxix and 1–50.

_____. 1973, *Custom and Conflict in Africa*. Oxford: Basil Blackwell.

Government of Pakistan. 1984a. *1981 Census Report of Punjab Province*. Islamabad: Statistics Division.

_____. 1984b. *1981 Census Report of Faisalabad District*. Islamabad: Statistics Division.

Gresham M. Sykes. 1969. 'Cases, Courts, and Congestion'. In *Law in Culture and Society,* ed. by Laura Nader. Chicago: Aldine Publishing. pp. 327–36.

Gulliver, P.H. 1969a. 'Case Studies of Law in Non-Western Societies'. In *Law in Culture and Society,* ed. by Laura Nader. Chicago: Aldine Publishing. pp. 11–23.

_____. 1969b. 'Dispute Settlement Without Courts: The Ndendeuli of Southern Tanzania'. In *Law in Culture and Society,* ed. by Laura Nader. Chicago: Aldine Publishing. pp. 24–68.

Haar, B. ter. 1948. *Adat Law in Indonesia*. Ed. by Adamson Hoebel and A. Arthur Schiller. New York: Institute of Pacific Relations.

Haberland, Eike. 1983. 'Historische Ethnologie'. In *Ethnologie eine Einfhhrung,* ed. by Hans Fischer. Berlin: Dietrich Reimer. pp. 319–44.

Haider, A. Sajjad. 1960. *Village in an Urban Orbit: Shah-di-Khui, a Village in Lahore Urban Area*. Lahore: University of Punjab.

Hartmann, Richard. 1944. *Die Religion des Islam: eine Einfhhrung.* Berlin: Mittler.

Hastrup, Kirsten and Peter Elsass. 1990. 'Anthropological Advocacy A Contradiction in Terms?' In *Current Anthropology* 31.3, 1990, pp. 301–11.

Helmken, Dierk. 1976. *Der Gleichheitssatz in der Praxis des Indischen Zivilverfahrens.* Wiesbaden: Steiner.

Hershman, Paul and Standing, Hillary (eds.). 1981. *Punjabi Kinship and Marriage.* Delhi: Hindustan Publishing Cooperation.

Hesse, Carla. 1991. 'Enlightenment, Epistemology and the Laws of Authorship in Revolutionary France, 1777–93'. In *Law and Order of Culture,* ed. by Robert Post. Berkeley: University of California Press. pp. 109–137.

Hoebel, E. Adamson. 1941. *The Cheyenne Way: Conflict and Case Law in Primitive Jurisprudence.* Norman: University of Oklahoma Press.

———. 1968. *Das Recht der Naturvoeker.* Olten:.Walter. (Translated from the original English *The Law of the Primitive Man.* Cambridge: Harvard University Press. 1954.)

———. 1965. 'Fundamental Cultural Postulates and Judicial Lawmaking in Pakistan'. In *American Anthropologist, Special Publication* 67.6, 1965, pp. 43–56.

Izmirlian, Harry (jr.). 1964. *Caste, Kin and Politics in a Punjab village.* Ann Arbor: University Micro-Film International (rep.) 1981.

Jettmar, Karl. 1972. 'Kann Entwicklungshilfe die Stuetzung einer Status-Quo-Politik vermeiden?' In *Sozialer Fortschritt durch Entwicklungshilfe?* Ed. by Friedemann Bhttner. Mhnchen: Claudius. pp. 78–93.

———. *Das Eigentumsrecht der Kazachen.* Wien. (unpublished).

Keiser, Lincoln. 1991. *Friend by Day, Enemy by Night! Organized Vengeance in a Kohistani Community.* Fot Worth: Holt.

Khan, M. Ayub. 1959. *Speeches and Statements of Field Marshal Mohammad Ayub Khan President of Pakistan.* Karachi: Pakistan Publications. 2,1959.

Khanna, Hans R. 1985. *Judiciary in India and Judicial Process.* Calcutta: Sarkar.

Koepping, Klaus Peter. 1981. 'Probleme der Ethik der Ethnographie in Theorie und Methode'. In *Grundfragen der Ethnologie: Beitrge zur gegenwrtigen Theorie-Diskussion,* ed. by Wolfdietrich Schmied-Kowarzik und Justin Stagl. Berlin: Dietrich Reimer. pp. 93–106.

_____. 1993. 'Ethik in Ethnographischer Praxis: zwischen Universalismus und Pluralistischer Autonomie'. In *Grundfragen der Ethnologie: Beitrge zur gegenwrtigen Theorie-Diskussion,* ed. by Wolfdietrich Schmied-Kowarzik und Justin Stagl. Berlin: Dietrich Reimer. pp. 107–108.

Law Reform Commission Report. 1959. *The Report of the Law Reform Commission 1958-59.* Karachi: Government of Pakistan Ministry of Law.

_____. 1970. *The Report of the Law Reform Commission 1967-70.* Karachi: Government of Pakistan Ministry of Law and Parliamentary Affairs (Law Division) Karachi.

Loeffler, Reinhold. 1988. *Islam in Practice, Religious Beliefs in a Persian Village.* New York: State University of New York Press.

Luhmann, Niklas. 1989. *Legitimation durch Verfahren.* Frankfurt: Suhrkamp Wissenschaft.

Majumdar, D.N. 1959. 'Indian Anthropologists in Action'. In *Journal of Social Research* 2.1-2, 1959, 10-15.

Malinowski, Bronislaw. 1976. *Crime and Custom in Savage Society.* New Jersey: Littlefield, Adams.

Mead, Margaret. 1974. *Coming of Age in Samoa.* (orignal 1928). New York: William Morrow and Company.

_____. 1978 'The Evolving Ethics of Anthropology'. In *Applied Anthropology in America,* ed. by Elizabeth M. Eddy and William L. Partridge. New York: Columbia University Press. pp. 425–38.

Mitchell, J.C. 1983. 'Case and Situation Analysis'. In *The Sociological Review* 31(2): pp. 187–211.

Moon, Penderel. 1945. *Strangers in India.* London: Faber and Faber.

Moore, Erin. 1985. *Conflict and Compromise: Justice in an Indian Village.* New York: University Press of America.

_____. 1993 'Gender, Power, and Legal Pluralism'. Rajasthan, India. In *American Ethnologist* 20.3, 1993, pp. 522–42.

Moore, Sally F. 1978. *Law as Process: An Anthropological Approach.* London: Routledge and Kegan Paul.

Nader, Laura (ed.). 1965a. 'The Ethnography of Law'. In *American Anthropologist, Special Publication* 67.6, 1965.

_____. 1965b. 'The Anthropological Study of Law'. In *American Anthropologist, Special Publication* 67.6, 1965, pp. 3–32.

_____. 1969. *Law in Culture and Society.* Chicago: Aldine Publishing.

————. 'Styles of Court Procedure: To Make the Balance'. In *Law in Culture and Society*. Chicago. pp. 69–91.

Patel, Rashida. 1979. *Women and Law in Pakistan: An Exposition of the Socio-Legal Status of Women*. *Karachi*: Faiza Publishers.

Partridge, William L. and Elizabeth M. Eddy. 1978. *The Development of Applied Anthropology in America*. New York: Columbia University Press.

Pospisil, Leopold J. 1974. *Anthropology of Law: A Comparative theory*. New Haven, 1974. Translation (German) *Anthropologie des Rechts*. Mhnchen: Beck, 1982.

Post, Robert (ed.). 1991. 'Theories of Constitutional Interpretation'. In *Law and Order of Culture*. Berkeley: University of California Press. pp. 13–41.

————. 1991. *Law and Order of Culture*. Berkeley: University of California Press.

Redfield, Robert. 1962. 'Relations of Anthropology to the Social Sciences and to the Humanities'. In *Anthropology Today,* ed. by Sol Tax. (rep. 1970). Chicago: University of Chicago Press. pp. 454–60.

Roberts, Simon. 1979. *Order and Dispute: An Introduction to Legal Anthropology*. Harmeondsworth: Penguin Books.

Rosen, Lawrence. 1989. 'Islamic 'Case Law' and the Logic of Consequence'. In *History and Power in the Study of Law,* ed. by June Starr and Jane F. Collier. Ithaca: Cornell University. pp. 302–19.

Rouland, Norbert. 1988. *Anthropologie juridique*. Paris: Presses Universitaires de France. Translated into English by Philippe G. Planel as 'Legal Anthropology' in 1994. London: The Athlone Press.

Salisbury, Richard F. 1974. Foreword to *A Bangladesh Village, Conflict and Cohesion* by A.K.M. Aminul Islam. Cambridge: Schenkman.

Scheppele, Kim L. 1991. 'Facing Facts in Legal Interpretation'. In *Law and Order of Culture,* ed. by Robert Post. Berkeley: University of Carlifornia Press. pp. 42–77.

Schlesier, Karl H. 1974. 'Action Anthropology and the Southern Cheyenne'. In *Current Anthropology* 15.3, 1974, pp. 277–83.

Schott, Rhdiger. 1983. 'Rechtsethnologie'. In *Ethnologie: Eine Einfhhrung,* ed. by Hans Fischer. Berlin: Dietrich Reimer. pp. 181–204.

Slocum, W.L., Jamila Akhtar and Abrar Fatima Sahi. 1960. *Village Life in Lahore District: A Study of Selected Sociological Aspects.* Lahore: University of the Punjab.

Stavenhagen, Rudolfo. 1971. 'Decolonializing Applied Social Sciences'. In *Human Organization* 30.4, 1971, pp. 333–59.

Starr, June and Jane F. Collier (eds.). 1989 *History and Power in the Study of Law. New Directions in Legal Anthropology.* Ithaca: Cornell University.

Steul, Willi. 1981. *Paschtunwali: Ein Ehrenkodex und seine rechtliche Relevanz.* Wiesbaden: Steiner.

Tax, Sol (ed.). 1959. 'Action Anthropology'. In *Journal of Social Research* 2.1-2, 1959. pp. 1–9.

Vining, Joseph. 1991. 'Generalization in Interpretive Theory'. In *Law and Order of Culture,* ed. by Robert Post. Berkeley: University of California Press. p. 1–12.

Walsh, Cecil. 1929. *Indian Village Crimes with an Introduction on Police Investigation and Confessions.* London: Benn.

――――. 1930. *Crimes in India with an Introduction on Forensic Difficulties and Peculiarities.* London: Ernest Bern.

Westermarck, Edward. 1933. *Pagan Survivals in Mohammedan Civilization.* (rep. 1973) Amsterdam: Philo Press.

Willigen, John van. 1991. *Anthropology in Use: A Source Book on Anthropological Practice.* Boulder: West View Press.

Wulff, Robert M. (ed.). 1987. *Anthropological Praxis. Translating Knowledge into Action.* Boulder: West View Press.

INDEX